A Life in Oxford

A Life in Oxford

ANTHONY KENNY

JOHN MURRAY

Albemarle Street, London

The extract on pp. 136–7 from Anthony Powell's
Journals: 1982–1986 (Heinemann) is reproduced with the kind
permission of the author and Reed Consumer Books Ltd.

© Anthony Kenny 1997

First published in 1997
by John Murray (Publishers) Ltd.,
50 Albemarle Street, London W1X 4BD

The moral right of the author has been asserted

A catalogue record for this book is available from the British Library

ISBN 0-7195-5061 0

Typeset in Monotype Garamond
by Servis Filmsetting Ltd, Manchester

Printed and bound in Great Britain by
The University Press, Cambridge

Contents

To Robert and Charles

I

Bachelor Don

THE OXFORD OF the 1930s has been described in many a memoir and novel. Oxford in 1964, when I returned there as a don after leaving the priesthood, was much closer to the Oxford of the 1930s than to the Oxford of the present day. The University was, as it had been for centuries, a loose federation of twenty or so self-governing colleges, most of them for men, and all of them confined to a single sex. Senior Common Rooms were close bodies of a couple of dozen dons, half a dozen of whom might reside in college. The predominant ethos was that of the Arts tutor, who thought of himself primarily as a teacher, who had probably never troubled to obtain a doctorate, and who – though he might well write a book or two – thought of research as something that went on in laboratories on the fringes of the University. Undergraduates wore gowns not only to lectures and to meals in college Halls, but also to individual tutorials or when making business calls on college officers. Colleges closed their gates in the evenings, and the hours for visiting between the sexes were strictly regulated. After hours the only way in for late returners, and the only way out for overstaying visitors, was a climb up and down drainpipes and over walls topped with broken glass.

Having left the Church, I found that the only secular profession for which I was qualified was that of philosopher: I had acquired an Oxford doctorate in the subject in 1961, and my thesis when published had been well received. A philosophy post in Oxford, therefore, seemed the most promising prospect. There was – and is – no Philosophy Department or Faculty in Oxford; philosophy is taught as one of several groups of disciplines making up BA courses called 'honour schools'. The two contexts in which it was mainly studied and taught in the 1960s were the honour schools of Literae Humaniores ('Mods and Greats', which consisted of ancient history, literature and philosophy) and Philosophy, Politics and Economics ('PPE'); a few

students combined philosophy, instead, with psychology and/or physi-
ology ('PPP'). Each college would have a Fellow as Tutor in Philosophy,
and a few had more than one. The philosophy Fellow would collaborate
with the tutors in ancient history and literature, or the tutors in politics
and economics, in the education of their Greats or PPE pupils.

These two honour schools were regarded as apt preparation for a
career in the Civil Service or in public life. Greats tutors would explain
to their pupils how the three parts of their course would provide three
universally useful and necessary skills. The literary element would
enable them to express themselves with clarity and elegance; the
philosophical element would give them a mastery of abstract and logical
thought; the historical element would give them facility in the evaluation of documentary evidence. The world of Graeco-Roman antiquity,
it was claimed, had provided a uniquely favourable microcosm for the
practice of these skills. The surviving corpus of texts was sufficiently
modest to be mastered within the four years of the course, which then
consisted of five terms of literature followed by seven terms divided
between history and philosophy. Moreover, classical culture, while it
had inspired many generations of our forebears, and explained many
features of our own tradition, was sufficiently remote to enable those
who absorbed it to transcend the prejudices of the current age.

In many colleages there were more Greats and PPE pupils than a
single philosophy Fellow could teach, and to help out a short-term post
would be created. Assistants of this kind were (and are) known as
'college lecturers'; often two colleges, each of which wanted only a part-
time lecturer, would combine to offer a single appointment which
would pay a basic living wage and provide free meals and accommodation. Exeter and Trinity Colleges advertised such a lectureship towards
the end of 1963: I was elected to it, and moved into rooms in Exeter at
the beginning of 1964, as an assistant to Christopher Kirwan in Exeter
and to Bede Rundle in Trinity.

The teaching duties of a college lecturer can be quite heavy, and
during my first term I gave 16 hours of tutorials a week, mainly on
moral philosophy and Aristotle's *Nicomachean Ethics*. Oxford titles are
commonly misleading, and a lecturer was not obliged to lecture (just as
a Reader does not earn his keep by reading). However, I was happy to
join Kirwan in a seminar on Aristotle's *Metaphysics*. I quickly noticed
differences between the pupils of the two colleges. Those from Exeter
were more likely to be bright and earnest grammar-school boys,
whereas a pupil who missed tutorials in Ascot week or turned up in
morning dress was more likely to be a Trinity man.

Though I lived in Exeter, in a set of rooms on the Turl once occupied by Sir Hubert Parry, I was a member of both senior common rooms. As the terms of my appointment allowed free dinners at Trinity and one free meal a day at Exeter, I normally lunched at Exeter and dined at Trinity. Lunch was austere, with the Fellows reading newspapers, as at a boarding-house breakfast; dinner was a more gracious affair, with excellent food – cooked, it was said, by twin-brother chefs who took it in turns to preside in the kitchen but who had not spoken to each other for years after a falling-out.

Exeter was presided over by Sir Kenneth Wheare, a genial political theorist who had designed short-lived constitutions for many of the former British colonies in Africa. The Common Room was – it was said – divided into two factions, each led by an elderly bachelor. The more conservative was headed by Dacre Balsdon, a mannered classicist of the old school, the more liberal by Sir Cyril Hinshelwood, an expert on gas-phase kinetics. During my own brief stay at Exeter I was not much aware of faction (Balsdon was on leave), and was able to enjoy without complication the friendship of Hinshelwood. As resident bachelors we were thrown a good deal on each other's company, and I admired the breadth and depth of his cultural interests, from classical literature to contemporary painting.

At Trinity, at least in the Common Room, the most notable presence was that, not of the President, the publisher Arthur Norrington, but of the senior history Fellow, Michael Maclagan. He was a member of the College of Heralds, Slains Pursuivant I believe, and cut a handsome dash when wearing his playing-card uniform. He was almost always to be found staying on for wine and dessert after dinner, advising the younger fellows and lecturers about vintage port, and teaching us the meaning of words such as *solera*. Trinity had been a Jacobite college, and the back gate of the College onto Parks Road was never to be opened until the Stuarts came back into their own. Napkins were laid in the Common Room each night, but without finger bowls: Maclagan explained that this was because a Hanoverian magnate visiting the College in the eighteenth century had noticed that Fellows drinking the Loyal Toast held their glasses over the bowls to show that they were drinking to 'the King over the water'. The bowls were henceforth forbidden, but the napkins that had accompanied them remained, as a silent protest against their removal.

Trinity contained enough young bachelors for post-dinner Common Room to be a regular event. As the port and madeira circulated the master of the revels was John Kelly, then a young law don, later a Senator in Dublin and, briefly, Attorney-General in a Fine Gael government. He was an incomparable raconteur; an admirer of P.G.

Wodehouse, he knew by heart many of his funniest passages, and connoisseurs held in high esteem his rendition of Gussy Fink-Nottle's prizegiving speech. When the days lengthened, the Common Room often adjourned to the garden for croquet in the twilight.

My stay was short: as a college lecturership is a transitory job, holders are encouraged to apply for long-term Fellowships. A vacancy at Balliol from October 1964 had been brought to my attention before I took up my lecturership, and I was offered it early in the year. My letter of resignation to Exeter and Trinity accordingly followed soon after I took up my lecturership there, and from October 1964 I became a Fellow of Balliol on a salary of £2,750 per annum.

After Exeter and Trinity, Balliol seemed at first solemn, stern, almost sombre. One of the first colleges to be founded in Oxford, it was two centuries older than Exeter and three centuries older than Trinity. However, it had preserved fewer of its ancient buildings than either, and was predominantly a mass of undistinguished or oppressive Victorian architecture. Rooms were scarce, and from my comfortable set at Exeter I moved to three unconnected undergraduate rooms, a bedroom, a teaching room, and a drawing-room, at the top of a cramped staircase. Dessert was taken in the Senior Common Room only on guest nights. Above all, the College took itself very seriously as an academic institution. It preened itself – not wholly realistically, as I came to discover – on a tradition of plain living and high thinking.

On my first morning I was given my copy of the College Statutes; as a Fellow I was now to share, on equal terms, the government of this ancient corporation. My set of keys included a master-key for the College back gate and the Master's Field. I did not yet know this was the name of the College sports ground some minutes away on Jowett Walk, so when at lunch I found myself next to Thomas Burrow, a very senior and very taciturn Fellow, Professor of Sanskrit for many years, I asked him, 'Can you tell me what is the Master's Field?' There was a pause. 'Constitutional law, if I remember rightly,' came the reply, 'but it's a long time since he did any work.'

The Master, Sir David Lindsay Keir, was indeed the author of several texts on constitutional law and history, dating from his pre-war years as a don at University College. He had since been Vice-Chancellor of the Queen's University at Belfast, and at the time of my arrival had been Master of Balliol for fifteen years. The election to succeed Lord Lindsay in 1949 had been difficult: conservative dons supported an erudite and exquisite Latinist, Roger Mynors, while those who regarded themselves as progressives favoured 'Red Robert' Birley, the unconventional Headmaster of Eton. When it became clear that Birley was unlikely to win, some of the progressives put forward Keir as a compromise candidate, and he was chosen.

By 1964 he seemed an unlikely choice as a candidate of the Left. Most of the dons regarded him as a reactionary autocrat, and Governing Body regularly voted against any measure he brought forward. During my first year as a Fellow we voted away what remained of the Master's powers to nominate to scholarships and fellowships, and replaced magisterial discretion with committees of Fellows reporting to Governing Body as a whole. Though his Canadian wife was universally beloved, Keir was not popular. With hindsight, I see how meanly we treated him, ungrateful for his services to the College; he was devoted to its welfare as he conceived it, and had supervised a highly successful centenary capital appeal which by 1963 had raised a million pounds.

During 1964/5, however, the Fellows were more concerned with electing a new Master than being fair to an old one. I arrived in time to take part in the final stages, presided over by the Senior Fellow, Theo Tylor, Tutor in Law and Estates Bursar. Tylor was an awesome figure, a chess grandmaster with a gravity of seniority which was only enhanced by his blindness. His speeches, explaining the annual accounts to Governing Body or introducing new members to the Senior Common Room, were full of precise dates and detailed statistics; it was always difficult to tell whether these were quoted from memory or read from braille notes concealed in his coat pockets. Any young Fellow who inadvertently sat in his favourite chair in the Common Room was in danger of being crushed as he lowered his enormous bottom into its accustomed place, assumed to be vacant.

Despite Tylor's prestige and authority, the election bid fair to be as difficult as that of 1949. Voting preferences among Fellows were influenced not only by the division between left and right, but also by that between arts and sciences. The two internal candidates were R.P. Bell, a chemistry Fellow in the College since 1933, and Christopher Hill, a Fellow since 1938, internationally known as a Marxist historian. Both were respected tutors, but Bell was thought to lack flair, while some Fellows could not stomach Hill's long membership of the Communist Party (terminated in 1956 in response to the Soviet repression in Hungary). As in 1949, a third candidate was introduced, by Fellows on the right who thought (correctly) that in a straight vote Hill would defeat Bell. Robert Birley very sportingly agreed to try his luck for a second time. When he dined in College I found him most impressive, and worthy of support, but when it became clear that he would not command sufficient votes I joined the majority which eventually elected Christopher Hill.

In contrast to Keir, Hill was generally liked by the Fellows, and as Master retained the affection even of those who disapproved of his politics and his policies. His election reflected the largely left-looking make-up of Governing Body at the time. The leftward tendencies of Balliol dons were, it must be said, anything but radical; apart from Christopher himself, no member of the SCR regarded himself as a Marxist, and in national politics most of us were typical Labour voters on the centre or right wing of that party. 'Being on the Left' in Balliol had less to do with socialist theory than with favouring progressive educational policies in College and University. We worked to admit more working-class students, to widen the variety of courses on offer, to relax some of the traditional disciplinary and ceremonial regulations, and to encourage the co-education of men and women – ambitions and ideals many of which, distasteful as they may have been to Keir, had been cherished by previous Masters such as Sandy Lindsay and Benjamin Jowett. In a certain sense the election of Hill, Marxist though he was, could be seen as a return to tradition after an interregnum; and this explained why his supporters included dons who in national politics were old-fashioned Conservatives.

One such was Christopher's history colleague, the medievalist Maurice Keen, whom I saw often in my first year since we were both resident bachelors. At a time when it was taken for granted that dons would make an effort to share some of the non-academic life of their pupils, only a few found time to befriend undergraduates outside their own subject. Maurice did, and I constantly admired the number of his friends among undergraduates far beyond the history school. He was (and is) one of the few surviving examples of the ideal of an Oxford tutor: devoid alike of malice and ambition, a warm and unthreatening presence in any gathering of junior members, and an agent of peace in the SCR. When first we became acquainted, he and I were a little wary of each other – perhaps an unconscious reflection of our common but divergent Irish ancestry, his Southern Protestant and mine Northern Catholic.

I was puzzled by Maurice's votes in Governing Body on matters of College policy; while conservative more often than not, they did not seem to demonstrate a coherent political attitude. Then I came to realize that his vote was determined by loyalty to whichever person or institution he had known longest. Hence he would often support Master Hill against such as myself even if, on the particular issue, I was championing the more conservative cause. It gradually dawned on me that this was an entirely appropriate attitude for an expert on the feudal system; it had the pleasing consequence that the longer I knew Maurice the more I could count on his support.

In the early 1960s, before the years of the student revolution, the Junior Common Room at Balliol was somewhat to the right of the Senior Common Room. When Governing Body voted to allow women to dine at High Table, members of the JCR, invited to extend the courtesy to women undergraduates, declined with disdain. Among the junior members of the College were several who later became prominent as Conservative politicians or theorists – Chris Patten, Roger Freeman, Adam Ridley, and Patrick Minford. Of that student generation, only Bryan Gould rose to a like eminence in the Labour Party.

Prominent among the Balliol dons, and influential in shaping the College ethos, were the tutors in the PPE school, the group I joined when I became a Fellow. Balliol was unique among Oxford colleges in having not one or two but three philosophy Fellows; and though there was some overlap, a sharp distinction was made between Greats philosophy and the philosophy that went with politics and economics. Richard Hare, the well-known moral philosopher, shared the Literae Humaniores teaching with the ancient historian Russell Meiggs and the classicists Robert Ogilvie and Jasper Griffin. As one of the PPE philosophers I joined Alan Montefiore, who had taken the initiative in recruiting me to the College, to become part of a team which included the Hungarian Thomas Balogh and the Viennese Paul Streeten as economics tutors, and the American Bill Weinstein as politics tutor (joined in 1966 by Steven Lukes). 'You'll make a change', Alan said, 'from the international Jewry which has hitherto run this Honour School.'

I did not have much chance to work with Balogh and Streeten. October 1964 was the month of the general election which brought Harold Wilson to power after thirteen years of Conservative rule. When Wilson made his victory speech, Tommy Balogh, a close adviser during the election, was visible at his shoulder. One of the decisions taken at my first Governing Body meeting was to grant leave of absence to Tommy so that he might advise on economic affairs in the Cabinet Office, and Paul Streeten soon followed him, to join the Ministry of Overseas Development. Their tutorial duties were taken over by Wilfred Beckerman, already in College as a Research Fellow, and by a series of lecturers. Several of these too, in their turn, were enrolled to advise the Wilson administration.

Philosophers were not in such demand, and Alan remained as the presiding genius of the Balliol PPE school, a tutor of enormous conscientiousness, sympathetic and fair-minded to a fault. Whenever his less tolerant colleagues were minded to discipline some idle wastrel of a pupil, Alan was indefatigable in finding extenuating circumstances for the delinquent: a broken home, perhaps, an inadequate schooling, or a trace of mental illness. The final decision on any such issue almost always reflected his judgement. In any argument, when less saintly tutors got bored or lost their tempers, Alan's smiling and untiring patience would carry the day. Not only in the PPE school, but in the College as a whole, his views prevailed. As Tutor for Admissions in these years he was in a position to influence the make-up of the college. His devotion and energy, and the resonance of his views with those of Christopher Hill, meant that he was swiftly appointed to many committees powerful in college affairs. 'This college', grumbled one Fellow of conservative temperament, 'operates on the principle of balance: each committee must contain at least one Montefiore and at least one non-Montefiore.'

The balance to be struck was between two visions of the College whose contrasts were most patent when it came to the selection of commoners during the annual admissions season. All could agree, with enthusiasm, on the academically brilliant schoolboys who had distinguished themselves in the scholarship examination, but there was often more than one opinion about the qualities to be looked for in the commoners, candidates for entry to the college who had failed to achieve scholarships.

Hugh Stretton, a Fellow of Balliol in the 1950s, has left a vivid description of the divisions between the Fellows in his time.

> The Left suspected that the Right's idea of a decent commoner was an amiable, well-connected public-school dunce, keen on rugger and beagling but usually too drunk for either, likely to pass without effort (or qualifications) into the upper-middle ranks of government or business, to the ultimate detriment of British power, prosperity, and social justice, but sure to turn up to Gaudies and quite likely to donate silver or endow a trophy or two. The Right suspected that the Left's idea of a decent commoner was a bespectacled black beetle from a nameless secondary school who would speak to nobody, swot his solitary, constipated way to an indifferent degree, then forget the College the day he left it for a job in local government, where his chief effect on the national life would be as a chronic claimant on, and voter for, the National Health.

While the Admissions Tutor was Alan Montefiore (1962–67) and after him Bill Weinstein (1967–71), a marginal candidate such as Stretton envisaged the Left favouring was far the more likely to be admitted.

By this time Balliol no longer held its own independent scholarship examination; instead, the colleges of the University were divided into three groups which conducted joint examinations. A candidate applied to a group, within which he could specify an order of preference among the colleges. The number of scholarships a college could offer was predetermined by the size of its various honour schools; each college marked the papers of the candidates who had placed it first, and had an unquestioned right to offer its scholarships to the best of those candidates. But it could not then simply go on to offer commoners' places to the best of the other candidates whose preference it was. An exercise known as 'spreading the cream' came into operation, designed to handicap particularly favoured colleges – such as Balliol – and distribute talent broadly between the colleges. For example, once Balliol had awarded its scholarships, other colleges in the group were free to offer scholarships to Balliol's potential commoners, and if they did so these candidates were obliged to accept, even though they had preferred Balliol and Balliol wished to admit them.

Oxford scholarships were originally intended to provide maintenance in college for poor students, and for much of the University's history the distinction between scholars and commoners was not so much between the clever and the not-so-clever as between the poor and the rich. But after 1945 scholarships ceased to operate as their founders had intended: when it became mandatory for local education authorities to support (subject to a means test) all students who had been accepted into universities, it no longer made sense to use scholarships to maintain poor students. Instead, they were pegged at the level of supplementary income allowed by the local authorities without financial penalty. To offer more would have led to the confiscation of part or all of a student's LEA award. So by this time scholarships served just three purposes: they were a mark of academic distinction, they provided pocket-money, and they became part of a system of intercollegiate trumping.

None the less the scholarship examination was a serious exercise, playing a part not only in the distribution of scholarships but in the overall award of places. In addition to scholarship examination marks, three other elements were taken into account by tutors in deciding whether to offer places: the actual or predicted performances in other examinations, such as A-levels; the strength of the references provided by teachers; and the interview for which each serious candidate was summoned. At Balliol, the interview programme for PPE made great demands on the tutors. Because of the size and prestige of the school, the number of candidates was large, with perhaps sixty competing for twenty places. If other colleges were to have an opportunity to exercise their trumping rights, all had to be seen within forty-eight hours, so that interviews continued from early morning to late at night.

Pupils admitted in December would come into residence the following October (or the October after that, if they were taking a gap year before university). PPE students on arrival spent two terms preparing for a preliminary examination, and it was my task to teach them elementary (mathematical) logic. Despite its routine nature, I found this teaching congenial on the whole. At least there could be no argument about whether a pupil had got something right or wrong, which was not always the case with the more contentious subjects taken after prelims, such as moral philosophy.

For the final honour schools there were two other compulsory philosophy subjects to be taught: 'logic', which really meant metaphysics and philosophy of language, and the history of philosophy, as rather selectively understood in Oxford. I taught Descartes, Locke, Berkeley and Hume; the optional Kant class was always taken by Alan, who had a remarkable gift for interesting even the dimmest pupils in that difficult philosopher. The round of tutorials was heavy for a young don still fresh to many of the topics; in my first few terms I often had to give sixteen or more, weekly, spread over several different subjects.

Arts fellows were employed both by their college and by the central University: by their college primarily to give tutorials to individuals and pairs, and by the University to give lectures open to the general academic public. In Oxford it has been traditional in Arts subjects for tutorials to be taken much more seriously than lectures; an undergraduate was not ill-regarded for cutting lectures which he found unhelpful, whereas failure to turn up for a tutorial very soon led to trouble.

Lecturing I have always found less demanding than giving tutorials. The activities of a tutor – handing out a reading list at the beginning of the week and at the end listening to and commenting on a pupil's essay – might appear less arduous than the delivery, to a large audience, of an hour's worth of original and polished text. But lectures can be on a topic of one's choice and specialization, whereas a tutor, in any given week, has to show a mastery of the contents of three or four reading lists, each designed to provide a pupil with a week's work. Lectures can be prepared at leisure, in the vacation, whereas the topic of a tutorial discussion cannot be predicted with precision before the pupil has delivered his essay. In a lecture, the teacher holds the initiative; in a tutorial, the pupil. This is, of course, what makes the tutorial, at its best, superior to the lecture as a method of teaching; but it is also what makes it a heavier load upon the teacher.

It was and is a principle of the Oxford system that pupils should not be examined for their degrees by their tutors. Tutorial teaching is arranged by colleges; final examinations are the responsibility of the federal University. This separation of powers has the merit that candidates in examinations have no incentive simply to regurgitate the ideas of their tutors. Moreover, it means that tutor and pupil are in alliance together to anticipate and defeat the wiles of the examiners in the Final Honour Schools. Within college, however, a tutor often sets and marks informal examinations: since pupils are supposed to do academic work in the vacations as well as in term time, they are subjected to examinations ('collections') on their vacation reading at the beginning of the following term. And in the last term before Final Honour Schools, there are mock examinations to be set and marked in the course of revision tutorials.

When the examinations had been completed, a week or two before the end of Trinity Term, the tutors give a dinner for the examinees. On these occasions, like Christmas Day in an officers' mess, the seniors were supposed to be willing to make fools of themselves to entertain the juniors. I still have vivid (though patchy) memories of my first PPE Schools Dinner, for a graduating year which included Adam Ridley (later an architect of Mrs Thatcher's economic policies) and David Boren (later Senator for Oklahoma). These worthy citizens were no doubt among those who left promptly when the formal dinner ended, but others stayed on into the early hours, and I recall playing croquet after darkness fell on a lawn lit only by red lanterns and winning easily by the simple expedient of moving the hoops to where my ball had gone, smiling encouragingly as some of my pupils, rather drunker than I, shied croquet balls and glass tumblers through my third-floor study window from the quad below. This called for greater skill than most could muster by that stage of the evening, and it was fortunate that the activity was interrupted by the Dean arriving to complain of the noise. I awoke next morning to find broken glass on my floor and, scrawled on my blackboard, most unfairly in the circumstances, 'Kenny is stingy with his brandy'.

After the end of term tutors would await, with almost as much impatience as candidates themselves, the eventual publication of the class list. Only in very exceptional cases did candidates fail, or receive a mere pass: what counted was whether you were placed in the first, second, third, or fourth class. (Some years later, after intense debate and much rewriting of university legislation, the fourth class was abolished and the second class split into two. This achieved little other than a renaming of the original classes as 'first, upper second, lower second, and third'.) In 1965 Balliol PPE achieved two firsts, ten seconds, and one third, a poor performance as untypical as that of 1967, when there were ten

Balliol firsts. That, it must be said, was a year when the examiners were chaired by Alan Montefiore; but as examiners have to disqualify themselves when their own pupils' classes are to be determined, all of us in Balliol were quite clear that Alan's chairmanship had not made any difference.

2

Oxford Philosophy

ABOUT THE YEAR 1960 the world of western philosophy could be mapped, without too crude a degree of over-simplification, by means of a simple diagram. You could represent the overall position by taking a square and dividing it into four. In the top left-hand quadrant, place the existentialism then in vogue in the western part of continental Europe; in the top right-hand, the analytical or linguistic tradition dominant in English-speaking countries on both sides of the Atlantic. In the bottom left-hand corner place Marxism, then the official philosophy of Eastern Europe and of China; in the bottom right-hand, the scholastic philosophy then taught throughout the world in the seminaries and universities of the Roman Catholic Church.

The location of these quadrants in the square represents the features in which these philosophies resembled and differed from each other. The philosophies in the upper part of the diagram shared a concern for the intellectual and moral autonomy of the individual: philosophy not as a set of authoritative doctrines, but as a method of thinking (analysis) or a style of life (existentialism). The philosophies in the lower part were both historically linked to institutions whose primary purpose was non-philosophical, and shared a conviction that the most important philosophical truths had been settled once for all, so that they could only be expounded, never seriously called into question. The philosophies on the right-hand side of the diagram resembled each other in their interest in purely theoretical minutiae and in their close ties with systems of formal logic, while those on the left-hand side prided themselves on their practical commitment to the basic realities of human experience, such as work, power, love and death, neither having contributed significantly to the development of mathematical logic.

Oxford, when first I encountered it as a student at the end of the 1950s, was generally regarded as the centre of the analytic tradition, or at least of the less formal branch of that tradition known as 'ordinary language philosophy'. True, the two philosophers who were commonly regarded as founders of the analytic tradition, Bertrand Russell and Ludwig Wittgenstein, had both taught at Cambridge; true, the man whom many, then as now, looked on as the most influential living philosopher was the Harvard Professor, W.V.O. Quine. None the less, no other university in the English-speaking world could assemble such a collection of talent in the analytic tradition: Gilbert Ryle at Magdalen, John Austin at Corpus Christi, Herbert Hart at Univ. and H.H. Price at New College, together with a score of younger dons of international reputation, made Oxford the most exciting place in the world for a graduate student in analytical philosophy.

When I returned in 1963 there had been some changes. Price had retired and been succeeded by A.J. Ayer, who as a young don in his twenties before the Second World War had established a reputation as the leading English logical positivist. His return to Oxford was not universally popular: indeed, his election was railroaded through by the Vice-Chancellor against the votes of the senior philosophical electors, and both Austin and Ryle resigned from the electoral board in protest. Shortly after, Austin had died at the tragically early age of 48; in the Chair of Moral Philosophy he had been succeeded by a learned historian of logic, William Kneale. Despite the early signs of a brain-drain from Oxford to the US, Oxford philosophy was still in its self-confident heyday.

My own initial training had been in the scholastic tradition: as a seminarist attending the Gregorian University in Rome I had studied philosophy for three years and theology for four. I obtained neither pleasure nor profit from the philosophy course, based on Latin neo-scholastic textbooks and communicated through Latin lectures. Nor did I admire the philosophy lecturers, with the exception of a Dutch Jesuit, Fr Peter Hoenen, who taught cosmology and philosophy of science. Though we were officially learning Aristotelian and Thomist philosophy, in three years we read no actual texts of either philosopher, except for one book of Aristotle's *De Anima* and Aquinas' tiny pamphlet *De Ente et Essentia*.

It was, paradoxically, through the theology course that I learnt most of the scholastic philosophy which has proved useful in my later career as a professional philosopher. It was under the supervision of one of the theology lecturers, Fr Bernard Lonergan, that I wrote my doctoral thesis on linguistic analysis and the philosophy of religion, submitted to the faculty of theology, not that of philosophy. In the course of preparing this thesis I first came to close grips with the analytic tradition, and to write it I first came, as a student, to Oxford. Paradoxically, again, it was at Oxford that I first came fully to appreciate the genius of Aquinas, though the ground had been well prepared by Lonergan.

While working in Oxford on my Roman thesis I had also – for reasons to do with the funding of my studies – enrolled as a student for an Oxford D.Phil. The title of my Oxford thesis was 'The intentionality of psychological verbs': its purpose was to set out the logical structure of the language in which we express desire, intention, decision, and emotion. My work was very much influenced by the writings of Wittgenstein, and by discussion with two of his former pupils, Elizabeth Anscombe, then a Fellow of Somerville, and her husband Peter Geach, who taught in Birmingham.

No doubt it was on the basis of my D.Phil. thesis, published in 1963 as *Action, Emotion and Will,* that I was elected to my jobs at Exeter and at Balliol. It was wonderful to be able to join, on equal terms now, in discussion with the leading analytical thinkers. On some point of business I wrote to Gilbert Ryle, as 'Professor Ryle'; he wrote back 'Dear Kenny', and insisted that I must address him as 'Dear Ryle' – 'We are colleagues now, I am glad to say.' I was touched by this old-fashioned compliment, though with most of the other philosophers I revered I was already on Christian-name terms.

Elizabeth Anscombe invited me to give joint courses with her, and I discussed philosophy with her and Peter at their Oxford house during term time, and during the vacations at their summer shack at the Foxholes, a beautiful but primitive place in the hills where Shropshire meets Wales, where guests slept in tents, took cold showers at 6 a.m., and used an open-air privy under a fresco of the Last Judgement. Here, too, Elizabeth tried, in vain, to teach me horse-riding.

In Balliol I enjoyed keen philosophical argument with my Greats colleague, Richard Hare. Perhaps the most influential moral philosopher in Britain, he had worked out a toughly-wrought system which represented moral judgements as analogous to commands addressed to oneself and to the moral community. We shared a keen interest in the logic of imperative language, but I could not agree with his thesis that moral judgements could not be regarded as stating truths or falsehoods. His position was well entrenched, and he was skilled at anticipating and turning aside any criticism I could devise. I found it more rewarding to discuss such neutral philosophical topics as the nature of time, when his keen intelligence operated free of the constraints of publicly adopted battle-lines. We often walked along the sodden towpaths of the Thames, where he took most unfair advantage of his great height, launching a challenge just before striding across a puddle with his long legs, leaving me to think of an answer as I splashed through the muddy water, two steps to his one.

Though I returned to Oxford with an established position as a writer in the analytic tradition, large areas of the undergraduate syllabuses were unknown to me. I had never, for instance, read right through Plato's *Republic* or Aristotle's *Ethics*. It was not difficult to master Aristotle's ethical system: a lot was, unbeknownst, familiar to me through Catholic moral theology. Plato was much harder going, especially as I had to rely on hazy memories of A-level Greek while teaching scholars fresh from Demosthenes and Pindar in the Mods course. I suspect some of my brighter Greats pupils laid traps to find out the gaps in my knowledge.

However, I enjoyed Greek philosophy much more than the historical papers I taught the PPE students who were my main responsibility. In the PPE syllabus, the core authors were Descartes, Locke, Berkeley, and Hume. I could not relish reading and teaching their texts in English, nor could I accept the contrast drawn in histories of philosophy between continental rationalism and British empiricism. To this day it seems to me that Locke's importance – apart from his interesting conundrums on personal identity – is simply that he is the most intelligent and eloquent advocate in English of the mistaken ideas which are common to both rationalism and empiricism. Berkeley is an elegant writer who framed a number of other people's arguments in their most congenial English form. Hume is of greater importance, but principally because of his writing on causation, which stimulated Kant to some of his most insightful writing. In a university where the native language was not English, one would not, I believe, spend much time on any of the British Empiricists.

Initially, I took the same jaundiced view of Descartes. Early in 1964 an American academic, impressed by *Action, Emotion and Will*, approached me to write a popular textbook on Descartes for Random House. 'Why would anyone want a book on Descartes?' I asked Elizabeth Anscombe. 'His whole system could be written on the back of a postcard: he had only two ideas, both of them wrong.' 'If you think he is not worth writing about,' was the reply, 'you ought to do so in order to teach you better.' I accepted the contract, and the cure worked. A systematic reading of Descartes' work soon convinced me that he well deserved his status as father of the modern mind. He and Kant, in my view, tower above the three philosphers of the empiricist canon.

Much of my vacation time in 1964 and 1965 was spent reading in preparation for this book. Descartes is a marvellously skilful writer, his French and Latin prose so smooth that it goes down very easily at first reading – 'like a novel', as he said himself. His thought, however, is so carefully woven that a scholar can return again and again to his deceptively simple pages and find new texture in them. The works Descartes published in his lifetime can be read in a few days, though a modern reader who wishes to master his ideas must also read widely in his extensive correspondence.

I thoroughly enjoyed myself. In the winter vacation I worked through the elegantly printed and handsomely bound volumes of the Adam and Tannery edition of Descartes' works, late into the night in the fifteenth-century Balliol library, under the oddly comforting grunting of the College clock. In warmer vacations I carried the Pléiade pocket edition under the willows beside the river in the Parks, piecing together the philosopher's thoughts and seeing how his system fitted so wonderfully together.

My enjoyment notwithstanding, I continued, then as now, to think that the system is fundamentally mistaken. If you did want to put Descartes' ideas on the back of a postcard, you would need just two sentences: 'Man is a thinking mind'; 'Matter is extension in motion'. Everything in the system is to be explained in terms of this dualism of mind and matter. Indeed, it is because of Descartes that we think of mind and matter as the two great mutually exclusive and mutually exhaustive divisions of the universe we inhabit.

Both these great principles were mistaken. In Descartes' own lifetime his notions of matter and motion were shown to be inadequate, by themselves, to explain phenomena such as the circulation of the blood. His view of the nature of mind, as a locus of private consciousness only contingently connected with an animal body, endured much longer than his view of matter. Indeed, it is still the most widespread view of mind among educated people in the West who are not professional philosophers. In our century the theory was exposed as fundamentally incoherent by Wittgenstein, who showed that even when we think our most private and spiritual thoughts we are employing the medium of a language which is essentially tied to its public and bodily expression. But it is a measure of the enormous influence of Descartes that even those who most admire the genius of Wittgenstein think that his greatest achievement was the overthrow of Descartes' philosophy of mind.

In my book I tried to present Descartes' ideas in such a way as to bring out the internal richness and toughness of his system, while showing that it rested on assumptions which Wittgenstein had shown to be fundamentally untenable. Traditionally, there have been two major criticisms of Descartes: one, that his epistemology is fundamentally circular; the other, that he misrepresents the relationship between the mind and the body. I did my best to refute the first of these allegations, while bringing out the new force which Wittgenstein's work had given to the second.

In the course of writing the book I came to appreciate how many of Descartes' most interesting philosophical ideas are stated only obliquely in his published works and explained fully only in his correspondence – very little of which was then available in English. I therefore translated a selection of his letters, which with a brief commentary were published by the Oxford University Press in 1970, and have since been incorporated in the Cambridge University Press three-volume edition which is now the standard English version of Descartes' works.

On a visit to Paris shortly after finishing my Random House book, I remembered reading that Descartes' skull was preserved in the Musée de l'Homme. He had died in Sweden. Summoned there by Queen Christina, he was required by the busy monarch to give her philosophy lectures in the chilly pre-dawn hours. At his death, a victim of the Nordic winter, his body had been returned for burial in the church of Saint-Germain in Paris; but his skull had been retained, and returned to France only much later. I visited the museum and made my way to the place where the guidebook led one to believe it was to be found. There was indeed a glass case containing three skulls. One was labelled as Boileau's, the others bore names which meant nothing to me. A rather sleepy guide seemed surprised that Descartes' skull was no longer on view. He pointed out that the case bore the title 'Skulls of geniuses and of criminals'. I demanded to see the museum's director, and was eventually shown to his office.

The director received me genially in a room full of filing cabinets and bric-à-brac. It was a scandal, I complained, if scholars travelling from foreign countries to view the great man's skull found it missing from its appropriate place. 'Ah, *monsieur,*' he said, 'you have seen the case from which we removed it. It did not seem decent for the great Descartes to be displayed between two thieves – in spite, you understand, of the illustrious precedent.' 'So where it is now?' I asked. He went over to a filing cabinet labelled C–D, drew out a skull, and laid it in my lap. '*Voici, monsieur: le crâne de M. Descartes.*' The most striking feature of the skull was that it was scribbled over with Latin verses: inscribed, I learnt, by admirers during its sojourn in Sweden. I did not quite know how to react to the relic: should I kiss it, or kneel before it? I handed it back to the curator, asking whether it had any special characteristics. '*Non,*' he said sadly, '*un crâne tout à fait normal.*'

I tried out drafts of the Descartes book as lectures, using the audience's reaction as a guide to revision. This is a common practice: it is significant how many books by Oxford philosophers consist of eight chapters, one for each week of term and each taking fifty minutes to read aloud.

During 1965, because of a colleague's absence on sabbatical, I also had to give the standard lectures on propositional and predicate calculus for students studying symbolic logic. I was tickled to find myself lecturing to mathematicians as well as philosophers, despite having given up maths after O-level. I had always regretted being a mathematical ignoramus, so that it gave me an absurd pleasure to be billed on a mathematics lecture list. I have never quite lost the feeling that mathematics is the archetypal academic subject: pure exercise of intelligence unfettered by matter or emotion. But it was a good thing I did not have to give the logic lectures more than once, as I could not carry a proof of any length in my head sufficiently well to reproduce it on a blackboard.

At the time, I believed many problems in philosophy could be resolved by the application of methods of mathematical logic. This belief was fostered by my admiration for Arthur Prior, a New Zealander and Professor of Philosophy at Manchester who, with his wife, had befriended me while I was a curate in Liverpool. Arthur did indeed combine great skill as a logician with keen philosophical insight in a way unsurpassed by anyone else I have met since; I now think my exaggerated respect for the philosophical importance of mathematical logic was engendered by his unusual and personal talents.

I had kept in touch with the Priors, and often wished they were closer at hand. In June 1965, on the retirement of William Kneale, the Oxford Chair in Moral Philosophy fell vacant, and Arthur applied. Though he was primarily a logician and metaphysician, he had written respected works on moral philosophy, and electors to Oxford professorships customarily sat rather loosely to the formal descriptions of the chairs. Elizabeth Anscombe also applied; but the successful candidate was my Balliol colleague Richard Hare.

This left a vacancy in Balliol for a Greats philosophy tutor and I saw an opportunity to move from being responsible for the PPE philosophy syllabus, with which I had never been wholly comfortable, to becoming part of the Greats team. My colleagues agreed; the vacant Balliol Fellowship was advertised as a non-classical philosophy post. I was very pleased when Alan Montefiore suggested trying to head-hunt Arthur Prior for it, and delighted when he agreed to come, in spite of it being technically a downward step from his Manchester professorship. It was an enormous pleasure to have him as a colleague from October 1966.

On Hare's departure I moved into the teaching room he had vacated at the top of Balliol's winding, turreted staircase III. Long and narrow, with a view over our front quad at one end and Trinity's garden at the other, it was larger than my earlier study, but neither grand nor cheerful: it was once used by the BBC for a ghoulish Graham Greene film about an undergraduate attempt to raise the spirits of the dead.

On becoming a Greats tutor, I acquired a new set of immediate colleagues. The senior was the Ancient Historian Russell Meiggs, the world expert on Roman Ostia, immediately recognizable throughout Oxford, and indeed Europe, by the then unfashionable length of his bristling hair. He was a remarkably effective tutor, who made friends of his pupils for life: wherever around the world I later met Balliol alumni, the first question they asked about the College was 'How is Russell Meiggs?'

Harold Macmillan once reported one of his own Greats tutors as saying: 'Nothing you will learn in the course of your studies will be of the slightest possible use to you in after life – save only this – that if you work hard and diligently you should be able to detect when a man is talking rot, and that, in my view, is the main, if not the sole, purpose of education.' That was one thing Russell gave his pupils: an ability to see through what he called the Higher Nonsense.

The other was an enormous zest for the discovery of detail in the pursuit of an academic goal. He displayed this in his own work, be it on the Athenian Empire or the history of timber in ancient times – drawing on every scrap of evidence, whether from literary texts, inscriptions, or physical remains lingering on the spot. All round the world others were drawn into the chase. Many a legend tells of Oxford colleagues on classical hillsides or in secular forests meeting a shepherd or a lumberjack who said, 'If you are from Oxford you must know Meiggs.' Letters and postcards from the corners of the earth brought morsels of evidence, and diplomatic bags contained specimens relevant to his research.

It was not only Russell's Classics pupils who became and remained friends. Whenever he crossed the quad he would stop for a brisk word, a pointed joke, with half a dozen students met at random; whatever subject they were studying, all could recognize Mr Meiggs. He was the Warden ('Praefectus') of Holywell Manor – a Balliol annexe which was almost a college within a college. Running the Manor brought him into contact with students from home and overseas, graduate and undergraduate, male and female, artists and scientists.

A shrewd judge of character, who took pains to inform himself about the lives of his colleagues and pupils, Russell never indulged in malicious gossip. The unkindest thing I ever heard him say about anyone was, 'That man has never looked a tree in the face in his life.' But he was so fearless in putting candid questions, and was himself so free of humbug, that conversation with him could be like a cold shower washing off one's pretence and superficiality. In this respect his Balliol colleagues owed him every bit as much as his pupils.

In many ways Russell made me think of Dr Johnson. He had some of the same endearing eccentricities, and he exhibited to his colleagues and pupils that hatred of self-deception which led Johnson to say to Boswell, 'My dear friend, clear your mind of cant . . .' Above all he had the same ability to rise, by sheer power of will, above the recurrent threat of melancholy and the burden of disability and illness. Russell and I taught the classicists during the last two years of their four-year course, taking them over from the 'Mods' dons, Robert Ogilvie and Jasper Griffin, who taught them Greek and Latin literature for Honour Moderations, the taxing half-way examinations which were then taken before moving on to philosophy and ancient history.

Robert Ogilvie, when I first knew him, seemed to incarnate the legendary Balliol ideal of effortless superiority. Already the author of several books, including a very learned commentary on Livy, he always appeared completely at his ease in the company of his pupils, and entered into every aspect of their lives. He took in hand my education as a tutor, and lent me a book in which he had written a chapter on how to do the job. He often seemed to fit in his kindnesses to me between more important engagements with people I had never heard of, but clearly should have. The fullness of his life showed itself in his clothing – he might wear tails in chapel, or squash clothes at a tutor's meeting, clearly about to leave for some function of greater moment.

Jasper was junior to Robert, without a comparable academic reputation as yet; but I found him more formidable as a scholar, completely at home in the Greek and Latin classics, and apparently with almost total recall of the literature of several other languages. He was an intellectual giant, but a gentle giant: while fearsome in exposing any false pretensions among his colleagues, he never used his learning to bully his less gifted pupils. A fastidious stylist, he published little in his early years, though his learning was often at the service of less gifted writers. He was capable of deep affection and strong dislikes, both gracefully concealed beneath a veil of epigrammatic courtesy. I became, and remain, very fond of him.

We Greats tutors were fortunate in our pupils. One of the first philosophy students I encountered when moving to Balliol from Exeter and Trinity was Jonathan Barnes. I quickly found it a tough intellectual challenge to respond to his essays in tutorials: it was something of a relief to discover that he was not a typical Balliol undergraduate, but quite exceptionally able. In one of my first Governing Body meetings we voted to allow him to marry: scholars still needed permission to do so if they were not to forfeit their scholarships. Jonathan must have been one of the last to be jumped through that particular hoop.

There were many pupils of very high calibre reading Classics or PPE. Several I taught in my first years at Balliol now have an international reputation as professors of philosophy or classics: Kit Fine, for instance, Stephen Clark, Norman Daniels, Oliver O'Donovan, Christopher Pelling, Richard Jenkyns and Antony Price. Others made their reputations elsewhere, such as Paul Findlay at Covent Garden, Philip Spender at *Index on Censorship*, and Christopher Hitchens as author and journalist. Balliol continued also to attract highly talented graduate students in philosophy, such as Malcolm Schofield, Ralph Walker, and Anselm Müller.

At this time many UK philosophers were being tempted by offers from expanding departments in American universities. Though I had never been to the States I too began to receive inquiries, and was particularly attracted by invitations from the Universities of Chicago and Pennsylvania. I wrote to an American friend setting out the pros and cons.

> Philosophers in US Universities are better paid and worked less hard in term time than we are here. On the other hand I think we have advantages here – there is much more security of tenure and much less rat-racing up the hierarchy here. (A college fellowship is for life, if you want to keep it, with salary rising according to age – so once you are here you're free from further ambition and worry, if you don't want a professorship.) The pupils here, I gather, are on the average brighter than in any single American university – at least in this College, which collects some of the cleverest – and Oxford, I imagine, is architecturally more beautiful, and certainly older, than any American university. Then the college system is very congenial – you meet colleagues from every discipline each day at free meals, and you have free rooms, or a free house if you are married. So I think there's a good deal to be said for both systems.

Action, Emotion and Will continued to do well. One day the philosophy manager of Blackwell's bookshop told me my books sold better than any other philosopher's except Wittgenstein; perhaps he said that to all his authors. In May of 1965 a professor from Stanford, whose name was quite new to me, called on me at Balliol and told me he had been writing a full-length review of my book for the *Journal of Philosophy*. He was particularly taken with my treatment of the logic of adverbs. In the event, the review turned into a much more important article: his own solution to the problems on human action I had addressed. He was Donald Davidson, and had at this time only recently switched disciplines, comparatively late in life, from psychology to philosophy; he was to become one of the best-known philosophers in the US.

While links between British and US philosophy were very close, there was still in the 1960s a great divide between Oxford philosophers and those across the Channel. Alan Montefiore was fluent in French and anxious to build links between the two traditions: he set up an arrangement whereby each term two philosophers from the École Normale Supérieure would exchange with two from Oxford. One of our regular visitors was Jacques Derrida, not yet world-famous as the founder of deconstructionism, but already coming to prominence through works such as *Grammatologie*. At this time he was less arrogant and histrionic in style than he later became, but even then it was not easy for either of us to get much out of the other's writings; the most rewarding form of communication was to read closely together the text of some philosopher we both revered, such as Descartes.

Sadly, this attempt to bridge the gap between analytical and continental philosophy was brought to a premature end. In 1970, in the aftermath of the Paris *événements*, riotous students at a *bal prolétarien* burnt part of the library of the École Normale, and the funds which had supported our academic exchanges were used instead to fill gaps in the library.

During the 1960s, however, the philosophical blocks represented by my four-part diagram had begun to crumble, fissure and shift. The Second Vatican Council, inaugurated in 1962, led within the Roman Catholic Church to a period of liberalization; in the course of this, neo-scholasticism lost much of its canonical status, and by the next decade the staff of a seminary was likely to be as well versed in existentialism as in Thomism. Simultaneously, classical existentialism was losing ground where once it had held sway; Heidegger's influence went into severe decline, and Sartre, in the latter part of his life, was more interested in Marxism than in his earlier battles against essentialism.

Whereas in the 1950s and early 1960s there had been an almost impenetrable barrier between Anglo-American and Continental philosophy, by the end of the 1960s Germany, Italy, and (after the death of Franco) Spain had become more hospitable to analytical methods. Simultaneously, the philosophical ideas engendered in France by such as Derrida were finding favour in Britain and the US, if more commonly in departments of literature than of philosophy.

Analytical philosophy, too, began to alter from the simple squaring-off of the 1960s. The most obvious changes were a decline in self-confidence and a movement of centre of gravity. In 1960 Oxford was the unquestioned centre of the analytic movement, and philosophers came from the US to sit at the feet of Oxford philosophers. Analytic practitioners prided themselves on being the heirs of two philosophers of undoubted genius, Russell and Wittgenstein, and saw their task as being to exploit this happy endowment and share it with the rest of the philosophical world. In the years since the 1960s the leadership of the analytic movement has shifted definitively across the Atlantic, though no single American university has inherited the dominant role once enjoyed by Oxford. The tradition of Russell and Wittgenstein no longer commands universal respect; but no newer genius has emerged to succeed to an equal, uncontested esteem. Russell and Wittgenstein redefined the nature of philosophy, by placing the study of language at its heart, and by convincing their adherents that the task of philosophy was to study the way we express our thoughts, and to make those thoughts clear by tidying up any confusions in the language in which we express them. Some philosophers have resiled from these insights, but no one has succeeded in offering a superior definition of the nature of philosophy.

During the 1960s Anglo-American philosophy ceased to present even the appearance of a unified school. The label 'linguistic philosophy' had, indeed, always been a confusing one. 'Philosophy is linguistic', I wrote in an article in 1966,

> can mean at least six different things. (1) The study of language is a useful philosophical tool. (2) It is the only philosophical tool. (3) Language is the only subject matter of philosophy. (4) Necessary truths are established by linguistic convention. (5) Man is fundamentally a language-using animal. (6) Everyday language has a status of privilege over technical and formal systems. These six propositions are independent of each other. (1) has been accepted in practice by every philosopher since Plato. On the other five, philosophers have been and are divided, including [contemporary analytical philosophers]. In my own view (1) and (5) are true, and the remainder false.

As the 1960s developed, and the centre of gravity shifted from Oxford to the US, analytical philosophy in a certain sense became more linguistic, in that a major task of philosophy became the construction of a systematic theory of language. But the theories of language which became fashionable after the entrance of Davidson onto the scene were far removed from the philosophy of language presented by the ordinary language philosophers of the Oxford of the 1960s.

3

Engagement and Marriage

ONE OF THE Oxford philosophers I saw quite often was Brian McGuinness of Queen's: we shared a Catholic background, and a keen interest in Wittgenstein. Brian's wife Rosamund, known as 'Corky', was an American musicologist, a graduate of Vassar College. In the Easter vacation of 1965, at the end of my second term at Balliol, the Vassar madrigal singers came to Europe, and performed at Oxford. Keen to ensure them a respectable audience, Corky sent round invitations to Brian's colleagues: 'Come and hear some beautiful music sung by beautiful girls, and meet them at a party afterwards.'

The Trinity philosopher Bede Rundle and I went, listened to the Byrd and Tallis and Monteverdi, and joined the singers at the McGuinness's house in Moreton Road. I was struck by one of the sopranos, Nancy Caroline Gayley from Swarthmore in Pennsylvania; the next night, Bede and I took her and a friend to dinner. The madrigalists went on to London; I followed, and spent much of the next few days with Nancy, in parks and museums. By the time the group left for home, ten days after our first meeting, I was firmly in love. Nancy and I agreed to write.

Nancy was in her senior year at Vassar, a music major who had taken some philosophy courses; she was twenty-two, twelve and half years my junior. Her family were Presbyterians, much involved with the church community, of which her father was an elder. After her BA she was considering graduate studies in theology.

We wrote regularly, almost daily, throughout Trinity Term. I spelt out my past history, described the life of a Balliol don; Nancy's letters took me day by day through her final term at Vassar; we discussed our common interest in theology. As May wore on, my own became more explicitly love letters. I was silently amused when Corky McGuinness, at a later party for philosophers, said: 'Very different from the last party, isn't it? – I bet all those young American girls made you feel very paternal.' Nancy was more cautious, and not until July did she say in so many words that she was in love with me. But long before then we had agreed that I should come and spend part of the long vacation with her family. To pay my fare I arranged to give lectures at three American universities: Penn, Pittsburgh and Brown.

We spent idyllic weeks together in August and September, partly at the Gayleys' house in Swarthmore, partly at a family holiday home on the ocean in New Jersey. Nancy's mother Betty, a warm, self-sacrificing person, shared Nancy's musical and artistic interests but always thought of herself primarily as a home-maker. Hank, Nancy's father, was an advertising copywriter in Philadelphia, but unhappy that his considerable verbal skills were being used to no higher purpose; he could be overbearing to his family. But since his war service he had been a great Anglophile, and he enjoyed the company of academics – why else choose to live in a college town like Swarthmore? – so I was on a good footing with him from the start. Nancy's two younger sisters, Stephanie and Sandy, were both still at Swarthmore High School.

I was made to feel a part of the family, and of the close-knit Swarthmore community. I was charmed by the grey fieldstone and abundant trees of the little town, and loved the relaxed, friendly way families overflowed into each other's houses. It seemed very different from my own solitary and cloistered upbringing. But though Hank and Betty made me most welcome, they were also wary: where was this rapturous relationship going to lead? The differences between Nancy and myself in age, nationality, and religion, all spoke against the wisdom of a marriage.

It was, indeed, highly imprudent of me to have fallen so deeply in love that I wanted to be with Nancy for the rest of my life. When I was laicized, I was not released from the official requirement of celibacy; and despite my long-standing scepticism, I had not yet made any definitive break with the Catholic Church. Sooner or later I would in any case have had to put an end to this twilight state of half-Catholicism; but it would have been kinder to do so before entangling Nancy in the complications of theology and canon law.

When Nancy saw me off from Boston Airport after my last lecture at Brown, it was agreed between us that she would come to stay with my family in Cheshire at Christmas. Between September and December, we would try to disentangle the theological issues and decide whether we could marry with clear consciences; if so, we would become engaged at Christmas.

The daily letters exchanged during the autumn were a strange mixture of passionate emotion and theological disceptation. We compared at length the Presbyterian and Catholic positions on issues of Church government. Neither of us wished to convert the other: indeed, it would have been impudent of me to seek to recruit someone else to a religion I had myself long been on the point of leaving. Biblical texts flew to and fro, and we agreed that the hierarchical structure which divided the two churches could not be established from the New Testament; this was important, because it meant that the authority whose legislation prohibited me from marrying could be rejected without a rejection of Christianity.

But an unexpected difficulty arose. Whether or not the legislation imposed by canon law was binding, Nancy held that if I had actually taken a vow of celibacy, that was a promise to God, not to the Church, and ought to be kept. My reply was that I had done no such thing: monks and nuns vowed celibacy, but parochial clergy like myself were merely bound to it by an arbitrary law of the Church. (This was, and is, standard Catholic teaching.) But then I discovered in my files a paper I had signed on becoming a subdeacon (the stage at which the obligation of celibacy is imposed) which looked on the face of it rather like a vow. I sent it across the Atlantic, and for several letters we argued about its implications. In the end I convinced Nancy that it was not a vow but an oath: a statement on oath that I was freely accepting the obligations Church law placed on me. The distinction between a vow (a promise to God) and an oath (calling God to witness to the truth of a statement) is commonplace among Catholics; but I think that for a while Nancy suspected it of being a Jesuitical sophistry I had dreamt up on the spur of the moment.

Support came from an unexpected angle. I reported my troubles to Arthur Prior, who earlier in his life had been a Presbyterian elder. I told him Nancy's opinion about the keeping of vows, and asked if this was a common Presbyterian view. No, he said: 'Calvin is very sharp and explicit', he wrote, 'on the non-binding character of priestly vows of celibacy, in his *Institutes*, and I have never heard of any Presbyterian theologians taking any other view. Mary's father [a minister] once married an ex-priest, and it is a thing I'm sure he wouldn't have thought twice about, though he was in fact more than ordinarily rigorous about promises.'

My mother, though she had not yet met Nancy, was enthusiastic about the idea of my marrying, but also quite clear how the religious problem should be solved: I must apply to the Vatican for a dispensation from celibacy. Very reluctant to have any more dealings with the Vatican authorities, I did however write to a friendly canon lawyer in Rome to ask what the procedures were. I described his answer to Nancy:

> I had a letter from Orsy, the Jesuit in Rome. He says it is unlikely that I'll get
> a dispensation from the Pope. The procedure is this: I should write to my
> former Bishop, Heenan, and to the Holy Office. I am very unwilling to have
> any dealings with the Inquisition at all, and he says I would have to tell them
> all the reasons why I thought my obligation was unfair. I hate the idea of
> doing this – as you know, I find it hard to write even to you on this topic, let
> alone to the Cardinals of the Inquisition. Of course, I'd do anything, however
> revolting, if it made the difference between marrying you and not. But that
> depends on your position now about my vow or obligation. Write soon about
> it, so I can decide whether to write to the Holy Office or not.

However, the more I thought about this, the less I liked it. To apply for a
dispensation would amount to accepting an authority whose legitimacy
I had already rejected, and I was reluctant to do this, even to comfort my
family. Moreover, I was fairly certain that, provided Nancy agreed, we
would go ahead and marry even if the Holy Office turned down my
request. My priest uncle, Alec, played a great part in my life. I asked him
what it would mean to him and my mother if I married without a dispensation. He said, 'It doesn't make any difference to us if it doesn't
make any difference to your own conscience.' I asked him, 'If I decided
with a clear conscience that I should get married not in a Catholic
church, would you come to the wedding?' and he said, 'Like a shot.'

In fact, in the later 1960s and the 1970s many ex-priests received permission from Rome to marry, or had their irregular marriages recognized by the Curia. But in the long term I was glad I had not succumbed
to the temptation to apply for a dispensation, which would have prolonged my entanglement with a Church whose authority I had long
since ceased to venerate.

Nancy had now started a graduate course in theology at Drew
University. Our relationship did not have a good effect on her academic
progress. On the one hand, the theology she was studying was heavily
influenced by a continental style of philosophy which did not keep easy
company with the analytic philosophy she was becoming familiar with
from my writings and those of my Oxford friends. (Not that she necessarily found analytic philosophy congenial: she was repelled by an
article of one of my colleagues which contained the sentence 'We in
Oxford are content to be the heirs of Plato and Aristotle'.) On the other
hand, the schizophrenic nature of our correspondence took its toll. At
the end of October I wrote, accompanying a theological treatise on the
Church and the Kingdom of God:

> In previous letters I've expressed the same impatience as you about waiting
> until Christmas [to decide to be married], and also given reasons why we
> *should* wait. It seems to me that the decision can only be honest if based on

actual theological *work*, not just on what I feel or am inclined to say about the Roman Catholic Church. This may seem very tedious and arid but its very aridity should be some sort of guarantee of objectivity. Remember, darling, that you already believe that what we want to be true (viz., that the RCC is false in its claims) *is* the truth, so you must think we can only *gain* by going into it as fully as possible. My dearest, whom every day I long for, I keep on wanting to say, as you sometimes do, 'oh let's be married and forget about the theology' – but we both know in our better moments that that isn't right. On the other hand, one can't go on teetering for ever, that's not fair to either of us, and that's why we set Christmas as a deadline. I'm very sorry, though, that you can't work. I did try so hard not to upset your academic plans – and in spite of that I've made havoc of them! I'm afraid I don't find it hard to work. This is largely because my work is teaching and just has to be done, I have to say *something* to my pupils and audiences. But because of you I actually work much *better* – I'm teaching in a more lively and interesting manner than I've ever done before, I can feel it and see it in my pupils' faces and work. This shows, I think, that the real me underneath doesn't believe we shall ever be separated, however hard the theological me tries to keep an open mind.

When I re-read the anguished correspondence of the autumn of 1965, it seems almost a miracle that we have now had thirty years of happy and uncomplicated marriage together. But perhaps the two are connected: a relationship that could survive the torment of our trans-atlantic courtship could survive anything.

Even when Nancy arrived in England in December there were some days of gloom and despair. But by Boxing Day we had resolved our uncertainties, and became engaged to each other by a stream in a wood near my family's house in Hale Barns. Mother and Alec were delighted with Nancy, and kept to themselves their lingering regrets that we were not to have a Catholic marriage. The date of the wedding was now fixed for 2 April 1966. Nancy had decided to withdraw from her unsatisfac-tory theology course at Drew and concentrate on preparation for married life.

The last term of our epistolary courtship was much more cheerful. I told my Balliol colleagues of my plans to marry, and they were gratify-ingly enthusiastic. Balliol owned a number of houses for married fellows, which were awarded on seniority. Hare's promotion to the Professorship of Moral Philosophy meant that he would migrate from Balliol to Corpus Christi and vacate his college house in St Margaret's Road. The Engineering Fellow, Alasdair Howatson, had become a Fellow shortly after me, but had long been married and had a family; like me, he was unprovided with a house. Christopher Hill adjudicated that since the Hares were not leaving until after April 2nd I would be the senior married fellow when the house fell vacant, and accordingly had the prior claim.

I was rather uncomfortable about this, as the house was large for a newly-married couple with no children and hardly any furniture. But the matter never came to an issue, because our problem was solved by the Priors. On a visit to Oxford in preparation for Arthur's coming to Balliol as a Fellow in October, they had bought a small house. They offered us the use of it rent free and furnished between our wedding and their arrival. It was ideal, and would give us time to look around to find a house that suited us. The Fellows in the Senior Common Room clubbed together to buy us an antique wooden chest, and so we had at least one item of furniture of our own.

It took some time for us to settle where our marriage should take place. The natural choice would have been the Gayleys' own Presbyterian Church in Swarthmore, but Hank and Betty suspected Mother and Alec might be uncomfortable about a wedding in a non-Catholic church, and it was finally agreed that the ceremony should take place in the drawing room of their house; a family friend who was a Presbyterian minister would officiate, and Alec would take part in the ceremony.

As soon as Hilary Term ended I went to stay first with Nancy in New York and then with her family in Swarthmore, to have the required pre-marriage medical test, and apply for a licence. (I resented being asked to state my race on the licence form, and refused to do so; but it does not seem to have invalidated the marriage under Pennsylvania law.) As I knew no one outside Nancy's family, there was the problem of a best man. Hans Oberdiek, of the Philosophy Department at Swarthmore, had never met me but knew my writings, and volunteered.

We were married according to the Presbyterian rite, and Alec pronounced a blessing he had written.

> In the presence of God the Father of us all these two children of his who are so dear to him, and so near and dear to us, have declared their love and pledged their loyalty.
>
> Through the one who said, 'Where two or three are gathered in my name I am there in the midst of them', we all pray together for their happiness and for their peace. We pray that their love may grow broader and deeper still with every joy they share – and every sorrow.
>
> And now in the place of a father to one and of a second father to the other, standing by the side of their dear parents, with a full heart I pray God to bless them.
>
> My dearest children, I wish you this blessing through God's beloved son and sign you with the sign of his cross. And may God teach you to help each other to his eternal truth and to everlasting life.

Nancy's family and friends outnumbered mine by more than fifty to one, but there were telegrams of good will from friends in England, and on my return I found many letters of congratulation. Of the numerous Catholic friends who wrote to me, only one rebuked me for marrying; some years later he came out as a homosexual. But the Catholic philosophers to whom I had been closest, Elizabeth Anscombe and Peter Geach, were deeply saddened by my rejection of the Church's authority.

Our honeymoon was spent partly in Paris and partly in a cottage in Welshampton, on the border between Wales and Cheshire, which the Priors had placed at our disposal; back in Oxford, we took further advantage of the Priors' generosity, moving into their house in the Paddox for Trinity Term while we looked for a house of our own. From Charles Caine, the Bursar of St Peter's College, we finally bought an expanded labourer's cottage, its beamed central part dating from the early nineteenth century. It was near Farmoor, on a lane off the road to the Eynsham toll bridge, built by the lawyer Blackstone so that travellers could avoid the highwayman-infested Wytham Woods route. There were no neighbours within half a mile; the cottage backed on to one farm and faced another, and we had a glorious view across the fields and woods towards the Cumnor hills until a disfiguring chain of pylons was constructed across our line of vision. It was good to savour the rural solitude, and to participate vicariously in the rhythm of farm life, but there were disadvantages. A car was necessary for work, shopping, and social life, and it was a constant battle to keep weeds from creeping into the garden from the meadows. Furthermore, the house needed constant attention, beyond my skills as a handyman.

No sooner had we settled in to Lane House than we had to leave it in the hands of visiting friends, for I had long since arranged a sabbatical term in Illinois for Michaelmas 1966. We went to Swarthmore for a wedding and then flew west to Chicago, where I taught two courses in the philosophy department of the University of Chicago, one on the philosophy of mind and one on Descartes. We lived in an apartment high up in a block of faculty housing overlooking the Midway, the broad lawn-lined highway to the south of the University of Chicago campus.

While we were in Chicago Nancy conceived but miscarried our first child. It was an unhappy time, but we were cheered in November by a visit from my uncle Alec, in the US for the launch of the American edition of the Jerusalem Bible, of which he was General Editor. He and my mother joined the family party at the Gayleys' for Christmas. Alec suffered a mysterious seizure in Swarthmore after Nancy and I had returned to Oxford, and tests when he came home showed cancer, but he recovered from the removal of a kidney to resume his teaching at Christ's College, Liverpool.

I was back in Oxford in time for consideration of those Rhodes
Scholars for 1968 who had made Balliol their first choice of college.
Among them was William J. Clinton. Having studied his papers, the
PPE tutors passed him on to his college of second choice. He told me
recently that he had been so happy at University College that with hind-
sight he was glad to have been found wanting by Balliol.

Nancy became pregnant again in the summer following; there were
no problems this time, and her mother Betty came to Oxford for the
birth of our first son in February 1968. My mother and Alec were
anxious that the child should be baptized, though they knew we did not
intend to bring him up as a Catholic; in a private ceremony in Lane
House, with Betty as godmother, Alec christened him Robert
Alexander. According to custom, I provided port for the Fellows of
Balliol to drink the health of mother and baby at Consilium, the communal dinner on Wednesday nights.

In August Nancy and I took a holiday in Rome with the six-month-
old baby, staying in a hotel which belonged to a former ballerina who
had befriended me when I was awaiting laicization in 1962. For the first
time Nancy saw the monuments and treasures which had surrounded
me during the eight years I spent as a student at the English College. In
the mornings we explored the city with the baby in his carry-cot, pic-
nicking on the Palatine or being crushed in the Porta Portese flea-
market by baby-loving Italians, gooing at Robert and advising us to
wrap him up more warmly and not leave him *nudo in scatola*. In the afternoons one of us baby-sat while the other went out. On our last day we
hired a car and drove through the Castelli Romani, around the lakes of
Albano and Nemi, and down to the sea at Anzio. In no time at all Nancy
fell in love with Italy, as I had, nineteen years earlier.

During 1969 Alec's cancer returned, with secondary tumours in the
brain. Gradually he wasted, impatient at first of illness and a difficult
invalid. Nancy and I drove to Manchester with the baby every other
weekend, to sit by his sick-bed in my mother's house at Hale Barns and
to do our best to console her. In his last days Alec became calmer, and
bore with dignity and even serenity the loss of his strength and the
fading of his wit and curiosity.

This year was further saddened by the death of my closest Oxford
colleague. Arthur Prior had now been three years in Balliol, and in the
autumn term took sabbatical leave with Dagfinn Follesdal's philosophy
department in Oslo. He liked Norway and found the students at his
seminars interesting; but severe rheumatism gave him broken nights
and tired days. Late in September he told me the optimistic diagnosis of
an Oslo doctor, and his own good response to treatment – 'I write to

you now as one of the miracles of modern medicine.' The letter went on to follow up an issue I had raised in modal logic, and to discuss the possibility of enlarging in some way the life of a spastic student attending his classes. It was very typical of Arthur in its combination of abstract energy and human sympathy, and it was the last I ever had from him. It ended euphorically – 'I can stand on one leg and put a sock on the other for the first time for months' – but ten days later he was dead, from heart failure. I travelled to Norway with his son, to join his wife and family and their Norwegian friends for his funeral. Since Arthur's death no other person has, for me, combined to the same degree personal friendship and philosophical companionship. To replace him as philosophy tutor, Balliol elected Bill Newton-Smith.

The following year, 1970, was one of birth as well as death. Summoned to the hospital delivery room at seven one October morning, I kept looking at my watch: I was due to give the first of the term's lectures on Wittgenstein at ten. Nancy says she asked me, 'If this baby doesn't arrive before 9.30, will you stay with me or go to your lecture?' and that I replied, 'Many more people would be disappointed if I didn't make the lecture'. Fortunately, Charles James arrived at 9.30, and I went off to give the lecture with a clear conscience.

Our second son was not baptized: poor Alec was at death's door, and indeed a few days after the birth he died. Charles's first outing was the drive to Liverpool for Alec's funeral at Christ's College. Shortly afterwards my mother moved to Oxford, to live near us and share in the raising of our family.

4

Once a Catholic

IN THE EARLY years of our marriage Nancy and I attended church fairly regularly, though we never joined any church community. When members of my family were with us, we went to Mass with them; at other times we went to the local parish church in Cumnor, sometimes to Orthodox or Presbyterian services in Oxford. We attended more Church of England services than any other, though with my Catholic and Nancy's Presbyterian background, neither of us ever felt really at home in an Anglican atmosphere. However, Church of England services seem to represent less of a commitment to any specific Christian dogma than the worship of any other denomination and this, to me, was a boon. But I have always felt most comfortable in the church of a community to which I really belong, such as a college chapel.

Unless one is a convinced Christian, why go to church at all? Of course, it is possible to attend a service purely as a spectator, for the sake of the music, or the architectural spendour. But between the pure spectator and the committed member of a specific denomination there are many intermediate positions. Unless one is a convinced atheist – which I have never been – one may feel a desire, and indeed a need, to say prayers. There is no more irrationality in an agnostic praying than in a traveller crying out for help in an emergency without knowing whether there is anyone within earshot. And what more appropriate environment for prayer than within a community of others gathered for the purposes of worship?

An unbeliever need feel no hypocrisy in listening to sermons or the reading of scriptures, or saying prayers such as the Lord's Prayer. Often the hymns sung in church express sentiments impossible to feel, but they are as impossible for many believers as for unbelievers or fellow-travellers. (The normal canons of sincerity of utterance seem to be relaxed by the verse form. Gilbert Ryle told me that he divided unbelieving friends in church into singing and non-singing atheists.) There are, however, limits to participation; to recite the Creed or receive Communion would, in my view, be not only a sacrifice of integrity on the part of the unbeliever but also an insult to the seriousness with which these actions are undertaken by believers.

The circumstances of my marriage had focused my attention on those aspects of Christian doctrine which divide Catholics from Presbyterians, but my underlying unease in relation to Christianity was much more fundamental than any denominational disputes: it concerned the existence and nature of God, as conceived by Christian philosophers and theologians, and as defined in the official documents of all the Christian Churches.

After laicization – while I was no longer a priest, but still a doubting Catholic – it seemed to me that the most important step to take was to examine the proofs of the existence of God to see whether any of them was valid. I felt I could do so more dispassionately now that I had rejected the Catholic discipline which made priests swear that, no matter what fallacies might be discovered in the arguments, God's existence was provable. I thought then that the best place to start would be the Five Ways of St Thomas: the five proofs of God's existence at the beginning of the *Summa Theologiae*. Aquinas with his extraordinary genius was, I felt, more likely than anyone else to have produced a valid proof. So I studied his arguments carefully, examining the validity of each step, attempting to supply gaps when they appeared, and to choose between alternative interpretations of ambiguous moves.

I presented my findings more than once in series of lectures in Balliol Hall, published in 1969 as *The Five Ways*. These were well attended, and the audience included foreign visitors to Oxford, several of whom have told me more recently how well they remembered them. (What seems to have been best remembered, however, was not any philosophical argument, but a pigeon which once came through the Hall windows and flew around my head, and which I shooed away, saying, 'I'm lecturing on St Thomas, not on St Francis'.) My conclusions were negative. None of the arguments, on close examination, seemed successful; I tried to pinpoint where each of the five ways was guilty of fallacy. I was disappointed to discover how frequently the arguments depended on a background of outdated Aristotelian cosmology, and began to question my initial supposition that the *Summa Theologiae* was the best place to look for arguments for God's existence; perhaps I should have made a closer study of the *Summa contra Gentes*; or perhaps I should have looked to philosophers other than Aquinas. Instead of doing either, however, I turned my attention from the existence to the attributes of God; or, perhaps, from proofs to possible disproofs of his existence.

At Oxford the endowed special lectureship called the Wilde
Lectureship in Natural and Comparative Religion is, by convention,
held alternately by a philosopher of religion and an anthropologist; I
applied for, and was elected to, this lectureship for the years 1969–72.
My obligation was to deliver eight lectures on Natural Religion in each
of the three years. I chose as my subject the traditional attributes of
God, lecturing on omniscience in 1970, omnipotence in 1971, and
benevolence in 1972. I addressed the topics as a historian and a
philosopher, not as a theologian – reporting the teaching of divines on
these topics, but not myself accepting or appealing to any religious
tradition as an authoritative guide to truth. The philosopher's task was
to examine whether the teaching of the theologians was or was not
internally consistent.

Questions of the greatest philosophical interest arose from omniscience, God's knowledge of all there is to know. I described how this
had been treated in the Bible, by the Church Fathers, and by scholastic
and Reformation theologians. Each lecture was devoted to a particular
class of objects of divine knowledge. How does God know the eternal
truths of mathematics and logic? How does he know the kind of truths
that we learn by experience? Is his knowledge in this area speculative or
practical? How is he aware of time, if he is himself outside time? Does
he know the past, the present, and the future? Does he know counter-
factual truths – that is, when p is not true, does he know what would be
the case if p were true?

The greatest difficulty in this area concerns the relation of God's
knowledge to the future free actions of human beings. If it is still an
open question whether I go to London tomorrow, then it seems that
God cannot know whether I will go to London tomorrow. For if he
knows, say, that I will *not* go to London tomorrow, then it is hard to see
how I can genuinely be free to go to London, since to do so would be
to make God's knowledge false, which is absurd. How are we to reconcile the omniscience of God with human freewill?

Over the centuries philosophers and theologians have wrestled with
this problem, and have sought to solve it in many different ways. Some,
such as Luther, have preserved divine omniscience by a flat denial of
human freewill. Others have preserved freewill by placing limits on
omniscience. Some have said, for instance, that God does not know
future human actions, but that this does not prevent him knowing all
truth, because there is not yet any truth of the matter about such future
events. Others, following Aquinas, have said that God lives in eternity
outside time and knows future events but not as future; I argued that
the implied notion of eternity was an incoherent one, and that if God

cannot tell the difference between past and future then his omniscience is very limited indeed.

The question whether omniscience is compatible with freedom may be seen as a particular instance of the question whether freewill is compatible with determinism, that is, the theory that everything that happens is determined in advance. Some philosophers have sought to provide a solution to this question by a subtle analysis of the notion of freedom. Freedom can be understood in more than one way: to use the philosophers' jargon, it can be understood either as liberty of indifference or as liberty of spontaneity. Liberty of indifference is the ability to act otherwise: the ability, when I do X, *not* to do X. Liberty of spontaneity is the ability to do what one wants: the ability to do X because I *want* to do X. Liberty of indifference is commonly thought to be incompatible with determinism. If it is determined that I will do X, then surely I cannot have any genuine power *not* to do X. Liberty of spontaneity, on the other hand, seems to be compatible with determinism: maybe I regularly do what I want to do, but perhaps my wants have been determined in advance by factors outside my control. So if we define freedom not as liberty of indifference but as liberty of spontaneity, then divine foreknowledge may turn out to be compatible with freedom, since God can know what I will do by knowing those factors which determine my wants.

Ever since the Reformation there has been disagreement within both the Catholic and the Protestant camps whether liberty of spontaneity, without liberty of indifference, is sufficient to constitute the degree of freedom necessary for human moral responsibility. I took the view, when I wrote my Wilde lectures, that it did. It was an uncertain matter whether human beings possessed liberty of indifference, but they clearly possessed liberty of spontaneity, and this was all that was necessary for responsibility. Since liberty of spontaneity was compatible with determinism, it was compatible with divine omniscience.

The theological notion of omnipotence is much harder to pin down than the notion of omniscience. Shall we say that it is the ability to do just anything? But God cannot sin. Shall we say that he has the ability to do whatever he wants, or whatever he can, or whatever is possible? All these definitions turn out to be inadequate or circular. In my lectures the most coherent definition I could produce was very clumsy: 'God is omnipotent' is equivalent to 'For all p, if it is logically possible that God brought it about that p, then God can bring it about that p.' I was prepared to argue that omnipotence, thus conceived, was a coherent notion.

In fact, the notion of omnipotence is not only philosophically complicated, but also theologically comparatively unimportant; the word *omnipotens*, or 'almighty', as it occurs in the Creeds, has more to do with God's being ruler of all than with his being able to do everything. My 1971 lectures turned out to be a contribution to logic rather than to natural theology. In analysing the notion of power, I was able to show that all the formal logics developed up to that time were incapable of analysing ordinary sentences containing the word 'can' in simple contexts such as 'I can swim'.

'Benevolence' was the theme of my third series of lectures. Traditionally, God is omniscient and omnipotent: but he is not omnivolent. In the 1972 lectures I set out to analyse the notion of the divine will, as I had analysed the notions of the divine intellect and the divine power. Once again, I began with a historical account of theological discussions. In creating the world, does God act freely or by necessity? Is God responsible for the evil in the world? Does God will the damnation of sinners? Does he take pleasure in it? Does he always act for the best? Once again, the lectures were much taken up with general philosophical analysis of the relevant notions, in this case notions such as desire, will, and goodness.

The lectures were well attended and well received. Both philosophers and theologians could learn something from them: I could offer the philosophers the knowledge of theological ideas I had learnt at the Gregorian, and the theologians the techniques of logical analysis I had learnt at Oxford. Several members of historical and literary faculties also came, and stayed. But the Wilde Lectures as delivered were too disjointed and inconclusive to be publishable; I continued to work on them, and they developed, in the end, into two books quite different from each other. The first grew out of the reflections on the general nature of power and will contained in the lectures on divine omnipotence and divine benevolence. I came to believe that the human will is essentially the ability to act for reasons. Accordingly, if we are to understand the will, the two topics which need most carefully to be studied are the concept of ability, and the nature of practical reasoning. Both are topics on the borderline of philosophy and logic.

There is a well-established branch of logic, known as modal logic, which offers a formalization of the notions of possibility and necessity. This was studied extensively in the Middle Ages, and rediscovered in the present century, restated in symbolic form, as an extension of the mathematical logic founded by Frege and Russell. The word 'can' is used in ordinary language to cover both ability and possibility; it occurs in contexts such as 'I can speak French' as well as in those such as 'sea creatures can be mammals'. This makes it tempting to think that ability is merely one form of possibility, and that modal logic is adequate to provide a formal analysis of human and other abilities.

In fact, it is easy to show that this is not so. It is a law of standard modal logic that if p, then possibly p; but it is not the case that if I do a particular thing I have the ability to do that thing: once in a while, for instance, I may hit the bull's eye, but by luck, not because I have the appropriate ability or skill. Another law of standard modal logic is that if it is possible that either p or q, then either it is possible that p or it is possible that q, and vice versa. Once again, the corresponding law does not hold with regard to ability. If I am given a pack of cards and asked to pick out a card which is either black or red, I have the ability to do so; but, not being a conjuror, I don't have either the ability to pick out a black card on request or the ability to pick out a red card on request.

Just like ability, practical reasoning is a topic which is ill-served by straightforward symbolic logic. This, too, is easy to show. Practical reasoning is reasoning about what to do; and a simple piece of such reasoning is this:

> I'm to be in London at 4.15.
> If I catch the 2.30 train I'll be in London at 4.15.
> So I'll catch the 2.30 train.

There is nothing wrong with this as an everyday piece of practical reasoning; yet in the ordinary logic used in theoretical reasoning, 'q. If p then q. So p' is not a valid argument from, but a well-known fallacy, exemplified in the following argument:

> If whales are fish, then whales can swim.
> Whales can swim.
> So whales are fish

The differences between practical and theoretical reasoning arise from the following facts. Rules of theoretical reasoning are designed to preserve truth: if we follow them we will never pass from a true premise to a false conclusion. But practical reasoning has as its purpose not the discovery of truth, but the formation of plans for the achievement of our goals. Rules of practical reasoning exist not to preserve truth, but to preserve something else which I called *satisfactoriness*. They exist to ensure that we never pass from a plan which is satisfactory to our purposes to another plan which is unsatisfactory to them. A large part of the logic of practical reasoning, then, must consist of a logic of satisfactoriness.

In the late 1960s and early 1970s I worked hard trying to develop two formal systems, one for the logic of ability, one for practical reasoning. In various articles I published prolegomena to such endeavours, but was never able to develop a fully regimented system with the appropriate syntax and semantics. To this day I do not know how far this was due to my own very limited skill as a symbolic logician, or how far to some intrinsic intractibility of the concepts I was trying to formalize.

In 1974, however, I worked up the philosophical insights which I had tried in vain to incarnate in logical form into a book focused on the traditional topic of the freedom of the will, and presented as a sequel to *Action, Emotion and Will*. In that book I had developed a theory others later called 'The Imperative Theory of the Will': drawing on Aquinas and Wittgenstein, I had argued that there was a logical kinship between wishes and commands, and that the formation of an intention could be looked upon as the mental utterance of a command to oneself. This idea was now developed much further.

The key idea of the new book, entitled *Will, Freedom and Power*, was that the quasi-commands which constituted intentions should be seen as conclusions of practical reasoning, and that the freedom of the human will was a consequence of the special characteristics of practical reasoning. Borrowing a piece of legal jargon, we can describe the difference by saying that practical reasoning is *defeasible* in a way that theoretical reasoning is not. In theoretical reasoning, if a conclusion follows from a certain set of premises, it will continue to follow no matter how many other premises are added to the set. But it often happens in practical matters that while it may be reasonable to adopt plan q in order to achieve goal p, it would no longer be reasonable if further goals were added to p. Taking a hovercraft may be a satisfactory plan with a view to the goal of getting to France; it may no longer be a satisfactory plan if the goals include not only getting to France but also avoiding seasickness. Following Aquinas once more, I argued that basis of the freedom of the will was this defeasibility of practical reasoning.

In *Action, Emotion and Will* I had skirted the topic of determinism and left aside the question of its relation to human freedom. Now I argued that freedom and determinism were compatible with each other. I no longer distinguished, as I had when giving the Wilde Lectures, between a liberty of spontaneity which was compatible with determinism, and a liberty of indifference which was not. Liberty of indifference and liberty of spontaneity, I now came to see, were inseparable from each other. A full understanding of the nature of wanting showed that the ability to do what one wants implies the ability to act otherwise. A full understanding of the nature of ability showed that the ability freely to act otherwise is the ability to act otherwise if one wants to. However, both liberty of indifference and liberty of spontaneity, I now argued, could be reconciled with determinism.

An act A is determined if it occurs as a result of circumstances C which are a sufficient antecedent condition of its occurrence (C is a sufficient antecedent condition of A if there is a covering law 'whenever C, then A'). Freedom and determinism can be reconciled, I now argued, if we define freedom of action in the following way. An agent does X freely at time t provided the following four conditions are fulfilled:

(1) he has the ability to do X
(2) he has the ability not to do X
(3) he has the opportunity to do X at t
(4) he has the opportunity not to do X at t

I argued in my book that no one had ever shown that the fulfilment of these four conditions entails that my doing X at t is undetermined in the sense that it falls under no covering law and has no antecedent sufficient conditions.

I was not, here, arguing for the truth of determinism; I was at the time agnostic on this issue. I was merely criticizing one argument used to prove that determinism is false: namely, the argument that since (as I agreed) we know we are free, then determinism must be false since determinism is incompatible with freedom.

Will, Freedom and Power, while it developed much of the material of the Wilde Lectures, left on one side their major concern: it hardly mentioned God. But I continued to work on the theological implications of my developing ideas, given opportunities to do so by invitations to lecture in the Divinity School at Princeton and in the Philosophy Department at Cornell, where I gave modified and abbreviated versions of the Wilde Lectures.

The most stimulating environment for my development of these ideas was a summer Institute on philosophy of religion at Calvin College, Grand Rapids, Michigan, sponsored by the National Endowment for the Humanities in 1973. The purpose of such summer Institutes was to bring young faculty in small and isolated colleges together to attend lectures by, and join discussion with, international leaders in particular fields. Along with Peter Geach, Terence Penelhum and others, I was chosen as one of the lecturers. Calvin College was built around the seminary of the Christian Reformed Church, a small, theologically conservative and intellectually highly-powered Christian denomination influential in southern Michigan. We guest lecturers were entertained in princely fashion in the Manor House of the campus; my own suite had three rooms, five beds, and a pink marble bathroom, while my senior colleagues enjoyed appropriately greater grandeur; in our spare time we listened, fascinated, to the Watergate testimony on television. The presiding presence at the conference was Alvin Plantinga, who from the tiny department at Calvin had established a formidable international reputation. He was well-known for his exposition of the Free Will Defence to the Problem of Evil, and for having flogged new life into that long-dead horse, the ontological argument for the existence of God.

The three weeks of that conference were among the philosophically most happy and fruitful of my life. The students were keenly demanding, but also immensely appreciative. An audience of young faculty members is the most gratifying possible for a lecturer: they are brighter and better informed than students in the average graduate class, but unlike a senior faculty audience they are still keen to learn and have not yet hardened into particular professional stances. I had long known how stimulating a colleague Peter Geach could be but, not for the first time, I had to make peace between him – with his way of declaiming biblical texts in response to ill-thought-out questions – and his audience; they soon came to appreciate him. Getting to know Plantinga was richly rewarding, and the start of a long friendship. He was a hero to the conference from the first day: a tall, blond, athletic, second-generation Friesian who gave courses in mountain-climbing, he had something to offer to every student. His lecturing technique was very like his climbing technique: first make sure of the position you are in before you take the next step, then take it swiftly and confidently.

In mid session I wrote to Nancy the following account of the conference:

> I am having, philosophically, a splendid time. The monastic air-conditioned office they have given me is sufficiently uncomfortable for there to be nothing to do but work in it, and sufficiently comfortable for one to be able to work long stretches in it without freezing, melting, suffocating etc. The other speakers, especially Peter and Alvin, are very stimulating, and I've now got about two-thirds of my Wilde Lectures into a state that is approaching publishable, and am getting a lot of encouragement . . . Moreover I'm currently in a state of heady euphoria because I think I have just solved the problem of freewill and determinism . . . I have had this sort of thing often enough before to know that there must be a snag lurking somewhere, but it survived a good deal of fire in this afternoon's discussion.

Since this was an Institute on philosophy of religion, the topic of freedom and determinism arose, as in the Wilde Lectures, in the context of God's knowledge and power. If freedom was compatible with determinism, then God, by determining human beings, could know what they would do. This removed any inconsistency between freewill and foreknowledge. But this, I argued, was insuffient to reconcile human freedom with the attributes which Christians traditionally ascribe to God. In tribute to our hosts at Calvin I took as a text the statement of the Belgic Confession:

> We believe that the same good God, after He had created all things, did not forsake them or give them up to fortune or change, but that He rules and governs them according to His holy will, so that nothing happens in this world without His appointment; nevertheless God is neither the Author of nor can be charged with the sins which are committed.

On that basis I sought to convince the assembled philosophers of religion that there could not be any such thing as the God described in that confession.

If determinism is false, and free actions are contingent, I argued, there can be no infallible knowledge of future free actions, since such knowledge appears to demand acquaintance with the state of affairs in question or with some other state of affairs necessarily connected with it. On the other hand, if determinism is true, then God is the author of sin, because if an agent freely and knowingly sets in motion a deterministic process with a certain upshot, then the agent is responsible for that upshot. Certainly, the truth of determinism would not make everything in the world happen in accordance with God's intention; but agents are responsible for their merely voluntary as well as their intentional actions, and in a totally deterministic world the distinction between causing and permitting would have no application to God. Since determinism is either true or false, there cannot be a God who is not the author of sin but infallibly knows future free actions.

In spite of the talent assembled, no satisfactory answer was presented to this dilemma, and I continue to believe that it is an effective disproof of the existence of God as God is conceived by traditional theology.

The Wilde Lectures were given their final form in the summer of 1978, and published under the title *The God of the Philosophers*. Much was dropped: in particular, what was left of the lectures on benevolence, after they had been exploited for *Will, Freedom and Power*, was difficult to disentangle from matters that were the province of the historian of dogma rather than of the philosopher of religion. *The God of the Philosophers* fell into three parts, as had the Wilde Lectures; but the first two parts corresponded to the lectures on omniscience, with the topic of foreknowledge expanded to make a section on its own. The third part was a drastic abbreviation of the lectures on omnipotence. At the end I summarized my conclusions, as they had firmed up at the Calvin conference.

> If the argument of the previous chapters has been correct, then there is no such being as the God of traditional natural theology: the concept of God propounded by scholastic theologians and rationalist philosophers is an incoherent one. If God is to be omniscient, I have argued, then he cannot be immutable. If God is to have infallible knowledge of future human actions, then determinism must be true. If God is to escape responsibility for human wickedness, then determinism must be false. Hence in the notion of a God who foresees all sins but is the author of none, there lurks a contradiction.

This conclusion, though firm, was limited. Only one concept of God had been shown to be untenable; there might be others, for all I had shown, that were no more different from the God of the Bible than the deity of scholastic and rationalist philosophy was. That question I left open.

From the agnostic standpoint of *The God of the Philosophers* the differences of doctrine between Catholics and Protestants, and indeed between Christians and Jews, appeared comparatively unimportant. However, I continued to take a special interest in developments within the Roman Catholic Church, and to be grateful for much that I had learnt from it while I was a member of it. I retained the friendship of priests who had been colleagues of mine in Rome: in particular Jack Kennedy, my closest confrère at the English College, now teaching theology at Christ's College in Liverpool where Alec had ended his career, and the Murphy O'Connor brothers, mountaineering companions in Italy and Switzerland. The elder, Patrick, came sometimes to Oxford for convivial evenings away from his work as a prison chaplain in Portsmouth, and the younger, Cormac, then chaplain to the Bishop of Portsmouth, kept in touch throughout a career that was to lead to the Rectorship of the English College in Rome and the Bishopric of Arundel and Brighton. In Oxford, one of the shrewdest people to discuss philosophy with was a Dominican theologian at Blackfriars, Father Herbert McCabe, of whom I had first heard during his days as an undergraduate at Manchester with Alasdair McIntyre, Robert Bolt, and Jack Kennedy's brother Frank.

Only once do I recall being snubbed by one of my clerical friends. Monsignor W.T. Heard lived in the English College in Rome: he had been my confessor while I was a student, and we had become quite close in spite of the age gap between us. Now he was a Cardinal and Dean of the Rota, or head of the Vatican judiciary. He was made an honorary Fellow of Balliol, where he had been an undergraduate in

1903, and we Fellows subscribed to have his portrait painted by Derek Hill. At the party to present the portrait and hang it in Balliol Hall, the Cardinal affected not to recognize me, among a group of Fellows assembled to greet him, and turned his back firmly. The portrait hung in the Hall until five years after his death; then the Fellows displaced it, and I hung it in the Lodgings when I was Master.

Much more frequently, priests would tell me they shared some of the doubts and concerns that had led me to leave the Church. In the 1970s several former colleagues also left the priesthood; a number received permission to marry, and continued as Catholics. Others remained priests while simply giving up Catholic beliefs which strained their credulity. It became quite common for priests in good standing to express, publicly as well as privately, hostility to Papal teaching on contraception, and disbelief in the Virgin Birth of Jesus.

Throughout the 1960s and 1970s three-cornered arguments of an extraordinary kind often took place, between atheist philosophers, liberal Christians, and conservative Christians. Some traditional doctrine would come up for discussion – it might be the belief that Jesus rose from the dead, leaving an empty tomb. Atheist philosopher and liberal Christian would agree that this doctrine was, in any literal sense, false. Atheist philosopher and conservative Christian would agree that any Christian should believe the doctrine to be true. I often found myself, in discussion with Catholic friends, arguing two corners of these triangles together: urging them that as Catholics they *ought* to believe a certain proposition, but also arguing that they *ought not* to believe it because it wasn't true. This was a paradoxical way of bringing out the illogicality of the attitude of many Catholics to their Church's claims to authority. In a *New Statesman* review of a book by liberal Catholics raising objections to Catholic teaching, I put it thus:

> Let us suppose the Vatican Council were to declare that despite past teaching, artificial contraception is not intrinsically immoral. How could the Roman Catholic Church ever be taken seriously again as a moral authority? If a doctrine taught so solemnly, and at a cost of such suffering, can turn out to be mistaken, what reliance can be placed on any other moral doctrine? If the use of contraceptives is ever permissible, it is surely frequently obligatory: in that case many of the faithful must have been kept for years from the performance of their duty by the teaching of the Church.
>
> If [these Catholic writers] are in the right, then at any time during the last fifty years a man would have been morally and religiously better off outside the Roman Catholic Church than within it. For as a result of being a Catholic he has been seriously misinformed about the nature of marriage, about the authority of the Bible, about the place of the Church and the sacraments, and

about the justice and judgements of God. And if this is so, what rational ground has anyone for being a Roman Catholic at all?

Catholics like to say, 'Once a Catholic, always a Catholic'. Taken literally, this is plainly false. It is not the case that everyone who has once accepted the authority of the Catholic Church always, consciously or unconsciously, accepts it in their heart. But it is true that if you have once been steeped in Catholicism, you retain for ever a certain cast of mind, and a certain cultural tradition. For my part, I am content that it should be so. The Catholic tradition is rich enough in all conscience, and many of the finest minds in European history have contributed to its adornment. I find that the classics of Catholic culture such as the works of Aquinas speak to me more through the force of their own pages than ever they did when imposed by Papal encyclicals. The tawdriness of many of the positivist and materialist alternatives to Christianity is more palpable now that I can read the texts which propound them whenever I want than when I was protected from them by the Index of Prohibited Books.

5

Revolting Students

IN MANY UNIVERSITIES throughout the world, the 1960s began peace-fully and ended in riots. According to the official history of the University of Oxford,

> Oxford's student radicalism did not begin in the mid 1960s with attempts to mimic Berkeley; it began with national developments in the late 1950s, and with local difficulties in the early 1960s. The latter reflect the fact that Oxford's rules adjusted only slowly to Oxford's broadened intake and to changing attitudes among the young. 1961 saw the proctors banning reviews of university lectures in *Isis* and St Hilda's expelling an undergraduate found with a man in her room; in 1962 the proctors censored *Isis* for discussing sexual relations; in 1964 they ran into further trouble over censorship and protests against apartheid. In the summer, angry undergraduates pioneered an unsavoury tactic by telephoning proctors in their homes.

I was well aware of the proctors' problems in 1964. The Junior Proctor was Brian McGuinness, in whose house Nancy and I first met. Brian and his fellow Proctor had disciplined some junior members who damaged the car of the South African Ambassador on a visit to Oxford. They were therefore identified, in the minds of some students, as friends of apartheid against whom any action was justifed; and in fact the protesters adopted more unsavoury tactics than are described in the official history. The proctors' addresses and telephone numbers were widely distributed (for instance, in nearby US airbases) as those of brothels. For a while it was difficult for the McGuinnesses to get an undisturbed night's sleep.

However, student unrest in Oxford in the mid 1960s was still modest, the tactics of student reformers generally law-abiding, indeed legalistic. The Student Representative Council had given evidence to the Franks Commission in 1965, and when that Commission failed to recommend student representation in university government, a group of junior members petitioned the Privy Council against the newly proposed statutes. The petitioners believed junior members should sit on university committees, a view supported by a majority of senior members polled on the question in 1968. Prominent among the petitioners was Michael Burton, the President of the Balliol JCR, and he received help and advice from some of the law tutors in the College. He was one of the leaders of the moderate majority among the students; but there was a radical minority large enough to organize an aggressive demonstration against the proctors in June 1968.

In imitation of their counterparts in Paris and California, radical students covered the walls of the city with anti-authoritarian graffiti. Slogans such as 'Women in Labour keep Capital in Power' gave way to 'Matriculation makes you blind'. Balliol's Broad Street walls provided a popular site for revolutionary fervour, wit, and bad taste. 'Mercurius Oxoniensis', a satirical historian who described the troubles in seventeenth-century style in the *Spectator*, wrote in November, 'The walls of Balliol coll. are today chalked from top to bottom with the canting slogans of the sect, all of them treasonable, most obscene, many illiterate, thretening destruction or perverse usage to loyall subjects. Indeed that whole coll. is now little other than an extroverted privy-house: the scribblings which there, through shame, are writ inwardly being here shamelessly publish'd to the world.'

The petition to the Privy Council was withdrawn when the University agreed to set up a committee to discuss relations between junior members and the central University. This committee met, chaired by the noted jurisprudent Herbert Hart, through much of the academic year 1968/9, and took evidence from many bodies, though the radical students refused to testify to it.

In Hilary Term 1969 I was due for sabbatical leave; Nancy, Robert and I spent Christmas 1968 with the Gayleys, who had just moved from Swarthmore to Ithaca, New York, where Hank was now working in the Development Office of Cornell University. Then we went westward, with a lecture stopover in Chicago, to the University of Washington. People told us we would find the Seattle winter just like England – always raining; luckily this was untrue, but Seattle was like England (and unlike New England), in that the first hint of snow was enough to disrupt the entire traffic system.

I quickly discovered that Oxford's student troubles were mild in comparison with those of a typical American university. The major issue at UW was the university's maintenance of an officer training scheme, which was unpopular, there as elsewhere, during the Vietnam war, detested by most students for a mixture of moral and personal reasons. Aggressive processions marched past the philosophy building,

chanting; bomb threats and bomb scares sometimes necessitated clear-
ing the lecture rooms. On my first day some of the pupils enrolled for
my course came to ask whether I believed in democracy in the classroom. This turned out to mean, would I give everyone an A for the
course? I said I could not guarantee this without having seen their work
first; whereupon some decided to switch to other courses.

If this kind of thing had been happening in Oxford, I would have
been most distressed, but as a visitor I could take a detached view, and
enjoy the comparatively light teaching schedule arranged for me; I
could also benefit from the occasional day's holiday when the department was closed because of a bomb scare. Every Friday I commuted to
Eugene and repeated my seminar at the University of Oregon; these
visits were not pleasant, because the department was then dominated
by a doctrinaire philistine version of analytic philosophy under the auspices of Frank Ebersole. My time at Eugene cured me of any lingering
infatuation with 'ordinary language' philosophy. More agreeable were
trips in March to lecture on the being of God in Iowa City, and on intention and morality at the University of Missouri.

We were back in Oxford for Trinity Term, one much enlivened
academically by the presence of Noam Chomsky as John Locke
Lecturer. Throughout the term he was much in demand around the
country to give lectures, whether on linguistics or politics; but he came
to Balliol from time to time for discussions with students, and I was
very impressed by the extreme care and courtesy which he showed in
answering even the most foolish question from the most junior undergraduate. Towards the end of the term my book on the *Five Ways* was
published, and the proofs of my Descartes book arrived for correction:
the text had done yeoman service in lectures on two continents.

At about the same time the long-awaited Hart Report was published. While not accepting the radical claim that a university should
be run as a democracy of faculty and students, Hart recommended the
setting up of joint committees of junior members with Council and
the General Board, and faculty committees of senior and junior
members to deal with academic matters. A Rules Committee, composed equally of junior and senior members, was to lay down disciplinary rules and to appoint a Disciplinary Court to deal with major
University offences – replacing the traditional unfettered discretion of
the two University Proctors. Official recognition was given to a
revamped Student Representative Council, with Michael Burton as its
first President.

The Hart Report brought a temporary peace in the student troubles.
In June 'Mercurius' could report that the wall-scribblings had dis-

appeared: 'Even Balliol coll. is now clean, at least on the outside, which is all that honest men look on.' While grumbling at the number of proposed committees, which were likely to clog business, he gave qualified approval to the Hart Report, '200 pages in octavo, with judicious reflexions, excellently writ: which, though misliked by some as too yielding, have damped the more factious spirits and much relieved such of us poor college tortoises as are in no great hurry for change.' But he lamented that the High Tables of Oxford were still 'divided betwixt young ninnies, crying for novelties, and old jellies, quaking and yielding to them'.

During the troubles in the wider University, individual colleges were pressed to relax discipline and allow student participation in government. There were differences between college and college: Merton undergraduates saw no need for change; those at Balliol were disgusted by its slow pace. On the merits of the Hart reforms, Balliol SCR was sadly divided.

One of the members of Hart's committee was Robert Ogilvie, now Senior Tutor. I do not know how enthusiastically he signed on to its recommendations, for though he was a popular tutor who lived on very easy terms with his pupils, he was no great believer in democracy in College decision-making, whether by junior or senior members. As Russell Meiggs later put it tactfully in an obituary notice, Robert while Senior Tutor had

> the responsibility of drawing up agenda for College meetings and guiding discussion on central issues. This was a delicate operation. A governing body of equipollent intellectuals needs a special kind of leadership. Robert was sometimes surprised by the strength of the opposition which his proposals encountered, but he was reasonable in argument and there is no doubt that meetings became more business-like and shorter.

Christopher Hill felt, with some justification, that his Senior Tutor often took upon himself decisions which should have been those of the Master and Fellows. Unlike Robert, Christopher was a firm believer in student participation in government, and was keen to scrap rules such as gate hours which he regarded as outdated. There was, therefore, some coolness between the two, and it may have been a relief to Christopher when Robert left in 1970 to become Headmaster of Tonbridge.

However, during these troubled times the most difficult relationship was not that between the Master and the Senior Tutor, but that between the Master and the Dean, who was also the Chaplain. Frank McCarthy Willis-Bund was an Irish Protestant clergyman with an eighteenth-century horror of enthusiasm, whether in its religious or its political form. He had been Dean since 1952, and a remarkably effective holder of that office in the terms in which it had been traditionally understood. I quote Meiggs again:

> In a society which tends to feed on gossip, not uncommonly spiced with malice, he was the most discreet of men. What he heard in private remained private. His classification of crimes was tolerant and fair. He was essentially conservative, but not political, and his friendships with undergraduates were wide-ranging. Though outwardly reserved he could sing music-hall songs with the VicSoc and talk nonsense with the Arnold and Brackenbury.

Frank dispensed justice quietly, briskly, and – according to the lights which had governed Balliol for generations – fairly.

Now, however, all was changing, and the Master and many of the Fellows were urging a faster pace. Personal discretion was out of fashion: rules must be made by committees and enforced by joint courts. Marxist undergraduates complained that Frank's justice was class justice: he had one standard for public school boys (whose misbehaviour counted as 'juvenile high spirits') and another for the products of state schools (whose offences violated basic decencies). Frank hated committees, and disdained to defend himself against these charges. The role of Dean became bitter; he felt he had lost support where most he should have expected it.

On my return from Seattle I found myself placed on a newly instituted Joint Disciplinary Committee: I had been rash enough, in my sabbatical report, to boast that I had lived through student revolt in its violent transatlantic form. The committee's job was to draw up an agreed code of rules and to set up disciplinary procedures for their enforcement. Energetic JCR participation on the committee meant that the code was minimal in content, and the creation of new joint courts and JCR deans was less a reinforcement of discipline than a fetter on decanal activity. It was my job to write the report of the committee in Trinity Term and, in the following Michaelmas Term, to pilot the new disciplinary system through Governing Body. In a rash piece of democratic enthusiasm we had voted that College rules should be binding on senior as well as junior members – a principle bitterly resented by some Fellows, though in fact most of the forbidden deeds were outrages elderly dons were unlikely to perpetrate. For better or worse, the College approved our new code with little amendment.

Underneath, not a great deal changed. Delinquents could choose to be dealt with by the new College Court or by the Dean; those caught red-handed in some juvenile offence would often opt to be dealt with summarily by Frank, rather than brought before a court containing their peers. But a few disciplinary cases were turned by JCR deans into well-publicised political confrontations. The Boat Club in particular was regarded by the JCR left wing as politically unsound, and JCR deans would leap in to prosecute if they thought Frank was too indulgent during celebrations at the end of Eights Week.

Much of the work of a dean is non-disciplinary. Frank, while sparing in attendance at meals in the SCR, would prowl around the College late at night, comforting the lonely and sorting out the financial problems of the improvident no less than rebuking the noisy and the drunken. But even here he felt that his authority was being undermined by the reforming Governing Body. A new office was set up, of College Counsellor: four Fellows were to be chosen by a vote of the junior members. I was one of the first four. Neither my counsel, nor my three colleagues', was often asked, and those who did usually wished to make a political protest rather than genuinely seek advice. Frank took the creation of this office as a slur on his own role. The Sunday after the first counsellors were appointed, he preached a sermon in the College Chapel on 'The role of the counsellor in the Old Testament'; it centred on the story of Achitophel as counsellor to Absalom, and dwelt on the evil end to which both men came.

My role on the Joint Disciplinary Committee initially placed Frank and myself in opposite corners: but during this period we became quite close. I soon found that my most important task was to reconcile Frank to the new system, and to defend him against allegations which he was too proud to refute himself. Almost always, when I looked into charges of unfairness and favouritism brought against him, I found them to be calumnies. One so outraged me that I wrote an open letter to every junior member exposing the malice of the JCR politicians.

This meant, of course, that I began to have my own troubles with the JCR officers, and during Michaelmas Term 1969 an unconscionable amount of time was spent debating with them on committees. However, there was no internal disruption in the form of demos and sit-ins. The President of the JCR, Martin Kettle, was a member of the Communist Party and preferred a skilful use of the rule book to the strong-arm tactics favoured by some of his Trotskyist colleagues further to the left. Indeed, in the battles between junior and senior members, he could display an old-world chivalry. By way of apology for the trouble he had caused me during the term, he invited Nancy and me to let in the New Year of 1970 with him and other members of the JCR Committee, in a cottage owned by his family in Great Langdale in the Lakes. The invitation recalled, in miniature, the Christmas truce in the trenches in the war of 1914–18, and we accepted with alacrity. After a pleasant weekend in the Lakes and a lively party, I returned to continue sparring with the JCR members of joint committees.

Throughout the following term, relations between students and their teachers reached a new low point throughout the University, and indeed nationwide. In February students occupied the offices of Warwick University and claimed to find in the files evidence of political bias in undergraduate admissions and letters of recommendation. In the same month a protest against repression in Greece led at Cambridge to a violent protest causing serious injuries and great damage to property. Warwick's fever spread to Oxford, and there was much agitation about files. The Delegates' room in the Clarendon Building was occupied for a week – not so much in the hope of finding files, as to demonstrate how suitable the building was for a Central Student Union, for the better organization of revolution.

I thought it important that senior members should show they were not intimidated by student mobs, so I went into the Clarendon Building to face the throng. I discovered that copies of a Proctors' Memorandum were being handed round with a sense of great outrage; I do not now recall its contents, but the disciplinary demands seemed harmless enough, and I stood on the table to address the students and convince them of the reasonableness of the Proctors' stand. Only days later did I discover that the memorandum was a spoof concocted by the revolutionaries to bring the Proctors into disrepute.

But another more senior don was determined to defeat the radicals at their own game. His public denunciations of the students' folly had marked out Warden Sparrow of All Souls as a target. Balliol wall, now once more a bulletin board for the left, bore in large letters: 'Are not two Sparrows worth one farthing?' When the Oxford Revolutionary Socialist Students left their banner unguarded outside All Souls, the Warden popped out of his Lodgings and captured it; when they requested it back for their next demonstration, he returned it, neatly furled; when it was unfurled as the march began, it was found to read 'Oxford Revolutionary Socialist Sillies'.

In Balliol, Robert Ogilvie moved files from the Senior Tutor's office to his home in St Cross Road. Frank McCarthy was asked to produce his own decanal dossiers. 'I have no files', he replied, 'but I know which of you are the trouble-makers and shall gladly tell any prospective employers who ask me what I know.'

In 1970 the Conservatives under Ted Heath won the general election. Heath had once been an organ scholar at Balliol, and had remained a loyal alumnus, often particularly helpful in persuading first-rate performers to give their services to the Balliol Musical Society. When he became Prime Minister, Christopher Hill sent a telegram from the Balliol SCR – 'Political congratulations from some of us, personal congratulations from all of us.' – but was wary of laying on any College celebration of the event.

However, in the course of 1970/71 Christopher went on sabbatical, leaving as Vice-Gerent, or acting Master, a South African Fellow in Mathematics, Jack de Wet. Jack's political views were well to the right of Christopher's, and he had been an exact contemporary of Heath's at Balliol: he seized the opportunity to invite Heath to dine with the Fellows in the SCR. Most of us, whatever our political views, much looked forward to the opportunity of welcoming a distinguished Balliol man as Prime Minister.

Shortly before the visit, the Government signed the Simonstown Agreement with South Africa, thus making Heath a target for anti-apartheid demonstrators, inside and outside Balliol. On the morning of the visit it was discovered that during the night the great plate-glass windows of the SCR had been painted with 'Fuck Heath', and graffiti daubed on several College walls. The Bursar and his staff had to work in a frenzy to make the common room presentable for the evening's guest; as they began the cleaning they found the wallets of two members of the JCR Committee, one containing the bill for the graffiti paint. The Vice-Gerent summoned the JCR President and Treasurer and showed them the graffiti and the painted windows. Had they any idea who could have been responsible? None at all. Was it not a terrible disgrace? Heads were nodded, appropriate tutting noises were made. 'Well, then', said Jack, 'how do you explain the presence of these wallets and this bill?'

Disciplining the perpetrators had to wait until after Heath's visit; in the meantime, we were clearly threatened with a significant demonstration during the dinner itself. Gates could be locked, and the lodge patrolled to keep out non-Balliol demonstrators, but the involvement of the JCR Committee in the night-painting showed that our own members felt sufficiently strongly on the Simonstown issue to brave any sanction the College authorities might impose. Frank McCarthy called for, and obtained, twenty police from the Special Branch to reinforce decanal authority.

When it came the demonstration was brief, but very disorderly. After the Fellows and their guests had taken sherry in the Master's Lodgings, the Special Branch men had to clear a way for them to cross the quad to the SCR. The scuffles were so violent that one Fellow was put off his dinner and went home, crying 'Thugs!' It became clear only later that it was the police, not the demonstrators, to whom he was referring.

As we crossed the quad between the scufflers I found myself next to Heath. 'This is a new experience for us,' I said, 'but I expect you're quite used to this kind of thing.' 'Never seen anything like it before in my life,' he replied. But once we were inside the SCR and dinner had begun, he chatted urbanely and energetically, as if nothing untoward had happened.

Governing Body had to decide what to do with the delinquent students; the matter was too important for decanal discretion or the College court. Discussion was prolonged and divisive. In the end the JCR was made to pay collectively for the cleaning of the College, but only the two individuals identified by their wallets were punished: one, who was near the end of his course, was sent down; another was rusticated for the year.

Ten years later, in the middle of the Thatcher administration, a College gaudy was held to which members of that JCR Committee came, now as old members of the College. The Fellow, Oswyn Murray, who had the duty of welcoming them back, could hardly avoid referring to past events; elegantly, he observed that the sentiments once expressed by the JCR on the SCR windows were now (in the 1980s) more often to be heard in 10 Downing Street.

These years of student revolution were very difficult for Christopher Hill. As a Marxist Master, he was caught between the revolutionaries and the conservatives. Right-wing dons would think him responsible, even if they did not say so to his face, for putting such crazy ideas into the heads of the young. Frank McCarthy believed, I am sure wrongly, that Christopher conspired with the revolutionaries to undermine decanal authority. On the other hand, whenever Christopher supported disciplinary measures, the Marxist students could reproach him with being a traitor to the movement: he should have been on their side, and here he was shoring up the reactionary bourgeoisie.

Perhaps for this reason, Christopher adopted rather a low profile at this time – especially at University meetings of Heads of Houses, many of whom placed at Balliol's door much of the blame for the troubles throughout the University. Mercurius Oxoniensis affected to believe that the Master was no longer alive, having been hanged by the fanatics in his doctor's robes: 'The late Master was hustled to his grave at midnight, very obscurely . . . The Proctors have forgiven the young men who hanged their Master, as doubtless ignorant of the statutes against murther.'

As a comparatively junior don with no College office I was much freer to enter into the fray than Christopher, aware as he was of the divisions within the Governing Body of which he was head. But this soon ended. In 1971 it was Balliol's turn to provide a Proctor, and Patrick Sandars, the physics tutor who had succeeded Robert Ogilvie as Senior Tutor in 1970, was elected. During the year of his Proctorship he would be in the full-time service of the central University: I was appointed Senior Tutor in his place.

6

The Chalet

SOME FOUR THOUSAND feet above the town of St-Gervais, on a spur of Mont Blanc called the Prarion, amid woods of pine and larch, there stands a substantial chalet. On some maps it is called 'Chalet des Mélèzes', on others 'Chalet des Anglais'. It dates from the first years of this century but replaces an earlier building erected by David Urquhart, a former British Ambassador to the Ottoman Empire.

Urquhart was a crusader in good causes, which he pursued in the light of a cluster of eccentric beliefs about human nature. One of his theories was that the human mind did not function properly at normal altitudes: below a height of five thousand feet, he believed, the brain was fuddled by an excess of oxygen. Another theory was that the key to the social problems of the nineteenth century was the Turkish bath. In earlier less hygienic centuries, he believed, though the rich had exploited the poor, they had not actually despised the poor because rich and poor had both alike smelt. Now, however, the rich had started to take regular hot baths, and to look down on the poor as the great unwashed. The solution was to build Turkish baths for the poor; that would make them actually cleaner than the rich, who misguidedly soaked themselves in tubfuls of their own dirty water. Accordingly, Urquhart campaigned for the installation of Turkish baths in Irish villages, and at Blarney, in County Cork, he published a magazine devoted to their propagation, entitled *The Diplomatic Courier*.

It was natural, then, that when in 1856 Urquhart came to build a summer home for his retirement years, he should build it in the Alps, comfortably above five thousand feet, and install within it a Turkish bath. From many parts of Europe and Asia distinguished visitors who shared Urquhart's devotion to world peace would arrive at the chalet by mule to discuss affairs of state – and affairs of Church, for Urquhart was a devout Roman Catholic. After his death in 1877 the chalet came into the possession of his son, Francis, who had spent his childhood summers there.

In 1896 Francis Urquhart became a Fellow of Balliol, the first Catholic to hold a Fellowship there since the Reformation. In term time in the College – where he was always known by the nickname 'Sligger' – he kept open house for his pupils and other undergraduates at all hours in his rooms overlooking the Martyrs' Memorial in St Giles; from 1891 he took groups of undergraduates to the chalet. Reading parties – in which pupils would spend some of the vacation with a tutor, partly on holiday and partly studying the texts on which they would later be examined – were a familiar Victorian institution in Oxford; but Sligger's reading parties acquired a quite special reputation. Those who disliked him regarded him as a snob and tuft hunter: but he combined an ability to spot and nurture those destined for a distinguished career with a concern to effect a mingling of the different social classes represented in Balliol, aiming, as he put it, to 'get the best men from the public schools and let them mix up with intelligent men from Birmingham, etc.' His chalet reading parties were intended to serve both purposes.

The original chalet burnt down in 1906. It was widely believed (but never proved) that the fire was started by the future Archbishop Temple, imprudently smoking in bed. Sligger had the chalet rebuilt, on a larger scale, still with a Turkish bath. Among those who joined his reading parties before the First World War were the future Cardinal Heard, several junior Asquiths, and the young Harold Macmillan (who was one of the 1913 party, and returned to St-Gervais in 1921 to spend his honeymoon in a chalet nearby).

Bound volumes, dating from the rebuilding of the chalet to the present day, preserve the names of those attending reading parties and photographs of the groups and their activities. Between the wars Sligger extended his invitations well beyond the walls of Balliol, and the guests include those who were later to be famous in many spheres, among them Herbert Hart, Richard Wilberforce, Cyril Connolly, Isaiah Berlin, Jo Grimond, and Quintin Hogg (later Lord Hailsham). The latter's description of the chalet in his autobiography *A Sparrow's Flight* is typical:

> These reading parties were among the most delightful experiences of my Oxford life. We travelled by train from Calais on a through coach to Le Fayet. We then changed to a rack-and-pinion railway known as the Tramway du Mont Blanc, which led to St-Gervais-les-Bains and a station known as Montivon. Then we walked by mule-path on to the chalet with our packs on our backs, leaving our luggage to be brought by mule-cart along the zig-zag path from the valley. We were expected to work on our academic studies both morning and afternoon. In the evening there were games on the rough lawn outside the chalet, and, more often alone but sometimes with companions, I

would scramble up the 600 feet which separated us from the rough top of the Prarion whence, on a clear day, you could see the whole range of the Chamonix Aiguilles . . .

The chalet itself was utterly delightful, smelling beautifully of pinewood . . . The view was spectacular, especially in the evening as the lights came out across the valley of Sallanches to the Mont Percé, through the hole in which the evening sun would shine as it was about to set. I look on the days I spent there as among the happiest of my life.

After 1932 illness prevented Sligger from going to the chalet; but his reading parties were continued by a number of younger dons who had been regular visitors since their undergraduate days at Balliol – Cyril Bailey, Frank Lepper, Christopher Cox, Roger Mynors, and Richard Pares. At his death in 1934 Sligger left the chalet to Roger Mynors, clearly feeling that he was the one most likely to continue the tradition of Balliol reading parties. During the war, of course, these were suspended, and between 1938 and 1952 no one from Oxford stayed at the chalet. After the war Roger Mynors lost interest in taking reading parties, and had cooled towards Balliol as a result of his disappointment in the Mastership election of 1949.

It was Giles Alington of University College who in the early 1950s began to make use of the chalet again – at first with small groups of friends, including married couples such as Peter and Ann Strawson. Later, joined by Frank Lepper of Corpus and Tony Firth and Christopher Cox, he organized something more like the pre-war reading parties. By the late 1960s it had become the custom that Tony Firth would preside over Univ. parties for one half of the summer, Christopher Cox over New College parties for the other half. Because the chalet had no electricity or internal water supply it was unusable except in the summer months, and the two groups took it in turns to open up the house at the beginning of July or close it at the end of August. Tony Firth, a middle-aged bachelor history tutor, shared the management of his parties with a barrister fellow of All Souls, Jeremy Lever. Sir Christopher Cox, originally a Balliol man, was an ancient history don at New College from 1926 to 1946 and then a civil servant in the Education Department of the Colonial Office and its successors, founding a string of universities in colonies on the verge of independence. Since 1970 he had lived in retirement in New College, taking a keen interest in the welfare of the undergraduates and keeping open house on the model of Sligger. Extremely sociable and garrulous, he became a well-known figure in the Prarion area; a neighbour there described his French as '*pas tout à fait correct, mais extrêmement riche*'.

In 1970 a group of my Balliol Greats pupils, who had heard and read stories of Sligger's pre-war parties, asked me why there were no longer any Balliol expeditions to the chalet. Would I be willing to take a party there? The only Balliol don with actual experience of the chalet was Maurice Keen – he and Tom Bingham had stayed there, with a family party, in the 1950s – but he disliked the Alps and was not keen to return. He advised me to approach Cox and Firth, who readily agreed to create a third slot during the summer months, to allow Balliol parties to visit the chalet as well. The timetable had already been drawn up for that year, so Balliol had to make do with the middle of September, when the days were short and could be cold; but it was agreed that in later years the three colleges should take turns at the beginning, middle, or end of the season.

However, Cox and Firth did not own the chalet, and to make use of it I needed the permission of Mynors, whom I barely knew, and who still kept well clear of Balliol, although he had been an Honorary Fellow since 1963. I wrote asking his permission to take Balliol reading parties; after a period of suspense I received a terse but cordial postcard giving me leave, and until I left the College I stayed at the chalet with Balliol students almost every year.

Once the pattern of the three colleges' reading parties had been established, Mynors decided to hand over the ownership of the chalet to a charitable trust so that it could continue in use without death duties being incurred as it passed from one owner to another. This was not a simple task, since the concept of such a trust is foreign to French law, and it took all the skills of Jeremy Lever, QC, to devise the appropriate legal mechanism. The chalet is now owned, in the first instance, by a French Société Civile. The two shareholders are the Chalet des Anglais Company and the Chalet des Mélèzes Company, English companies whose sole function is to own the shares in the French one. They in their turn are owned by a charitable trust, whose trustees are the direc-tors of the companies. The trustees only get their hands on the chalet, as it were, through two pairs of metaphysical gloves. The real business of the trust – the upkeep, repair and insurance of the chalet, the payment of rates and taxes to St-Gervais, and so on – is conducted at an annual meeting of the trustees. The first trustees were Christopher Cox, Jeremy Lever, Tony Firth, and myself.

One of the students who in 1970 asked me to renew the Balliol chalet connection was John Hare, the son of my former colleague Dick Hare who was now a professorial Fellow of Corpus. Dick and his wife kindly came along to show me, from their long experience in England, how a reading party worked. Another of the students who had suggested the party was a Czech, Anthony Klouda. He too was accompanied by his mother, and his father, who had been private secretary to Jan Masaryk (and was the last of his staff to see Masaryk alive before he fell to his death from the palace window in Prague in 1948). We were joined by two German philosophers from Heidelberg, Ernst Tugendhat and Lorenz Kruger, who were anxious to make contact with analytical philosophers. Half a dozen graduates and undergraduates made up the party – the ratio of senior to junior members was higher than on any of my later parties.

The route to the chalet in 1970 was not very different from that described by Hailsham. You took the overnight train from Paris to Le Fayet and transferred to the rack-and-pinion Tramway de Mont Blanc. You left this, half-way to its terminus at the Nid d'Aigle, at the Col de Voza, a steep twenty minutes' walk below the Hôtel du Prarion. From the hotel you dropped down on the other side of the spur via fifteen minutes of jeep track to a grassy path which crossed two streams (nick-named by classicist undergraduates the Oxus and Jaxartes), to come upon the chalet from above, looking down on its galvanized roof, its balconies of larch, and its primitive lawn surrounded by lupins. Though a great part of the lower slopes of Mont Blanc had been disfigured by ski-runs, ski-tows and *téléfériques*, the chalet was protected from these eyesores by the forests which surrounded it.

As in the 1930s, the chalet was heated by a wood stove (even in August the nights could be cold, and on rare occasions snowy) and all the water was drawn from a single tap in the kitchen, fed by a hosepipe poked into the stream some five hundred feet above the house. Cooking (and, later, refrigeration) was made possible by Calor gas in large blue canisters, whose replacement and replenishment in the valley was one of the major concerns of housekeeping. Lighting in the evening was by candle, or by Tilley lamps. Each new guest was solemnly warned against following the bad example of the Archbishop.

The main difference from the chalet of the 1930s was the lack of domestic service. Sligger wrote, and had printed, a set of rules of behaviour entitled 'The Perfect Chaletite', much of which was taken up with advice on how to treat the servants. In the 1970s there was no one to bring up your luggage by mule: you had to carry it all on your back. The Turkish bath was now a shower, operated from a cistern which had to be filled by hand with jugs of warm water. Shaving water was still brought each morning to the nine bedrooms, but by members of the party rather than by the Urquhart maids.

There was also a greater informality of dress. 'The Perfect Chaletite' laid down the occasions on which jackets and ties were to be worn, but in a generation which had to do its own laundry, jeans and T-shirts were the normal wear. There remained differences of ethos between reading parties: Christopher Cox's New College parties slept between linen sheets and ate off white linen tablecloths, all of which had to be carried down to St-Gervais to be laundered; Balliol parties preferred to bring sleeping bags and eat off the bare table.

I was the only one of the trustees who was married, and Christopher Cox was initially sceptical about the possibility of combining chalet and family life, but after 1974 we regularly went to the chalet as a family, often with Jonathan Barnes of Oriel, his wife Jennifer and their two children; one day I climbed to the top of the Brévent with the four children – a party whose median age was six.

In a normal year there was room for eight or ten students, in addition to the Barnes and Kenny families. Constraints on numbers mainly arose from there being only a single lavatory. Domestic chores were divided, and each member of the group would be given a title indicating his duties: M. le Bougie cleaned and replenished the candlesticks; M. le Bois was responsible for chopping the wood; M. Tilley had to learn the mysterious art of tending the paraffin lamps; and so on. The most unpopular duties were those of M. les Ordures, who had to dig a pit, fill it daily with trash, and cover it with earth before the arrival of the next party. Food preparation and washing-up were strictly determined by rota.

Breakfast was bread and jam and porridge: it was essential to have something warm on rising in the Alpine dawn. We had hot chocolate in the middle of the morning, and lunch was normally soup and cold pâtés and cheeses (in Haute Savoie, delicious and inexpensive). In the evening we always had a substantial cooked dinner. Nancy and Jennifer presided in the kitchen, but encouraged volunteer undergraduate cooks; these became more numerous over the years, as the New Man was born. Most undergraduates had one (rather expensive) party dish, but few were good at using up leftovers – essential if we were to keep housekeeping costs within the modest limits of the grant provided by Balliol from an F.F. Urquhart Memorial Fund.

Every few days a shopping party descended to the valley to fill knapsacks with meat and fruit and other perishables. Before each reading party arrived, non-perishables ordered in advance from the supermarket at St-Gervais were brought up to Col de Voza on the TMB, then ferried over to the chalet by the jeep belonging to the Hôtel du Prarion. Cheap, palatable red wine was ordered by the barrel from the vintner in St-Gervais, but we discouraged the use of spirits.

Since a reading party is a combination of holiday and seminar, different groups put the emphasis in different places. Balliol parties believed themselves to be more studious than those from Univ. and New College, but this may have been an illusion. Certainly we took the academic side quite seriously. On a normal morning, everyone was supposed to work at books related to their courses, or texts set for the party, either in their rooms or in the communal salon-cum-library with the wood stove. Afternoons were free, but after dinner everyone assembled as a seminar, and each member in turn would present a paper, or introduce a set text. The book set for the first reading party was Wittgenstein's *On Certainty*, chosen, in deference to our German guests, as a good text to bridge the divide between the analytic and the continental tradition in philosophy.

At the suggestion of the German philosophers, a written summary of each discussion (a 'protocol', they called it) was read out the following night to begin the proceedings. This custom was kept up in subsequent reading parties, and I now have a collection of thick exercise books recording twenty-five years of chalet discussion. Naturally, they vary in quality, but some of the best were sufficiently interesting to be typed out later for circulation to the participants.

In the afternoons one might play games. Cricket was hampered by the bumpiness of the lawn and interrupted by frequent searches for lost balls in the lupins; the golf course, laid out across the mountainside before the war, was now a vestige of its former self; but real tennis was played against the outside kitchen wall with energy and passion. Alternatively, one might walk up to the summit of the Prarion, or stroll around the side of the hill to admire the Mont Blanc massif from the goatherd's house at La Charme, or penetrate to the foot of the glacier of Bionassay and look into the blue chasms tucked into the gritty moraine. Urquhart, feeling that a constant view of Mont Blanc might destroy its magic, had the chalet built on the other side of the spur, facing north to the range of the Aravis. To see the massif you have to walk five minutes southward, but can then keep it in view for an afternoon; returning northward in time for dinner, you can enjoy the spectacular colours of the sunset on the other side of the valley.

As the afternoons were not long enough to take full advantage of the Alps, every three days or so, depending on the weather, we would declare a whole-day expedition, sending out the party in groups of various sizes to explore the massif. A popular expedition, to the Tête Rousse, involved taking the TMB to its topmost station, the Nid d'Aigle, walking for an hour up a rocky cwm, then for another hour zigzagging across an exposed arête until the Tête Rousse refuge was reached, across a snowfield. This walk is in fact the first stage of the normal route for an ascent of Mont Blanc, as far as it is possible to go without a rope, or crampons, or an ice-axe. Though it is not difficult and involves hardly any scrambling, it is sufficiently exposed to give the walker a sense of the high Alps and, on a fine day, a series of spectacular views both on the massif itself and towards a set of serrated ranges across the valleys into Switzerland and Italy. The height reached – about ten thousand feet – is just enough to emphasize the thinness of the air.

Other all-day expeditions involved descending to St-Gervais or to Chamonix and then reascending the ranges on the opposite side of the valley, and for most of these it was necessary to make use at some point of cars or buses or cable cars. Chamonix itself is a tourist town: 'The Perfect Chaletite', Sligger decreed, 'detests Chamonix', and its detestable features have increased and multiplied since his day. But there were delightful walks beyond it up to the Lac Blanc and the Lac Cornu which gave a glorious view of the entire Mont Blanc range. From St-Gervais one could go up the valley towards the Col du Bonhomme, the footpath pass into Italy, and explore the Miage and the Tré-la-Tête glaciers from les Contamines-Montjoie. A shorter walk on the other side of St-Gervais led up to Mont Joly, so called because it was sufficiently low not to have snow on its peak during the summer.

Serious climbing was not encouraged: I did not wish to be responsible for the safety of students whose mountaineering skill and experience I was usually in no position to judge, while an attempt on any of the summits on the Massif would necessitate an absence of more than a day and disrupt the party's schedule. Most novices, all agog on arrival to climb Mont Blanc but much underestimating the effort and time required, abandoned this ambition once they had been up to the Tête Rousse, returning suitably chastened. The serious and skilled I encouraged to postpone their climbing until after the reading party; the persistent but unskilled I advised to join the University Mountaineering Club and return to the Alps the following year.

On the last night each group organized a concert party (egged on by the junior Kennys and Barneses). Some welcomed the opportunity to give a further rendering of a party piece perfected for an undergraduate social club in Oxford, while others devised pieces of doggerel suited to the surroundings.

> Have you heard of Tony Kenny from a college on the Broad?
> Times were going hard with him – in fact the man was bored
> So he sent out invitations to each and every one
> As how he'd like to see them that summer on Mont Blanc.
> When writing out he was careful to suggest to them
> That if they wished to travel even lighter than a feather

All they had to bring was a copy of the Politics
'Cos the weather in the Alps is like English summer weather

Refrain:

With a rainfall o so cold, hands too numb to grip
Oh hadn't we the wind up us on Tony Kenny's trip.

This, and a string of other verses, were sung to the tune of *Phil the Fluther* in 1975, when the weather had been unseasonably stormy for over a week. The author had his limitations as a poet, but went on to a distinguished career in the Irish diplomatic service.

Life at the chalet would have been impossible without the friendship and generosity of our nearest neighbours, the Hottegindre family at the Hôtel du Prarion. There had been Hottegindres in the area since before Mont Blanc was first climbed, and the kernel of the Hôtel, the Pavillon, was the only building on the Prarion older than the chalet. In the 1970s the hotel was run by Max and Simone Hottegindre with help (between school and university terms) from their daughter and four sons, and from Simone's mother Madame Orset. As well as arranging for the delivery of provisions on our arrival, the Hottegindres supplied daily bread and milk besides serving as a post office. We became good friends, and were proud to be invited to the marriage of the eldest son George in St-Gervais, when guests in their wedding clothes were ferried by a specially-chartered service of the Tramway du Mont Blanc from church in the valley to the reception on the Prarion; we were also delighted to entertain Max and Simone in Oxford in 1974 when they came to help celebrate Christopher Cox's seventy-fifth birthday.

Some years we paid winter visits to the Prarion so that Robert and Charles could learn to ski. The chalet was unusable in December and January, so we stayed with the Hottegindres. The hotel was well provided with nursery slopes and friendly instructors; Robert learnt fairly swiftly, and Charles overcame his baby habit of wandering off towards the summit of Mont Blanc as soon as one's eye was off him. As the scope for advanced skiing from the Prarion is limited, and our sons in their teens soon overtook my own very modest abilities, they went elsewhere in pursuit of more adventurous pistes.

Everyone who has visited the chalet either loves it or hates it. Nine out of ten of those we took there loved it, and treasured an unforgettable experience. A few found the mountains depressing and the house claustrophobic, and would sneak off down to the valley in search of gin and tonic, but they were the exception – just as the days when we were kept indoors while rain and hail bounced off the roof were few by comparison with those when one could read and sunbathe on the lawn while listening to the tinkling of the stream. Reading parties provided not only a magnificent, if Spartan, holiday, but also a great environment for academic work. Senior members writing books often made such astonishing progress that one began to wonder whether there might not after all be something in David Urquhart's theories about the ideal altitude for the operation of the mind. Jonathan Barnes, who in the 1970s produced a two-volume study of the Pre-Socratic philosophers, wrote in his preface, 'The book was begun and ended at the Chalet des Mélèzes, a living reminder of a lost and better world.'

7

Senior Tutor

ALL OXFORD COLLEGES nowadays have Senior Tutors, but in Balliol the office was initiated only in 1947, and was until 1962 combined with that of Tutor for Admissions. After that, Senior Tutor and Tutor for Admissions shared an office on the ground floor of the old Master's Lodgings. In April 1971 I moved into this office beside Bill Weinstein, who was just coming to the end of his period as Tutor for Admissions. For the first time in my life I had a secretary to myself: hitherto, as a Fellow without a College office I had given copy-typing to the Fellows' secretary, but typed most of my own letters. I have had many secretaries since, in many jobs, but none ever as good as my first, Julia Hore. (She eventually went on to become Balliol's College Secretary, and the most important influence for good in the institution.)

The Senior Tutor is responsible for the academic administration of a college. Balliol was ruled by a Governing Body, consisting of all the Fellows (whether tutors, professors, or junior researchers) and chaired by the Master, but much of the general management was delegated to an Executive Committee of a dozen Fellows. The Tutorial Board, an assembly of the tutors meeting thrice a term, took both general decisions on academic policy, and particular decisions about the courses and disciplining of individual students; the Senior Tutor, as the secretary and executive officer of this body, had ultimate responsibility for arranging and monitoring the tutorial teaching of the junior members. In practice, the implementation of most decisions was delegated to tutors in individual subjects, and the Senior Tutor only intervened if some tutor neglected to make suitable arrangements. The Senior Tutors collectively formed a committee to achieve coherence in academic standards and policies between the colleges, agreeing the amount of teaching to be reasonably requested of college tutors and fixing standard rates for the payment of free-lance teaching by outsiders.

The Senior Tutor was an *ex officio* member of the Executive

Committee, which met weekly and conducted the greater part of routine College business. The other administrative officers on that committee were the Estates Bursar, with responsibility for the generation of College endowment income, and the Domestic Bursar, with responsibility for running the College's 'hotel' side. At this time the Estates Bursar was the lawyer Don Harris (who had already served the College as Senior Tutor in 1962–66), the Domestic Bursar 'Jacko' Jackson, a retired brigadier, wounded in the Aden campaign. The committee included, in addition to the Bursar and sometimes in opposition to him, the Dean, who had responsibility for discipline. In 1972 Frank MacCarthy was succeeded in that office by John Jones, a chemistry tutor, who held the job for twenty-five years. This committee was chaired by the Vice-Master, the holder of which office changed every two years. Executive Committee was subject to Governing Body, and its decisions could be recalled and overturned; but in practice much of the business left for Governing Body was more or less ceremonial. A really contentious item would be referred for discussion at Consilium, a one-hour informal meeting of Fellows held at 6 p.m. on Wednesdays. A straw vote taken at Consilium would normally be rubber-stamped by Governing Body: the constitution of the two bodies was, after all, identical. The Wednesday afternoon sequence of committees and consilia would end with a dinner in the SCR, which all Fellows were encouraged to attend. The theory was that any quarrels between Fellows which might have occurred during the conduct of College business would be healed before bedtime in the convivial atmosphere of this Consilium Dinner.

In the early 1970s much time in College committees was taken up with discussing relations between senior and junior members. Twice a term the Executive Committee held meetings with the JCR Committee. These were rarely productive, and often testy; Brigadier Jackson, in particular, found it difficult to endure with patience the doctrinaire posturing of some of the young men. (I once suggested to him that these encounters were character-building experiences. 'May we take it as a working assumption', he responded, 'that my character is already built?') The student reformers wished not just to meet with, but to sit as of right on, the Executive Committee. Christopher Hill was sympathetic, but failed to convince most of his colleagues of the merits of the proposal; they feared the kind of rhetoric typical of joint meetings would hold up urgent College business.

I stood somewhere in the middle between Christopher and Jacko: I was not in favour of putting junior members on Governing Body, or on Executive Committee, but I felt they should have more say in the running of their own lives than the patriarchal and military approach of

Jacko would have allowed them. As Senior Tutor I was anxious to keep on good terms with both wings of opinion among Fellows; my policy, as I explained in an unguarded moment to Jasper Griffin, was 'Vote with the Left and drink with the Right.' As merely a stand-in during Patrick Sanders's year as a Proctor, I felt my role was more to keep the machinery ticking over than to take initiatives in academic policy.

Meanwhile, I was able to continue with philosophical writing. I had been under contract with Penguin since 1967 to write an elementary introduction to the philosophy of Wittgenstein, but the MS was not completed until September 1971. The book, though written for the general reader and the undergraduate classroom, contained also some challenges to the contemporary orthodoxy among professional scholars. In particular I rejected the common view that Wittgenstein had fathered two unconnected philosophies, the rigid logical atomism of the *Tractatus Logico-Philosophicus* at the time of the First World War, and a more fluid ordinary-language version of analytical philosophy in the posthumously published *Philosophical Investigations*. I showed that this view was no longer tenable in the light of Wittgenstein's intermediate writings of the 1930s, recently published, and that his philosophical interests had remained remarkably constant while his ideas had developed in a continuous and organic manner. As usual, I tried out the chapters of the book as lectures in Oxford, and in January 1971 I was able to present its main ideas in four lectures to a graduate seminar at Cornell University in the presence of two of the most distinguished senior Wittgensteinians, Norman Malcolm and Max Black.

Wittgenstein was delayed in publication, as it had been in writing, and finally appeared in 1973. It was generously reviewed, and widely adopted as a textbook; over the years it was translated into Dutch, Spanish, German, Japanese and French – this last a version so atrocious that it was pulped after protests from Penguin and myself.

During the academic year 1971/2 I paid regular visits to Scotland to take part in a series of Gifford Lectures. At his death in 1887 the Scottish judge Lord Gifford left endowments to the universities of Edinburgh, Glasgow, Aberdeen and St Andrews for undogmatic lectures in natural theology; these were normally delivered as a set of ten lectures by a single lecturer, and by 1971 a series of solemn and weighty volumes on the shelves of university libraries enshrined the wisdom of august past lecturers. For the session of 1971/2, however, the Edinburgh Gifford Committee decided to recruit a circus of four lecturers to debate with each other on The Nature of Mind: Christopher Longuet-Higgins, a Royal Society professor in Edinburgh, was to represent the physical sciences, C.H. Waddington the biological sciences; I was to represent philosophy, and my colleague at Merton, John Lucas, theology. Each of us took it in turns to lecture, and after each series of four lectures there was one session of open discussion, making up the complement of ten.

I enjoyed these visits to Edinburgh: there was enough agreement between the four of us to make debate possible, and enough disagreement to make it lively. Each of us used different criteria to distinguish minds from non-minds. For Waddington, the mark of the mind was the pursuit of goals, while Longuet-Higgins, who was becoming increasingly fascinated by artificial intelligence, thought of the mind as the locus of a special type of programming. I conceived the mind as essentially the capacity for operating in symbols; while Lucas emphasized autonomy as the mind's defining feature. In our discussions, both public and private, we got on very well; and I particularly appreciated the opportunity to get to know Christopher. He and I often found ourselves in closer agreement than our two colleagues, and would repair to his favourite oyster bar to thrash out the nature of intelligence. During the course of the lectures John Lucas developed the argument – since made much more famous by Roger Penrose – that since the mind is capable of insights which cannot be captured in any algorithm, the mind cannot be any kind of computer.

Besides working on the Gifford Lectures I was also preparing for publication some posthumous works of Arthur Prior's. Mary Prior found among his papers a set of manuscripts intended for a book entitled 'Objects of Thought', and invited Peter Geach and myself to edit it. Ten of eleven planned chapters were extant, in various stages of completeness, and we were able to reconstruct a version of the eleventh; the book was published by OUP in 1971. We also put together a volume of *Papers in Logic and Ethics* to match the set of *Papers on Time and Tense* which Prior had published just before he died; finally, we learnt that in 1951 Prior had completed a manuscript of 220,000 words with the title 'The Craft of Logic'. This had never been published – OUP had demanded substantial cuts – and up to his death Arthur had mined it for other books and papers, but Geach and I were able to find sufficient original and unpublished material to make *The Doctrine of Propositions and Terms*. This and the *Papers* were published by Duckworth later in the 1970s.

Geach and I shared an admiration for Prior, and enjoyed working together on his papers, but when it came to writing introductions and annotations, there was a certain contrast between my bland philosophical prose and the more pungent style he favoured: John Lucas tells an apocryphal story of sitting beside me on a flight to Edinburgh and

seeing me edit Geach's 'Prior's work on this topic shows up the shoddi-
ness of the efforts of that fool Quine and that nincompoop Strawson'
into 'No philosopher has spent more time on the elucidation of this
topic than Quine and Strawson; but even their genius and devotion
failed to achieve some of the insights which Prior here displays.' Like
many myths, the story contains a kernel of truth.

When my year as Senior Tutor came to an end I was owed another
sabbatical term. My current academic project was the translation into
English of Wittgenstein's *Philosophische Grammatik*, which had appeared
posthumously in 1969. I was happy with my grasp of the thrust of what
Wittgenstein was saying in each paragraph, but not confident enough of
my German to publish the translation without having a careful eye cast
over it by a native speaker. The German philosopher I knew best was
Ernst Tugendhat, who had more than once been my guest at the chalet.
I offered to spend my sabbatical at Heidelberg, and teach his pupils
some courses, if he would agree to vet my translation.

Nancy and I and the children drove to Germany in April, spending a
week in Holland on the way. For the boys the major excitement was the
toy Lego village at Madurodam; for Nancy, the paintings in the Kröller-
Müller museum at Oterloo; for me, the church in Dordrecht where in a
Synod of 1618 the Calvinists had routed the Arminians in debates on
predestination and freewill. We all enjoyed a visit to the cheese town of
Alkmaar, where Descartes had lived in self-imposed exile from France
and where, in one of the boys' favourite picture-books, the cow
Hendrika had fallen into the canal.

In Heidelberg we moved into a small apartment in the newly completed University Guest House, supported by a Visiting Fellowship
awarded by the British Academy. Each week I produced my quota of
translation pages; at the weekends Tugendhat came round to go
through the text with me, correcting errors I had made and explaining
passages which had baffled me.

Translation has always been for me a task congenial as a relaxation
from real writing. In one's own work one may be depressed by writer's
block, or find onself having to tear up the work of weeks. As a trans-
lator, each day's stint has its reward; moreover, one can lay the task aside
for months and pick it up again without having lost the thread of one's
thoughts, as I had discovered in translating Aquinas and Descartes.

But if this was a relaxed time for me, it was not so for Tugendhat. As
Dean of a Faculty he was caught between vociferous radicals in
Heidelberg and rigid bureaucracy in the Kulturministerium of Baden-
Württemberg. At one time threatened by revolutionaries, he needed an
armed guard on his house; at another, he was reprimanded at Stuttgart

for adopting a negotiating stance of which the Minister disapproved. In these circumstances it was an extraordinary act of kindness to give so much time to helping me with my translation.

As in Seattle, so in Heidelberg I could see how mild our Oxford perturbations were by comparison with those suffered by academic colleagues overseas. The most surprising feature of the German scene was the way concessions wrung from the authorities by the threat of disruption were then formally incorporated into legislation. For instance, at Heidelberg there was an institution known as 'Tutorials' – not cosy one-to-one discussions between pupil and tutor (these, when held, were specifically described as 'Tutorials on the Oxford pattern'), but a form of counter-lecture. A professor would give his lecture, perhaps on the interpretation of Hegel, and then immediately one of the students would give a second lecture pointing out the erroneous bourgeois ideology contained in the professor's and contrasting it with the true Marxist position as seen by the students. The extraordinary thing was not that the professors had to put up with this, but that the tutorials were funded out of the education budget by the Christian Democrat government of Baden-Württemberg.

I wondered what the students would say about my own lectures, on Wittgenstein, but fortunately I was exempted from 'Tutorials'. Perhaps it was because I was only a visitor, giving a short course. But it is possible that what I had to say was considered insufficiently ideologically unsound to need correction – as I soon discovered, the Marxist students in my class thought of Wittgenstein as a fellow-traveller, which took me by surprise as radical students in England regarded him as a reactionary pillar of the status quo. But the Heidelberg revolutionaries may have found congenial Wittgenstein's notion of language games. This is the idea that in order to understand the meaning of any term it is no good looking at language alone, or at the thoughts going through a speaker's head: to understand how language functions, you have to look at the whole context of extra-linguistic social activity within which it is embedded. Wittgenstein's last work, *On Certainty*, left unfinished at his death, extended the notion of language-games to the body of scientific knowledge as a whole. It was not hard to see how this could be an attractive notion to those who saw contemporary Western science as a bourgeois phenomenon conditioned by the social pressures and distortions of capitalist society.

For any historically-minded philosopher, a term in Germany is an exhilarating experience. Not only was Germany the home of one who is universally regarded as among the greatest philosophers of all time, Immanuel Kant; but all lively twentieth-century philosophical traditions derive in one way or another from nineteenth-century German philosophy. As I observed in a BBC talk about my experience in Heidelberg,

> You can divide contemporary philosophers into four classes: if you want to find out which of the four classes a philosopher belongs to, you've only to ask . . . 'Who was the greatest nineteenth-century German philosopher?' There are four possible answers: he may name Hegel, or Marx, or Frege; or he may say, 'It all depends what you mean by great.' If someone gives you the last answer, you know you are dealing with a linguistic or analytical philosopher, and you need not have any more to do with him because he is a bad analytical philosopher. If he were a good analytical philosopher he would have answered 'Frege', without hesitation: because he would have accepted even his standards of greatness in philosophy from Frege himself.

In Heidelberg and in the other three or four German universities I visited I encountered three different groups of philosophers. The most vociferous, at least among the younger generation, were the Marxists, some harsh and doctrinaire, others broader and more humane under the influence of the Frankfurt school. Then there were those who specialized in analytic philosophy, like Tugendhat himself, and Günter Patzig at Göttingen, who had promoted a belated discovery in Germany of the importance of Frege. For the third and perhaps the largest group, the inheritance of Hegel was still paramount. Heidegger's influence seemed to be on the wane, and few of those I met regarded themselves as in any sense existentialist: but the hermeneutic tradition was alive and well, and Hans-Georg Gadamer, old and frail but still shrewd, was a benign and authoritative presence at faculty discussion groups. I took the opportunity to try, not for the first time, to get to grips with the thought of Hegel. I was able to attend the seminars of two of the finest Hegel scholars of the age, Henrich and Theunissen; but as in previous attempts, I failed to derive from the texts any philosophical benefit commensurate with the pain invested in the effort.

The pink stone of Heidelberg provided a marvellous background for a sabbatical spring, and life in the Gästehaus was congenial, though for the most part it was with fellow visitors, Japanese and American, that we enjoyed ourselves, rather than with our busy German hosts. I soon gave up my initial hope that time spent here would make me fluent in German. I could read it without difficulty, and understand spoken German with effort, but I was glad that my students were happy for me to give my seminar in English. When I was invited to give public lectures, my sponsors would sometimes assume that my profession of incomptence was mere modesty, and encourage me to speak German. To disabuse them, I adopted the practice of lecturing for the first five minutes in German. I would then pause and say to the audience, 'Now that you have heard what my German is like, would you prefer me to continue in German or English?' The vote was always unanimous for English.

Attached to the academic guesthouse was an imaginative play area, and our children enjoyed themselves. Robert was much spoilt with sweetmeats by the shop-keepers of the neighbourhood, while Charles (for the time being 'Kleiner Karl') spent his sabbatical in learning to speak his first words. Robert was impressed, and a little envious, that so many nearby towns seemed to be called after facets of Charles's life: his nap and his bath, for instance, had given their names to Karlsruhe and Karlsbad.

An advantage of a Trinity Term sabbatical is that it runs into the Long Vacation, giving one six months of time free from Oxford teaching. From Heidelberg, in June, we moved to Stanford, where I was to teach in a summer session. We rented from the poet Donald Davie a delightful house, all glass, oversize flowers, and hummingbirds. We entertained a stream of visitors from both sides of our family, and the children almost lived in the campus swimming pool. The northern California climate was quite blissful, at least on first acquaintance. My classes, in a room on the cool Spanish cloister which housed the Philosophy Department, were neither particularly demanding nor particularly rewarding. But the visit provided an opportunity not just for basking in the California sun, but also for picking some of the finest philosophical brains from among those gathered at the Research Institute in nearby Palo Alto.

I have come to look back on the Heidelberg–Stanford sabbatical as one of the happiest experiences of Robert and Charles's early childhood. Whether they enjoyed all the travel and upheaval I am not so sure, especially as the summer was rounded off with an Italian holiday on Lake Bracciano and a September reading party at the chalet. However, I returned to Oxford with a complete draft of the Wittgenstein translation, and after extensive scrutiny by Rush Rhees, the executor of Wittgenstein who had edited the German edition, the text of *Philosophical Grammar* was sent off to the publishers, Blackwell, early in 1973.

In the academic year 1972/3 there was a second series of Gifford Lectures in Edinburgh, this time on 'The Development of Mind', which we discussed in terms both of the individual development of the embryo and the child, and of the evolution of the human race and its place in the history of the cosmos. In my own lectures I drew on the Church Fathers Jerome and Augustine to discuss whether individual minds were inherited or created, and set out a number of difficulties which stand in the way of regarding the human mind as the product of evolution. I argued that there were features of human language which were *prima facie* inexplicable by natural selection; but in this I found myself isolated from my fellow lecturers. In both years the cross-talk at the sessions was intellectually lively, in a knockabout way, and we had no difficulty sustaining the enthusiasm of a large audience. But when our lectures and discussions were published, in two volumes of cold print, they seemed rather flimsy by comparison with the elucubrations of previous Gifford lecturers. As Gilbert Ryle remarked apropos – tartly, but justly – 'Good talking often makes poor reading.'

In Oxford, after the lull secured by the Hart Report, student agitation began again in Michaelmas Term 1973. It now focused on the demand for a central student union. The hard-core Marxists professed to aim at the overthrow of the capitalist system, and saw the bourgeois universities as the soft underbelly most vulnerable to attack. It was not sheer fantasy to imagine that the fabric of a social system might be torn apart by undergraduate misbehaviour: after all, the 1968 student revolution in Paris had nearly toppled de Gaulle, and student protests in the US had been one factor in producing national disillusionment with the Vietnam war. But so far the achievements of the Oxford radicals had been meagre: a degree of student participation in committee discussions and in the enforcement of discipline; a relaxation of some ceremonial rules; and a more permissive attitude to sexual relations.

The radicals decided the problem lay with the collegiate system. Because of it, there had been none of the great three-cornered confrontations between Students, Faculty and Administration which had torn apart universities in the US and on the continent. Members of JCRs, whatever their rhetoric, remained on terms of personal intimacy with their tutors; there were many occasions in the year, and not only on the river or the sports field, when, for example, a Trinity undergraduate would feel he had more in common with a Trinity don than with a Balliol undergraduate. The remedy for this disgracefully eirenic state of affairs – so the radicals argued – lay in setting up a central students' union.

The official leadership of the student body, university-wide, though to the left of many JCRs, was not commonly drawn from the extreme radicals; indeed, it was because the Student Representative Council was regarded as too moderate that there was agitation for a central students' union. The great majority of students did not share in the Marxist agenda; but from time to time they were willing to take part in a demonstration or a sit-in, partly as a lark, partly to keep the dons on their toes.

In November 1973 the Examination Schools – a perfect site, the radicals argued, to instal a central students' union – were occupied for a
week. Lecturers were, perhaps, not too distressed at having to cancel or
re-allocate their lectures, but the harassment of University police and
staff alienated many students who might otherwise have felt sympathy
with the radicals. A referendum after the sit-in showed that the majority of Oxford's students supported the moderate leadership of the
Student Representative Council. No one was disciplined by the
University for the occupation of the Schools and the disruption it had
caused; possibly the University authorities, caught unprepared, had not
collected sufficient evidence against particular individuals to bring a
successful prosecution before the disciplinary courts. But the Proctors
bided their time.

Despite their rebuff in the referendum, the radicals persisted. The
Balliol JCR was regarded by many throughout the University as the
focus of student radicalism. In fact, in 1972/3 the JCR had a right-
wing president, an Irish classicist named Patrick McDonagh, and
probably the majority of JCR members were no different from the
majority of students throughout Oxford. But other JCR officers were
radicals, and in JCR meetings there were enough activists willing to sit
through interminable procedural motions and filibusters until non-
politicized members left in bored frustration. During the last minutes
of a barely quorate meeting, inflammatory motions could be rushed
through, or direct action could be mandated in terms which were
deliberately kept vague. McDonagh had a difficult time, and did not
complete his year in office; he was succeeded by a graduate computer
specialist, Christopher Brickhill, who was more willing to go along
with the radicals.

The winter of 1973/4 was the miserable period in which the miners' ban
on overtime caused Prime Minister Heath to impose a three-day
working week. Throughout the country, embattled miners and left-wing
students made common cause. In Balliol buttery unfamiliar, burly,
middle-aged men were to be seen drinking with the JCR committee. On
7 February an election was called for the 28th; on 10 February the
miners began an all-out strike; on 13 February fifty students – in pur-
suance of the radicals' policy of designating possible sites for a student
union – invaded the Indian Institute building. This time the University
officials were ready. The intruders were forcibly expelled by members
of the administrative staff, proving that middle-aged men who had been
brought up on rugby were physically more than a match for their
juniors who had confined their sporting activities to pool. Though

there was still no central union as a launching pad for revolution, even a collegiate university had a central administration for a target: on 4 March rioters attacked the offices in Wellington Square, and were repulsed by the University police and staff.

The patience of senior Oxford at last snapped and the new – unwieldy – disciplinary statutes were put to work. Three dons and two students formed a court to try eighteen delinquents who had been personally identified. It was discovered that the Hart recommendations had failed to include any provision for dealing with contempt of court: the proceedings were constantly disrupted by shouting, singing and whistling members of the student public, often in fancy dress. After a highly embarrassing trial, more like the last night of the Proms than proceedings in a court of law, all the accused were found guilty and rusticated for a year.

Hart had provided an appeals procedure, to a court to be chaired by an outside QC; the appeals of thirteen were presided over by Patrick Neill, QC. No more protected against contempt than the previous judges, he kept order effectively by a severe use of his eyebrows. One sentence was reduced, the other appeals were dismissed. Now that it had been dealt with seriously, student disruption petered out. There were no further troubles of this kind for the rest of the decade.

I began to feel a certain distaste for the student generation. In 1974 a Senior Research Fellowship at All Souls was advertised, designed to support scholarship and writing, and involving no obligation to teach. It sounded attractive, and I applied. However, some time after the job had been advertised, Michael Dummett, a prize Fellow of All Souls, disqualified himself as one of the electors, and also applied. In competition with the most distinguished philosopher of his generation, no one else could hope to be chosen. Disappointed at the time, I have long since been thankful that my connection with Balliol was not severed at a time of temporary disillusionment.

The summer of 1974 brought academic encouragement, too: in July I was elected a Fellow of the British Academy. I had only a rather vague notion of the nature of this august body, but I did know that such an honour was the equivalent, in the Arts, of a Fellowship of the Royal Society for a scientist, and that many of the philosophers I most admired were already Fellows, so I was delighted to accept. At forty-three I was a comparatively young member of a body of senior scholars, and for some years I took very little part in the Academy's affairs.

After another family holiday on Lake Bracciano and a good September chalet party which reminded us that the company of undergraduates could be a delight as well as a bore, I returned refreshed for the new academic year at Balliol. Relations between senior and junior members resumed something much more like their normal tone.

The student troubles of the 1970s were painful and in some aspects disgraceful, but in the end they made surprisingly little difference – though this was not obvious at the time, and many dons worried that Oxford would never be the same again. The academic life of the University was very little affected: even during sit-ins, students took it in turns to leave for a couple of hours, to read essays to tutors, or make sure that experiments were progressing according to plan in the laboratory. Even the traditional ceremonial of the University survived intact: students still wear subfusc for matriculation and examination and take an oath not to light fires in the Bodleian. No major public ceremony, such as the conferment of honorary degrees at Encaenia, has ever been seriously disrupted.

Many new courses were introduced as a result of student demand in the 1960s and 1970s, and interdisciplinary honour schools multiplied. But though these changes were sometimes a response to dubious demands for 'relevance', syllabuses were never hijacked by temporary student fashion, as happened in some universities on the continent and in the US, and most of the courses have survived to the present day on their academic merits. They did place extra, sometimes excessive, burdens on teachers and libraries, but almost all dons would be prepared to defend the academic value of their content and the rigour of the standards to which they are examined. The need for extra fee income and benefactions in the 1980s was to prove more of a threat to academic standards in Oxford than student power had ever been.

The one obvious and permanent change which came about was that the Oxford authorities ceased to make any attempt to control the sexual lives of junior members. Gate hours were universally abolished; the midnight lock-out was succeeded by lodges open all night, or the issuing of keys. Rules forbidding the presence of visitors of the opposite sex were repealed, or fell into disuse. Long-term cohabitation was still discouraged, but placed on an economic rather than a moral footing, with an insistence that rooms were let only for single-person occupation. It was not the threat of direct action that brought about these changes; long before the student troubles began, many dons had thought it wrong to enforce chastity on junior members, and colleges routinely installed contraceptive machines. Oxford merely kept pace with – in fact followed a little behind – changes in society as a whole; the permissive university was brought about by the permissive society. The Latey Report in 1967 had declared young people to be adults at 18, and in 1969 they were given the vote. Since most students were now officially adults, there was only a dubious legal basis for University and college authorities to claim to be acting *in loco parentis*.

Christopher Hill, always a great enemy of moralizing, proposed that in Balliol the traditional term 'moral tutor' should be replaced by 'personal tutor', since it was no part of a tutor's buiness to try to enforce a moral code upon a pupil who was another self-responsible adult. The Fellows agreed to the change. I mentioned it to one of my classics pupils. 'Oh,' he said, 'and did you all vote to halve the tuition fee as well?'

8

The Quantification of Style

AFTER COMPLETING *Will, Freedom and Power* in 1975 I began to dream of writing a comprehensive history of freewill, a subject which has never ceased to fascinate me, covering what had been said and thought not only by philosophers and theologians through the centuries, but also by lawyers, psychologists and physiologists in recent times. The task would be enormous, and would involve mastering disciplines I was unfamiliar with. I thought of it as something that would take about twenty years, to be taken up and laid down from time to time. I was aware by now that my talents were insufficient to make any significant original contribution to philosophy; but a work of historical philosophy such as this might have a permanent value in the philosophy of mind.

One day a colleague from another university, who had been a graduate student in Oxford with me, said, 'You would never write about philosophy of logic without knowing something about symbolic logic; how can you dare to write about philosophy of mind when you know nothing about artificial intelligence?' I did not think the parallel was apt then, and do not now; but I was stung by the remark.

I was not totally uninformed about artificial intelligence: I had met some of its foremost practitioners at a conference at Berkeley in 1970, and had read some of their writings. I knew the discipline was a special branch of computer science which aimed not simply to use computers to solve problems, but to write programs which would solve problems in the way human beings solve them. Artificial intelligence was related to computer science as the attempt to build a flying model bird is related to the building of an aeroplane. I had not been impressed by the writings of those who wished to use computers to mimic human mental operations, because they appeared to have a naïve and unphilosophical idea of the human mind itself. But I had to admit that I had not made a serious study of AI, and that indeed I had never myself made use of a computer.

I decided to remedy at least the latter defect, and took elementary courses in a chilly room in the old Atmospheric Physics building. At this time beginners still wrote programs and entered data by punching cards; and we had to punch the cards hole by hole, with a hand-held machine like a tree-pruner. Learning in this way was a slow business, but I persevered until I had mastered the programming language ALGOL68 and progressed to swifter and more elegant forms of data entry.

Naturally, I did not want to learn in a vacuum: I wanted to have a problem or problems which I could use a computer to solve. Fortunately, Oxford had a teaching officer, Susan Hockey, who gave classes on the use of computers in humanities scholarship. I enrolled in her course, and found her one of the best teachers I have ever encountered. She taught me how to use a computer to make concordances, and gave me a feel for the kinds of areas where the computer is useful to the scholar. Through her teaching and my own experience I came to have a sober appreciation of the strengths and weaknesses of computers, especially in the field of the humanities.

From time to time we read in the newspapers that the computer has solved some problem in literary history – it has proved that the Epistle to the Ephesians was not really written by the Apostle Paul, or discovered a new play by Shakespeare (the 'Play of Sir Thomas More'), or spoken the last word on the question whether the book of Genesis was written by Moses in person or was the work of a committee of latter-day Jewish scribes.

Claims of this kind are almost totally misleading. Most people have no experience of using the computer in literary studies, but have been much exposed to science-fiction films. When told that the computer has proved this and that, they are apt to imagine a robot gifted with a degree of intelligence far beyond that of any flesh and blood literary scholar and picture it settling, scientifically, problems which for centuries have baffled the amateurish methods of historians and philologists.

It is worth saying quite firmly that computers cannot *prove* anything. Computers cannot, in the literal sense, carry out even the simplest arithmetical tasks. It is often said that computers can carry out many calculations much better than human beings. But this is true only in the sense in which we say that clocks can tell the time better than human beings. That is, if you want to know the time, you do better to look at a clock than to make a guess in your head. But it is we human beings who use clocks to discover what the time is: a clock cannot tell the time, and would not know what to do with it if it could. The same goes for computers: a display or printout counts as a solution to a mathematical problem only because of the meanings of the symbols it contains, and the meaning is conferred on those symbols by the part they play in our lives. Computers cannot confer meaning on their output because they have no lives for it to play a part in.

This is a very general point about the limitations of computers. But there is an extra point in addition about the use of computers in literary contexts: computers do not solve literary problems even in the transferred sense in which they can be said to solve mathematical problems; all they do is facilitate calculation and provide additional data for scholars who use statistical methods in the study of style. Those who use computers in attempting to solve literary problems employ methods developed from those adopted by scholars long before computers were invented.

A scholar who has made loud claims for the powers of the computer to solve literary problems is the Revd A.Q. Morton, who in 1975 was the Presbyterian minister of the Abbey of Culross. In his book *Paul, the Man and the Myth* (1966) he had addressed the long-disputed problem of the authenticity of the Epistles of the Pauline corpus. Following previous work by W.C. Wake, he studied the length of sentences in the Epistles, and made extensive comparisons with sentence-lengths in other Greek authors. He showed that the variability in sentence-lengths between Epistles was beyond parallel in any of the other authors studied. On the basis of this, and of the frequency of occurrence of a number of common conjunctions and particles, he concluded that Romans, 1 and 2 Corinthians, and Galatians formed a homogeneous group which could be attributed to the Apostle Paul; between this group and the other Epistles there were a large number of significant differences, some of them larger than any differences known to exist in the writings of any other author, regardless of literary form or variation over time. The other Epistles, he suggested, might come from as many as six different hands.

I read Morton's book with keen interest: he has a vigorous and accessible style which can make the study of the authenticity of a text as exciting as a detective novel. Moreover, I found it a useful introduction to statistical argumentation, of which I had hitherto been quite ignorant. But I was sceptical about the confidence with which some of his conclusions were drawn.

At the time when I began to be interested in these matters, Morton's attention had turned to a number of classical Greek texts, in particular the works of Aristotle. In the early 1970s he claimed to have discovered the fingerprint of Aristotle – that is to say, a statistical test which would discriminate Aristotelian from non-Aristotelian texts. Using a number of such 'fingerprint' tests he claimed to have shown, for instance, that the *Constitution of Athens* was not a work of Aristotle; indeed, that it was 'so unlike his work that it is difficult to see how the suggestion that it might be Aristotelian would ever have gained support had it not been early assumed'.

I was most interested in this work, for it was on an Aristotelian problem that I intended to try my newly acquired computer skills. I knew that many classical scholars were very sceptical of Morton's methods; but I knew also that they were taken seriously by Professor Kenneth Dover, whom many regarded as the foremost Greek scholar of the age. I decided, before applying Morton's methods to my own problem, to make some checks of my own on his claims.

One of Morton's tests for Aristotelian authorship was based on the frequency of certain Greek particles (*de* and *gar*) as the second word in a sentence; another depended on the syntactic category of the final words of sentences. Sentences were divided into three classes: those ending in a noun, those ending in a verb, and those ending in some other part of speech. A comparison of samples from Aristotle with those from other authors shows Aristotle to differ from the others in that an unusually high proportion of his sentences end in parts of speech other than nouns or verbs.

I applied the tests Morton had devised, not just to samples of selected works, as he had, but to the hundred-odd works of the entire corpus. The result of my counting (in which I enrolled hapless students, friends, family members and chalet parties) was that though Morton had detected features which were characteristic of much that Aristotle wrote, to take these features as knock-down discriminators would mean excluding from the corpus works of unimpeachable authenticity. I sent my results to Morton. He replied with a genial and helpful letter, the beginning of several years of friendly correspondence which culminated in his securing my election to the Royal Society of Edinburgh in 1979. However, neither then nor later did I feel that he was sufficiently disconcerted by my results or suitably willing to revise his claim to have discovered the 'fingerprint of Aristotle'.

In 1976 I published what I had discovered in an obscure and now defunct journal – my first publication on stylometry, the name now becoming current for the study of quantified features of style. I have never encountered evidence to suggest that anyone other than myself ever read the article.

In computer-aided authorship attribution studies, the aim is to detect possibly unconscious features of style which are characteristic of an author and which run right through his works. The presence of these features will, it is hoped, indicate an authentic work; a forgery will be given away by their absence. Such features may be tiny and, judged by conventional concepts of style, insignificant features of a work; but taken collectively, it is claimed, they will constitute a reliable criterion of authorship. Ideally, a stylometric test of authorship should be a feature which is characteristic of all the known works of a particular author and which is unique to his works. However, features which are to be found in all, and only in, the works of a particular author turn out to be frustratingly difficult to come by, as my studies of the Aristotelian corpus illustrated.

Authorship attribution problems are easiest to deal with when they can be cast in the following form: in respect of the measured features, does the doubtful work resemble the work of candidate author A more than it resembles the work of candidate author B? A classic example of this kind of study was the work of the Harvard statisticians Frederick Mosteller and David Wallace on the Federalist Papers, a series of articles published in 1787 and 1788 to persuade the citizens of New York to ratify the US Constitution; some are known to have been written by Hamilton, and some by Madison, but the authorship of twelve was disputed.

Mosteller and Wallace looked for 'marker words', those which were particular likes or dislikes of the two authors. Madison and Hamilton differed consistently, for instance, in their choice between *while* and *whilst*. In the fourteen essays known to be by Madison, *while* never occurs, *whilst* occurs in eight; *while* occurs in fourteen of forty-eight Hamilton essays, *whilst* never. Thus, the presence of *whilst* in five of the disputed papers pointed towards Madison as the author.

However, such markers were few in number, and Mosteller and Wallace found it useful to look rather for words which were used by both authors with comparative frequency, but at different rates. Prepositions, conjunctions, articles – 'function words' whose frequency is almost independent of context – provided suitable instances. It was found, for example, that low rates for 'by' were characteristic of Hamilton, high rates of Madison; with 'to' the situation was reversed. After considering several thousand words, Mosteller and Wallace found twenty-eight with strong discriminating power, including the function-words 'upon', 'also', 'an', 'by', 'of', 'on', 'there', 'this', and 'to'. On the basis of comparisons between the rates of use of these words, Mosteller and Wallace felt able to conclude beyond reasonable doubt that Madison had written the twelve disputed papers.

Two features are noteworthy in the problem Mosteller and Wallace tackled. First, the potential authors were a closed set: there were only two candidates. Second, no assumptions were necessary about the variability of an author's style. The question was not, Is this essay *too* unlike Madison to be by him? It was, rather, Does this essay resemble Madison more than Hamilton?

The Aristotelian problem I wanted to address was similar in form to that of the Federalist Papers. The Aristotelian corpus contains two ethical treatises of parallel structure, the ten-book *Nicomachean Ethics* and the seven-book *Eudemian Ethics*. The problem they present is not one of authorship attribution, since nowadays most scholars regard both treatises as genuinely Aristotelian; the puzzle is that three books make a double appearance in the manuscripts through which they have been transmitted to us, once as books five, six and seven of the *Nicomachean Ethics*, once as books four, five and six of the *Eudemian Ethics*. For generations scholars have argued about the relationship between the two treatises: the twentieth-century consensus is that the *Eudemian Ethics* was a juvenile work and the *Nicomachean Ethics* represented Aristotle's mature system. However, many of the arguments for the superiority of the *Nicomachean Ethics* were based on the books which the manuscripts assigned to both treatises. The prior question, in my view, was to settle which was the original home of the disputed books; this I hoped to determine by using the computer to make a close stylistic comparison between the disputed books and each of the rival contexts.

At that stage in the development of information technology, a study of this kind involved considerable labour. When I began, there was no machine-readable text of the *Eudemian Ethics*; I commissioned a graduate student, Stephan Gruen, to prepare such a text for me by punching cards. As the work progressed, however, there became available a complete tape of the works of Aristotle, produced by the Thesaurus Linguae Graecae in California, and I gratefully made use of that. Using the COCOA programme I produced word-lists and concordances for all the books of the two treatises, as a basis for the statistical comparisons. When first I began making such calculations I used ALGOL68 programs I had written myself; later far more user-friendly programs became available from the SPSS package popular with social scientists. The computing was all done on the Oxford ICL 1960A mainframe computer, and involved frequent visits to the computer centre in Banbury Road, at various hours of day and night, to input data and collect armfuls of bulky print-out.

Like the Federalist problem, mine was a simple matter of assigning a disputed text to one of two competing contexts; did text A resemble text B more than it resembled text C? Again, it was a matter of empirical investigation to discover which features of vocabulary varied between the *NE* and the *EE* and which, therefore, were the features which should be investigated in the disputed books. However, the number of features which turned out to discriminate the *NE* from the *EE* was very much greater than the number of discriminants between Madison and Hamilton. Significant differences were found in particle use, in the use of prepositions and adverbs, pronouns and demonstratives, and in the preference for different forms of the definite article. Altogether twenty-four independent tests were carried out, which involved some sixty per cent of the total word-usage in the text. In twenty-three out of twenty-four cases the tests gave an unambiguous answer – that the common books, considered as a whole or in small samples, resembled the Eudemian treatise more than the Nicomachean one. The wealth of the material and the straightforward nature of the problem meant that very simple statistical methods were adequate to establish the conclusion with a high degree of probability.

This result, established sometime in 1976, was gratifyingly unexpected. If the disputed books belong with the *Eudemian Ethics*, then much of the argument for the superiority of the *Nicomachean Ethics* collapses. Moreover, chronological references in the disputed books are consistent with the view that they – and therefore, now, the *Eudemian Ethics* – belong to the final period of Aristotle's life. My results, therefore, pointed to a reversal of the consensus of some seventeen centuries, that the *Nicomachean Ethics* is *the* Ethics of Aristotle.

I supplemented my statistical studies with historical and philosophical research of a more traditional form. I discovered that – according to the admittedly fragmentary evidence which survives – from the time of Aristotle until the second century AD the *Eudemian Ethics* was given the pre-eminence which scholars have since given to the Nicomachean treatise. I selected a number of important ethical topics, such as the nature of wisdom and the nature of happiness, and showed that the teaching of the disputed books was more consistent with that of the Eudemian treatise than the Nicomachean.

The three strands of argument – historical, stylistic, and philosophical – were gathered together in a book entitled *The Aristotelian Ethics*, which I offered to OUP. After a long delay a favourable report was received from their reader, D.J. Allen, at that time the doyen of Aristotelian studies in this country. Seeing the book through the press was a nightmare: the amount of Greek in the text, and the number of statistical tables and graphs, gave great scope for error; the proofs had to be sent back many times, and many mistakes, both mine and the printer's, remain in the published text. Publication was so delayed that I began to worry lest my conclusions be anticipated by a team of scholars at Louvain who were studying the same problems with much more money and much more computer time. I hastened to read summaries of my results to universities in Britain and the US, from the Moral Sciences Club at Cambridge to the University of Texas in Austin, as an insurance against being beaten to the post by the Louvain team. It is unusual for a philosopher to have to worry about establishing priority in research, such a common problem in the life of a scientific researcher.

At last the book appeared, in 1978. It was widely reviewed, but many reviewers were clearly puzzled what to make of it. While most accepted, with varying degrees of reluctance, my claim to have shown that the disputed books originated in the *Eudemian Ethics*, many resisted the conclusion that this treatise therefore had as much claim to be definitive as the *Nicomachean Ethics*. My statistical argument received better treatment from the statisticians than from the philosophers, some of whom did their best to savage it in their reviews; the leading US stylometrist, Richard Bailey, held it up as model for statistical studies of authorship, and Mosteller and Wallace, in a second edition of their classic Federalist study, presented a summary of my book in an appendix covering the best recent work in the field.

Two other books grew out of the work I put into *The Aristotelian Ethics*. I had originally intended to include as part of the philosophical argument, along with the discussions of happiness and wisdom, a comparison between the treatment of voluntariness and practical reasoning in the disputed books and their rival contexts. The material, however, was so abundant and so complicated that it would have been out of proportion to the rest of the argument. Accordingly, I worked it up into a separate book, published by Duckworth in 1979 under the title *Aristotle's Theory of the Will*. Containing no statistical or historical argument, it was altogether a more humdrum and traditional piece of work than *The Aristotelian Ethics*, and perhaps for this reason was rather more kindly treated by philosophical reviewers.

The second book to be spun off from my long hours in the computer centre was something quite different. Susan Hockey's courses had made it clear to me that a humanist scholar had no reason to be afraid of the computer: handling machine-readable texts was a comparatively simple matter. The real difficulty in the use of the computer in analysis of style is the necessity for a mastery of statistics. Most humanists had, like myself, given up mathetmatics after O-level or its equivalent; few of us had ever been given any training in the use of statistics either for description or for argument. In the course of writing *The Aristotelian Ethics* I had worked my way through the statistics exercises in a number of elementary textbooks. All had been written for either natural or social scientists: there was no statistics textbook in English designed for the historian or the literary scholar. Accordingly, the examples to be worked through and the methods to be mastered often turned out to be only marginally relevant to the particular skills I wished to acquire. When I had finished my work on Aristotle, I therefore decided to write the text-book I wished I had had. My plan was to explain only those statistical techniques which were likely to be useful to the literary scholar, to take all the examples and exercises from literary contexts, and to write at a level, and move at a pace, which would present no problems for those who were starting from a base of O-level mathematics. I thought a conventional publisher might be reluctant to publish such an oddly con-ceived textbook; so I offered it to Robert Maxwell for Pergamon Press. He gave it a surprisingly warm welcome, but rejected the various titles I proposed. Though the statistical techniques explained in the book could all be worked with pencil and paper or pocket calculator, he insisted that it be called *The Computation of Style*; it would only sell, he told me, if the title contained some allusion to computers. Published by Pergamon in 1982, the book was kindly reviewed and occasionally adopted as a text-book for university courses; for several years it was the only textbook of statistics in English for the humanities scholar.

Later I returned once more to the stylometric study of Aristotle, and for the first time I did address the issue of authorship attribution. In 1981 the Symposium Aristotelicum held a meeting in Berlin devoted to a number of dubious works in the Aristotelian canon, *De motu animal-ium*, *Metaphysics* α and K, *Meteorologica* IV, and *Categories*, and I was invited to offer a paper on the possible contribution of stylometry to the ques-tion of authenticity. In it I took the twenty-four commonest particles, ascertained the frequency of each particle in each work, and thus con-structed the distribution of the works of the corpus in respect of each particle. Studying it in this way gave one an indication of the mean, and also an empirical measure of dispersion. One would hope that spurious works might reveal themselves by appearing at the edge of the distribu-tion. The results provided some evidence in favour of the authenticity of *Metaphysics* K and of the *De motu animalium*, while casting doubt on that of the other works under discussion. But I did not claim that this evidence amounted to a conclusive proof either way.

Indeed, after ten years' work on the Aristotleian corpus I came to the conclusion that no criterion or set of criteria yet suggested offered a plausible test of authorship. All that stylometry can do for authorship attribution, I concluded, was to offer additional evidence for and against authenticity, complementing rather than superseding traditional methods.

The general public can view with equanimity the success or failure of stylometric methods when applied to arcane questions of the authenticity of the corpus of a long-dead author. But stylometry is also increasingly being applied in quite a different context: that of the courts. It is sometimes a question whether a particular confession is the unaided work of an accused person, or a fabrication of a police officer. Stylometric evidence was admitted in such a case in 1974: a California court trying Patricia Hearst for bank robbery was asked to hear stylometric evidence to help determine whether she had composed the propaganda for the Symbionese Liberation Army which was part of the case against her. The trial judge refused the evidence on the grounds of 'the relative infancy of this area of scientific endeavor'. But since then such evidence has been admitted in English courts, and from time to time prisoners who allege that they have been incarcerated on the basis of fabricated confessions have written to ask me to examine the confessions and appear as an expert witness in the Court of Appeal. I have always refused, being in fundamental agreement with the Patty Hearst judge, that stylometry is not yet a science comparable to that which underlies fingerprinting.

The mind has no fingerprints, but the features which a stylometrician measures can fairly be compared, if not to a fingerprint, at least to a signature. A signature is something that can be altered or copied with an effort; and yet a signature is something characteristic of an individual, and we use it, along with other things, as a means of identification in practical life, and in many contexts it has legal effects. The computer may some day assist us to recognize the stylistic signature of an individual: but only when many more comparative studies of the degree of stylistic variation in the same person's life have been completed. The computer will never be able to detect the fingerprints of the mind; and the day when it will be able to read the mind's signature is still in the future.

It may be thought that these investigations into stylometry have been far removed from the interest in freedom and determinism which stimulated my first encounter with the computer. On the contrary: the statistical investigation of style provides an ideal microcosm for the study of the relation between freedom and determinism. For the choice of words in a literary text is a free human action if there is any such thing; and yet, within any literary text, a researcher will be able to find regularities which were totally beyond the ken of the writer whose work exhibits them. No other field of study so clearly exhibits the interplay between free choice and scientific law.

9

The People's College

T HE YEAR 1975 began for me in a dramatic manner, in Yugoslavia. A philosopher from Zagreb, Ivan Supek, had founded an Inter-University Centre at Dubrovnik, where faculty from universities in Eastern and Western Europe were invited for a week or two to lecture to an audience of students similarly drawn from both sides of the Iron Curtain. I was invited, with Philippa Foot from Somerville and a dozen other philosophers from the US and Scandinavia, to be a 'resource person' for the first part of the term beginning on 6 January, to lecture on History and Ethics. At the same time, the international Pugwash Group – initially a group of physicists from East and West meeting at Pugwash in Nova Scotia to share concerns about nuclear weapons – had decided to broaden its agenda and hold a symposium on Sciences and Ethics in Dubrovnik on 14–18 January, and Philippa and I were invited to read papers to the group.

Among the Yugoslavs expected to attend these events in Dubrovnik were eight philosophers from Belgrade, known as the Praxis group; the best-known among them were Mihailo Marcović and Svetovar Stojanović. These were critical and open-minded Marxists, in good standing with the League of Communists until 1968, at which time they were believed, rightly or wrongly, to have instigated student demonstrations. Since then President Tito had mounted a campaign to have them removed from their posts, or at least to have their activities curtailed; but for seven years attempts to dismiss or suspend them were unsuccessful because they were almost unanimously supported by their university colleagues, whose power at that time was considerable under the self-management laws then governing Belgrade University. However in 1974 the campaign against them hotted up, and the self-management laws were changed, so that all the external members – making up 50 per cent – of the University council were appointed by the Serbian government, instead of only half, as hitherto. This was widely seen as a prelude to the dismissal and, it was rumoured, the imprisonment of the Belgrade eight.

We Western 'resource persons' of the Inter-University Centre
debated whether we should call off our January courses in protest. But
it would have been difficult to boycott the courses at the Centre without
also boycotting the Pugwash Symposium, which seemed to present an
excellent opportunity to organize an international protest against the
harassment of the eight. In the days before our departure from England
it was unclear, amid the rumours, what had actually happened to our
colleagues in Belgrade. Philippa and I prepared a protest document, to
be circulated to all those attending the Pugwash conference if it turned
out that the philosophers had been imprisoned or prevent from attending. We carried in our suitcases cyclostyled copies of the protest for distribution, which made us nervous while passing through Customs.

No one, however, searched our luggage; and no sooner had we
passed safely through Immigration than we saw Mihailo Marcović
among the welcoming party, so the cyclostyled pages became scrap
paper. The conference and the lecture courses passed off without incident.

In due course, however, the eight philosophers were suspended
under the new law. Through the good offices of Sir Alexander Glen, a
loyal old member of Balliol who had been with Tito's Partisans during
the war, I was able to make a very full protest to the Yugoslav
Ambassador in London, while other colleagues protested around the
world. All international protest was able to achieve was a comparatively
humane suspension: though the eight were forbidden to teach or take
part in university government, they continued to be paid a salary, and
were allowed to write and travel. Later in the year Marcović paid a visit
to Oxford, where he stayed with us at Lane House, to talk philosophy
with me, to sing with Nancy, and to play chess with Robert. He was on
his way to a visiting professorship in Pennsylvania.

From state Communism in Yugoslavia I came back to student
Marxism in Balliol. In the aftermath of the student revolution, too
many aspects of the College remained affected by the left-wing agenda
of an influential element among the students. JCR meetings spent a lot
of time in voting support, and sometimes funds, to whatever national or
international causes were currently in favour with the International
Marxist Group or the Socialist Workers' Party. The physical premises of
the JCR were in a state of considerable disrepair, not only because funds
which might have been spent on maintenance and redecoration were
dissipated on the purchase of multiple copies of the *Morning Star* and
donations in support of the Neasden Five, or whoever were the most

recent victims of fascist oppression; it was also deliberate policy that Balliol JCR should express a proletarian ethos – the common room must resemble a rundown inner city pub, not a gentleman's club.

Balliol had long had an honourable tradition of trying to attract students from a wide variety of backgrounds, holding it quite wrong that Oxford should draw such a large proportion of its intake from the public schools which formed such a small proportion of the educational system of the country as a whole. In my early years as a Fellow great efforts were made to broaden the College's intake, by open days, by visits of dons and students to state schools, by invitations to their sixth-formers to sample a week in College before deciding whether to apply. Christopher Hill, with Alan Montefiore and Bill Weinstein as Tutors for Admissions, had worked devotedly on these recruiting drives, enrolling public-spirited undergraduates to take part in them. Very gradually, the imbalance between state and independent schools began to be redressed.

Now, somehow, all this had gone sour. Instead of developing into a community where class was unimportant, the official JCR for a time turned into a battlefield where everything was seen in terms of class. To be taken seriously in JCR politics an undergraduate had to be, or pretend to be, working class. Many products of public schools either ignored the JCR and enjoyed their social life elsewhere – perhaps at the Union, boycotted as elitist by the official JCR – or else adopted protective colouring and behaved in an aggressive pseudo-proletarian manner. Paradoxically, after the Labour Secretary of State Shirley Williams abolished grammar schools in favour of comprehensive education, the proportion of students coming from independent schools actually increased, reversing the gains made by state schools in the previous decade. (In 1975 the proportion between independent and maintained sectors was 50/50; by 1979 it was 60/40.) But many candidates who might, in other circumstances, have been expected to apply to Balliol no longer did so. Old members would bring their sons up to Oxford, take a look at Balliol JCR, then encourage them to apply elsewhere.

Much College energy was wasted in trying to enforce discipline in the underground snug that was the JCR bar. The Fellows devoted much time to devising regulations and concluding concordats to ensure that the Dean's writ ran in the bar so that the Bursar could keep it and its facilities in a sufficiently decent state to be usable by conferences in the vacations. It was instructive for Fellows to read the graffiti in the loos at the end of term, before they were hosed down and whitewashed for the use of strangers.

However, it is easy to exaggerate, in retrospect, the College's problems in the late 1970s. We were comparatively free from trouble concerning drugs. No doubt marijuana was used in College from time to time in spite of college rules, but the worst drug scandals in Balliol antedated the era of student power. In 1965 Joshua Macmillan, grandson of the Prime Minister, was found dead in suspicious circumstances; the verdict at the inquest was misadventure, not suicide, but it came out that he had been a heroin addict. Howard Marks, a popular physics student of the 1964–8 generation, began at Balliol the career in the international drug trade which led to his being sentenced by a Federal Court in Miami to twenty-seven years' imprisonment for smuggling.

During this period no student commited a disciplinary offence which the College judged worthy of sending-down. Of course, this can be interpreted in more than one way: tutors are perennially reluctant to terminate the careers of their pupils. When a rustication or expulsion was on the agenda at Tutorial Board, even conservative dons, who in principle favoured the strictest enforcement of discipline, turned into prisoners' friends if their own pupils were in jeopardy, finding the most implausible extenuating circumstances for their misbehaviour.

Academic offences, such as plagiarism, continued to be punished severely, and we maintained our rule that anyone who failed to pass preliminary examinations at the second attempt should be sent down. But in some subjects excuses for postponing tutorials were too readily accepted, and the end-of-vacation examinations, called collections, were treated rather perfunctorily. Internal academic incentives, such as scholarships and prizes, were matters of contention since the radical students, and some of the dons, disapproved of them as smacking of elitism. Other colleges, which regarded these matters more seriously, overtook Balliol in the competitive league of academic performance known as 'the Norrington table' which graded colleges in accordance with the proportion of First, Second and Third classes obtained in final examinations.

Between 1964 and 1978 Balliol's position in the league declined. Here again, it is important not to exaggerate: the decline was only a relative one. The number of Firsts remained high in absolute terms, usually between twenty and twenty-five per cent and always well above the University average. This no doubt reflected the unusually high academic calibre of Balliol entrants as much as it represented 'value added' during their time with us. Over these years, the University average showed a gentle increase; but if Balliol's Firsts were above average, so were its Thirds. The proportion of Balliol Thirds did indeed reduce steadily in the years after 1964, but not so swiftly as the rest of the University, and

Balliol's tally, once below the University average, was now just above it. In 1978 the decline halted, and for the next few years Balliol's position within the Norrington table remained fairly stable.

After the Hart Report Balliol, like other colleges, began to allow student representation on decision-making committees. On some, such as the Library Committee, the junior members were useful and constructive. But on more powerful committees JCR representatives tended to see their role as that of Trades Union representatives asserting the rights of their constituents against oppressive employers. This was, of course, to reverse the actual economic relations between students and dons: it was the students (or those who were paying fees on their behalf) who were employing the dons to labour for their benefit. But this underlying absurdity did nothing to staunch the committee rhetoric.

Balliol had an unusually large number of committees. A reform drafted by Don Harris in 1968 had broken up a small number of large College committees and replaced them with a larger number of small, specialised ones. This was a good idea; but over time so many members had been co-opted to one or other committee that by the mid 1970s we had a large number of large and unwieldy committees. Initially, students were given places only on sub-committees which directly affected their welfare, such as the Disciplinary Committee and the Domestic Committee, and so on. But there was an insistent demand that they should take places on the Executive Committee, to which these committees reported and which was in effective charge of the day-to-day running of the College. Christopher Hill, whose principled belief in the virtues of student democracy was a continuing triumph of hope over experience, more than once urged Governing Body to accept this student demand. But he was unable to persuade the majority of his colleages, and the matter rested for a while.

At the end of 1975 the Kenny family crossed the wintry Atlantic on the QEII to spend Christmas with the Gayleys in Ithaca, then move to Michigan for a sabbatical term in Ann Arbor. The garden of our house perched high above the river, near the beginning of the Pontiac Trail, was under snow for nine-tenths of our visit. We were somewhat out-of-the-way, but if you wanted to go anywhere, you could pick up a telephone and the City would send a bus to collect you. Robert and Charles experienced their first American schools.

Of the many sabbaticals I have taken in American universities, this was the one I enjoyed least. The members of the Philosophy Department were very civil and very gifted, but I did not feel at home in an atmosphere where philosophy of mind was regarded as armchair neuroscience. Moreover, there seemed to be nothing that resembled a departmental or collegiate common room where philosophical issues could be informally discussed. I gave forty lectures for a course on the history of seventeenth- and eighteenth-century philosophy, and while working on them first came to a basic understanding of Kant's *Critique of Pure Reason*, which I had never taught in Oxford. As usual on sabbatical, I gave individual lectures in other North American universities, near and far: in Charlottesville, Kalamazoo, Philadelphia, Ottawa, St Louis, Los Angeles, and Gainsville, Florida.

Trinity Term, back in Oxford, was much more congenial. Alvin Plantinga was at Balliol for the year as a Visiting Fellow, and we gave a joint class on philosophy of religion. I was an examiner for the B.Phil., the graduate taught course in philosophy – a task less arduous and more rewarding than examining in a major honour school: most of the reading was not of handwritten examination papers but of typed and bound theses, and gave one a feel for the philosophical problems which were exercising the minds of the brightest graduate students.

I had been appointed to succeed Patrick Sandars as Senior Tutor at the beginning of the academic year 1976/7, and as a Senior Tutor has less freedom to determine his own timetable than other tutorial fellows, living out in Farmoor had its disadvantages. We moved into a College house at 7 Mansfield Road, in easy walking distance of the College offices and also much more convenient for the family. Both boys had had their early schooling in Cumnor, but now Robert was at New College School and Charles at the Squirrel, both in Oxford. Our new house had been built for the College in 1924 by the architect E.P. Warren; it was double-fronted and pleasant, much larger than Lane House, with an ample attic floor which the children could have to themselves, to play Dungeons and Dragons or lay out elaborate train tracks. It was set too close to the road in front but at the back a long garden gave most conveniently onto the Balliol tennis courts and cricket field.

Living in the centre of the city posed security problems from which we had been exempt in Lane House, but not all were very serious. One Sunday morning we found the car had vanished from the garage: it turned out that someone who missed the last bus had simply borrowed it to get back to Cowley. We had to go to the police station and sign the inventory of its contents – 'three chocolate biscuits, four toy cars, assorted Lego, two road maps, one torch, etc.'

At the same time as I became Senior Tutor I was appointed to a research lecturership in philosophy funded by the Radcliffe Trust, which provided for a reduction in my teaching duties to give me more time for writing. A further reduction given by the College to all its officers in compensation for their administrative duties meant that I had only a minimal tutorial stint of four hours a week, with more time than at any other period of my life for philosophical study and writing.

Almost as soon as I took up office as Senior Tutor there was a crisis in the College. Christopher once again proposed to place junior members on the executive committee. I objected, as did every other College officer. It was not that we were all opposed, in principle, to junior members taking part in the government of the College; some were, and some were not. But we all felt that, given the truculent attitude of left-wing JCR committees, junior member participation at that time would be a recipe for fruitless argumentation and endless posturing.

Christopher enjoyed recounting how Lord Lindsay, when Master of Balliol, defeated in Governing Body by twenty votes to one, said to the Fellows, 'It appears we have reached an impasse.' On this occasion, Christopher himself displayed Lindsay-like characteristics, threatening to resign as Master unless Governing Body voted junior members onto the executive committee. This caused great consternation. Unlike Lindsay, Christopher was not alone in the stance he had taken; but even those who agreed with him were unwilling to vote for any measure under a threat of resignation.

An emergency meeting of the Fellows was called. Since, of necessity, it had to take place without the Master, it was felt it would look mutinous to hold it within the College; Bill Williams offered Rhodes House as a venue. Fellows waxed eloquent and indignant; but however much we disagreed with him, we were all too fond of Christopher simply to vote him down and accept his resignation. A compromise was worked out, which it fell to me to propose to him.

Nothing could be done, I told him, if he insisted on threatening to resign; the Fellows would not discuss the issue further under moral pressure. However, if he unconditionally withdrew his threat, the Fellows were willing to set up a working party to look afresh at the question of junior representation on the executive committee. 'And suppose that working party comes up with the wrong answer?' I told him that was a risk he would have to take; but we would ensure that the working party contained representatives of both schools of thought among the Fellows.

Christopher accepted, with good grace, the proposed compromise, and in due course the working party recommended a modified version of his proposal: the senior members of the executive committee who were not College officers would be balanced by an equal number of junior members. Because of the presence of College officers on the committee, Fellows would have a clear majority over students; on the other hand, if a sufficient number of Fellows and students on the committee felt College officers had gone wrong, they could vote to overturn their decisions. Governing Body (on which students were not to be represented) retained the right to overturn decisions of the executive committee.

The structure of governance thus set up remained in force for more than a decade. Towards the end of my own time as Master I was able, in rather different circumstances, to persuade Governing Body to remove junior members from the executive committee and return to the system in which the government of the College was restricted to its Fellows.

While Christopher's crusade for student government was not popular with many Fellows, he had almost all of us behind him on another issue about which he felt equally deeply. Long before he became Master he and a number of other Fellows had urged that Balliol should admit women as well as men. In 1964 New College had expressed the wish to become a mixed college, a proposal coolly dismissed by the Franks Commission. The possibility of one college deciding unilaterally to admit women was ruled out by the requirement that any change in a college's statutes which affected the University must be approved by the central University authorities, and many dons who were in favour of mixed colleges were also worried that the admission of women to the men's colleges would have an adverse effect on the existing women's colleges. Movement towards mixed colleges was therefore slow.

Impatient of the delay, the Fellows of Balliol invited St Anne's College to allow some of their graduate students to share with Balliol graduates the accommodation in the Balliol Annexe in Holywell Manor; the joint graduate institution set up in 1969 was the first mixed residential accommodation in Oxford. For some years Balliol's interest in co-education centred on this project, which was popular in both colleges.

Meanwhile, other colleges were pressing on with plans for full co-residence. In May 1972, after discussions between the five women's colleges and five of the men's colleges, Council put forward a scheme whereby Brasenose, Hertford, St Catherine's, Jesus and Wadham should, between them, be allowed to admit a hundred women annually for the next five years, after which the scheme would be reviewed. Until 1977 the University intended to 'withhold its consent to the alteration of the statutes of any other men's colleges designed to permit the admission of women'. Balliol was unhappy not to be among the first colleges past the post, and there was some doubt about the legality of this interference in College autonomy. Lord Bullock, then Master of St Catherine's, recalls that the moratorium 'nearly led the Master and Fellows of Balliol to want to take the Vice-Chancellor of the day and myself to the Privy Council.' At all events, Council had no control over the composition of our fellowships, and from 1972 we opened these to either sex. Carol Clark was not only our first woman Fellow, but the College's first ever tutorial Fellow in Modern Languages. She remembers being universally welcomed into the Senior Common Room: 'The Fellows who had voted for women Fellows were naturally glad to see me; those who had voted against had all been brought up to be gallant and chivalrous to women, no matter where they were.'

Balliol grumbled about the delays imposed, but hoped to be among the second tranche of five colleges allowed to admit women, in 1977. However, the passing of the Sex Discrimination Act in 1975 weakened the power of the University to control the number of colleges which went mixed. Though official policy was that candidates applying to Oxford should have a choice between mixed and single-sex colleges, University College, not on the official list for the second tranche, unilaterally declared its intention to admit women. This was the signal for a rush in which all the men's colleges, fearful of losing out to competition during the admissions season, voted to change their statutes. The Fellows of Balliol did so in 1978. Almost all voted in favour, but with a feeling of disappointment that neither the College's long commitment to the cause of women's education nor its loyal (if reluctant) acceptance of the University's gradualism had given it any advantage over other colleges in the current stampede for co-education.

Public proceedings to elect a new Master had to begin in the academic year 1976/7. Christopher Hill was retiring as Master a year early, in 1978, to take up a Professorship at the Open University, and was on leave during Trinity Term 1976; the acting Master was Patrick Phizackerley. The statutes of colleges lay down in detail the procedure for the election of a head of house; but for many years the statutory procedures had been largely a formality, preceded by a long period of searching for and sifting candidates, ending with a declaration by the Fellows of the person they intend to elect when the statutes permit them to do so. I intended to keep a diary of the making of the new Master, but it lasted only two entries; that for 21 April 1976 reads:

> P.J.R. P[hizackerley] summoned P.G.H. S[andars] and self to discuss arrangements for election to the Mastership. He points out that though the official proceedings of the election (in the College chapel) are by statute presided over by the Senior Official Fellow [who was, at the time, the history tutor

John Prest], nothing is said in the statutes about the real election (in Consilium etc.). It is agreed that it should be pointed out to J.M. P[rest] that since the election is wide open at this stage it would be better to have someone clearly *not* a candidate (E.T. W[illiams] or failing him W.M. P[aton]) to run the election. A Consilium should be held this term to discuss, e.g., do we want an academic or a politician; what age should he be; is he to live in College; should he run committees; and in general what the *profile* of the new Master should be.

The College solved the problem of the clash of jurisdiction between the Senior Fellow (Sir Edgar Williams, Warden of Rhodes House) and the Senior Official Fellow (John Prest, the senior among the tutors) by entrusting the election to a committee chaired by Bill Williams and including, among others, John Prest, Patrick Sandars and myself.

It was decided that the search committee should first of all concentrate on candidates from outside the College and then, having selected one or two of the most promising of these, look within our own number for one or two to run off, as it were, in a final competition with the best of the outside candidates. The course which our deliberations took is recorded in a letter to my parents-in-law on 17 May 1977.

You will know that Balliol has been, slowly and inefficiently, in the process of electing a Master since last October. For most of that time we have been considering and rejecting, or being rejected by, candidates outside the Governing Body, and only quite recently have we turned to consideration of candidates from our own number. For some time there have been rumours both inside the College and in the newspaper, that I would be among the candidates (a little embarrassing as I was also on the committee to sift the external candidates); several people expressed the hope that I would, but only today have I definitely been asked to stand and have agreed to do so. There are four, possibly five, candidates on the short list: beside myself, a Balliol physicist, and two historians, one from York and one from All Souls, with perhaps also a Cambridge anthropologist. The decisive vote will be taken in four weeks' time, with the formal and ceremonial vote some six months later. I have no solid opinion as to whether I am likely to be elected: probably I am the strongest internal candidate . . . but there is also a strong party which feels we should elect an external candidate.

So we have been, and will be for at least another month, in some suspense. Neither Nancy nor I have set our hearts on my getting this job, and we will not be particularly disappointed if they elect someone else: it is nice even to have been considered for such a historic post, and I am very happy in my present position and will continue to be so. If I am elected, it will not make a very great difference to our lives . . . If I'm not elected, I'll continue as Senior Tutor for a few more years and then perhaps put in for one of the senior philosophy posts in the University.

Once I had announced myself, at the request of Jasper Griffin, Bill Newton-Smith, and John Jones, as a candidate for the Mastership, I naturally took no further part in the election proceedings. Outside candidates were invited and dined and quizzed about their vision of the job. I was catechised rather by Fellows in individual interviews. The history tutors, in particular, were dubious at the prospect of the College being presided over by a philosopher, and pressed for another historian to succeed Christopher. At last, at the end of Trinity Term, the decisive vote was taken. I was elected, I believe, by a substantial majority. (Once Harold Macmillan asked me what the exact voting had been. He was at first incredulous, then rather scornful, when I told him I had never found out.) The historians were particularly warm in their felicitations: Maurice Keen left a bottle of champagne on my doorstep, and Donald Pennington was the first to congratulate me 'in the name', he said, 'of the no-longer-opposition'.

10

Into and out of the Lodgings

IN THE *Balliol Record* of 1977 Christopher Hill reported my pre-election in the following terms, in his Master's Letter:

> A newcomer to College life is a Balliol undergraduate newspaper called *Devorguila* (the eccentric spelling is not mine) . . . Number 4 – a special issue under the headline 'Kenny Rules O.K.' – hailed with proper enthusiasm the announcement of the name of my successor . . . I should like to record my own very great pleasure at being succeeded by a Fellow of the College who in the thirteen years since we elected him has become a personal friend and ally in many good causes. We both noted the irony that, at the first College meeting after the Fellows had announced their intention of pre-electing him, Tony Kenny and I found ourselves in a minority on an issue of principle on which he had spoken particularly eloquently. Not the first occasion for me to be voted down: probably not the last for him!

The issue in question was whether the College should continue to bank with Barclays, which was regarded by many senior and junior members as too heavily involved in apartheid South Africa; the junior members of the executive committee had urged a change the previous Michaelmas Term. Christopher had written to the manager of Barclays expressing concern about the bank's behaviour in South Africa. Executive Committee B (which, unlike the full Executive Committee A, consisted only of senior members) considered the manager's reply unsatisfactory, and recommended that the account be moved, but this recommendation (for which both Christopher and I had voted) was overturned by Governing Body at the final meeting of Trinity Term.

Part of the Long Vacation was spent in Colorado Springs, where I taught in a summer school supported by the National Endowment for the Humanities. Nancy's parents, and her sisters and their families, joined us for part of the time. We explored the Colorado Rockies, and Charles in particular showed a taste for cliff-perching which alarmed his mother and grandmother. Some old colleagues and pupils attended the school, and John Hare and I went up Pike's Peak, a strenuous walk up scrubby mountainside to a level of fourteen thousand feet, at which point one's sense of achievement is somewhat dampened by finding the summit covered with a large car park surrounding a food hall, reached by a freeway snaking up the mountain's far side.

When the new academic year began I decided to set, in advance, a term to my Mastership. At forty-six I was comparatively young to be elected, and if I served until retirement at sixty-seven I would remain in post for twenty-one years. In my view, such a long Mastership would not be good either for the College or the Master. Indeed, while I was still serving on the search committee I had objected to several candidates older than myself on the grounds that they were too young for the job. Accordingly I asked that my intention to serve as Master for no more than twelve years be minuted.

However, my last year as a Fellow was pleasant: it was relaxing to enjoy the prestige of the Mastership without any of its responsibilities. I resigned as Senior Tutor at the end of 1977 and Bill Newton-Smith was appointed my successor. I worked hard to complete the research and writing which I had undertaken as Radcliffe Lecturer. I was delighted to see that my own former tutor, Tony Quinton, had been elected at the same time to the Presidency of neighbouring Trinity. The newspapers remarked on the coincidence that two philosophers named Tony with American wives were to move into neighbouring Lodgings, and speculated whether this would bring to an end the traditional feud between the colleges.

There were important changes also in the lives of other members of the family. Robert, now a day-boy at New College School, had impressed the teachers with his ability, so we decided to submit his younger brother to the entrance examination. Delighted at the prospect of having both sons of the Master of Balliol as his pupils, the headmaster accepted Charles even though he was young for his class. However, though we did not yet know it, he suffered from dyslexia and at the end of a year he was asked to leave. We toured the Oxford region looking for a sympathetic school. One, highly recommended, caught fire while we were waiting for an interview. The headmaster assured us this was not an everyday event, but it did not seem a good omen. Eventually Charles was placed at Josca's School, where a precise awareness of each boy's potential was coupled with informality – everyone from the headmaster down was known by their Christian names. It suited Charles well, and he overcame his dyslexia and quickly regained lost ground.

A new addition to the household was a golden labrador retriever, christened Stigger, because he combined the sleekness of 'Sligger'

Urquhart with the bounciness of Tigger. Stigger grew up to be a wanderer, disappearing if ever a door was left open. He sometimes escaped into the cricket field behind the house to capture a bowler's sweater and be chased around the boundary. He liked socialising, and we were often invited by telephone, late in the evening, to retrieve him from The King's Arms or The Cape of Good Hope. Friendly undergraduates would haul him home from distant JCRs, looking well-fed, tired, and very pleased with himself.

The formal proceedings for my election as Master took place in the spring of 1978. On 15 June 1977 it had been minuted that 'the Fellows agreed to bind themselves to elect Dr A.J.P. Kenny as Master as soon as they are free to do so under the College Statutes', and at a College meeting on 13 March 1978 Governing Body resolved to exercise the power to pre-elect before Christopher's retirement on 30 September. When the College reassembled after the Easter Vacation (spent finishing *Aristotle's Theory of the Will* and taking the family on chilly cliff walks in Cornwall), a statutory meeting of Fellows was held in the College chapel on 26 April, at which I was pre-elected by a unanimous vote. The Senior Fellow, Bill Williams, took me to the Lodgings to present me to the Visitor, Lord Kilbrandon, bearing a document bristling with *whereases* and *now therefores* and stamped with the College Seal. I then made the statutory declaration of fidelity to the College, and we crossed the quadrangle in the spring sun to enjoy a celebratory lunch.

The year 1978 was, at any rate by one reckoning, the 2,300th anniversary of the death of Aristotle, and the town of Thessaloniki, in Aristotle's Macedonia, planned to celebrate the event in August with a grand international philosophy conference. I was among those invited, and we decided to combine it with a family holiday, driving to Greece through Yugoslavia and returning by ferry to Brindisi and up the Italian peninsula.

Shortly before the conference, the newspapers carried stories of a substantial earthquake in Thessaloniki. Reassuring letters from the city council saying that all the hotels but one were fully functioning omitted to mention that most people were camping in tents in the parks or sleeping outside the city altogether. One of my philosopher friends rang in a panic to suggest we should all write to say we were not coming. I pointed out that the citizens of Thessaloniki were bearing up well and quoted my colleague Jonathan Barnes, who regarded it as 'un-English' to pull out.

We drove through France and stopped at the chalet for a few days to show the ropes to Carol Clark, who was taking a group of modern linguists this year. One day's drive from the chalet took us through the Mont Blanc tunnel and across to Trieste. The red-roofed villages in the hills of Slovenia gave us a good first impression of Yugoslavia, but after Ljubyana the *autoput* began, surely the most terrifying highway in Europe at the time. A modest dual carriageway, with no shoulder hard or soft, it carried traffic of motorway density at motorway speed. Trucks of *Gastarbeiter* from Germany hurtled past on their way home to Turkey. The road was lined with abandoned, burnt-out lorries. All facilities along the motorway were unspeakably filthy, but at the end of the first day we were lucky to find a tolerable hotel in Belgrade. The second day reached a low point at Nis, the town of a thousand skulls, where we got lost and nearly ran out of petrol on a ring-road of unmaintained cobbles. But after Nis the road improved as the Turkish traffic went east to Bulgaria, and we moved into wooded countryside following a lovely mountain stream which flowed all the way to the golden fields around Pella, once the capital of Philip of Macedon.

It was 11.30 p.m. Greek time before we reached Thessaloniki and found a hotel room. As we went to bed, we looked down at the lanterns lighting the people camping in the squares; some of them were looking up at us – all of us wondered who would be feeling foolish the next morning. But though there were some minor trembles, the week passed without further serious quakes, and we were able to enjoy the conference and throw ourselves into the celebration of Aristotle.

Our Greek hosts were amazingly generous. A tour was organized to Pella, where we admired the reconstructed stoa and pebble mosaics, then on to the recently-excavated tomb where golden armour had been found which its discoverer claimed might be that of Philip himself: the greaves were of different lengths, as were Philip's legs, and one of the masks was made to fit a damaged eye, such as Philip had. Next we went to the traditional site of the school where Aristotle had taught Alexander, hollowed out of the red rock; and finally, as the guests of the Northern Greek Tourist Ministry, to a lengthy open-air lunch with folk dancing and singing, in which even the most staid philosophers joined. Charles ingratiated himself with the kitchen, then with many of our friends, by discovering where the wine was and keeping everyone well supplied.

During the working session of the conference I read a paper on Aspasius, a second-century commentator on Aristotle. I defended a rash theory which had occurred to me in the first flush of my stylometric discoveries, to the effect that it was Aspasius who had first put together the *Nicomachean Ethics* in the form in which they came to us. By rights, I claimed, they should have been called the *Aspasian Ethics*.

After the conference we spent a week in Athens, in the house of a family of American academics who had exchanged it for ours at 7 Mansfield Road. In Athens we admired that exquisite golden armour; if it was not Philip II's, it must have belonged to some other equally wealthy king. A helmet encircled with flowers bore golden bees so delicate that they trembled in the slightest breeze.

We should now have taken the car ferry from Patras to Brindisi and returned, at a leisurely pace, up the Adriatic coast of Italy. But at Patras we found the ferry colossally overbooked, and were turned away along with many other ticket-holders. After a night of rage and frustration we realized we had no option but to turn and drive all the way back up the hated *autoput*. At the end of the drive we consoled ourselves with a few days on the Lido in Venice. By agreement with the children, they looked round churches with us in the mornings and we took them to the beach in the afternoon.

In September we all went to Ithaca for the marriage of Nancy's sister, and after the wedding I went to Washington to meet the substantial group of Balliol alumni stationed there. The two Balliol senators, Paul Sarbanes of Maryland and David Boren of Oklahoma, hosted a luncheon in the Capitol.

When I finally became Master in October, my first duty was to greet the Balliol Society, the annual gathering of the College's alumni. More old members turned up than usual, to see for themselves what kind of strange being the Fellows had chosen. The national press took quite an interest in my appointment, and I had to answer many questions. How did I usually vote? Labour. What powers does the Master have? None but the power to persuade. What were my worries about the College? I singled out the recent increase in overseas fees, which might reduce the College's international intake, and the disappearance of the grammar schools, which might reduce the number of working-class undergraduates admitted to the College.

Max Beloff, then principle of the University College of Buckingham, wrote to *The Times* taking me to task for voting Labour in spite of deploring the effect on Balliol of the elimination of the grammar schools. I wrote in reply that any vote for a party, as a former Professor of Government should know, often represented the choice of a lesser evil.

On this particular issue I am not as sure as Professor Beloff thinks I am that what is bad for Balliol is bad for the nation. The Labour policy is inspired by a desire to reduce the class divisions fostered by past British educational practice. No doubt the full achievement of this goal would demand the abolition not only of the grammar schools but of the independent schools as well. I am not surprised, nor can I regret, that no Labour administration has felt determined enough to carry this through. The present policy may well force colleges such as Balliol either to lower their standards of admission or to draw fewer of their students from families which cannot afford private education. Personally, I shall much regret being faced with this choice. But an education policy is not to be judged by its effects on university education alone. We may all hope that the school education offered by the new comprehensives will be considerably better than that offered by the old secondary modern schools. Who am I to say that this advantage offered to a large body of the population should be outweighed by a disadvantage which results for Oxbridge colleges?

On taking office, I discovered that a number of quaint perquisites went with being Master. When my first monthly salary was paid in, I noticed from the accompanying chit that it included twenty-odd pounds for the gubernation of Huntspill. I had not previously had any idea that I was gubernator of Huntspill, or even where or what Huntspill was; it transpired that it was a Balliol living in Somerset, held in the eighteenth century by a Master of Balliol who was such a disastrous vicar that the parisioners offered to pay future Masters three hundred pounds a year, to be called gubernation money, on condition that they never again presented themselves to the living – all settled by Act of Parliament in 1778. I had no difficulty in fulfilling the conditions attached to this payment, but after a few years John Jones, at my prompting, persuaded the College to waive its right to the money in favour of Huntspill Church Building Fund.

The earliest of the Balliol College livings had been that of St Lawrence Jewry, beside the London Guildhall. The College lost it in 1951, when the advowson was assigned to the City of London, but the City continued to pay the College a corn rent for part of the Guildhall site, and a front row stall in the church marked with the College arms was reserved for the Master; occasionally I exercised my right to occupy it.

During much of my first term as Master my family was preoccupied with preparations for moving house. David Keir and his predecessors had lived in the Master's Lodgings on Broad Street, erected by Alfred Waterhouse during the rebuilding of Balliol in the 1860s. Christopher Hill, when elected Master, firmly refused to take his young family into 'that gloomy building'. Permission to live out was readily given, as the College was glad to have the use of the extra rooms: all the ground floor of the house was now offices, and the top floor had been turned into undergraduate rooms and given a separate entrance. The *piano nobile* and the staircase which led to it from the front door in Broad Street had been retained as a ceremonial area for the Master, with two bedrooms and a drawing room in addition to his study, and a dining room with a splendid fifteenth-century oriel window looking onto the front quadrangle.

When the Lodgings were cantonised in this way, the Master was assigned a house at 9 Mansfield Road. This dated from 1891, when Benjamin Jowett was planning an annexe for poor students on the western side of the Master's Field, to designs by Thomas Jackson. A Warden's house was the first part to be erected and like many of Jackson's buildings it was highly eclectic, combining Jacobean roof-lines with a small Byzantine cupola. It was called The King's Mound, because its garden contained part of the fortifications erected by Charles I to defend Oxford against Parliamentary attack during the Civil War. Before the rest of the annexe could be constructed Jowett died, and the Fellows lost interest in providing for poor students. Instead, it became a tutor's house, first occupied by the historian A.L. Smith (founder of a distinguished academic dynasty, and eventually the next Master but two after Jowett) and later by a succession of remarkable Balliol tutors. Though it had been assigned to the Master in 1964, Christopher never moved into it, preferring his College house in Northmoor Road. Nancy and I were keen to occupy it, however, at least while our children were young, keeping open the question whether, at a later stage, we might move back into the Lodgings in Broad Street.

The Lodgings and The King's Mound both needed redecoration, so it was not until near the end of Michaelmas Term 1978 that we moved in. Though the distance was short, it seemed as complicated as any other house move; perhaps more so, since for a few hundred yards one could not bring oneself to do really systematic packing. 'Moving one Pandora's box into another' was how Nancy described it.

I spent a good part of every day in the Lodgings; in the study overlooking the garden quad I dealt with correspondence and interviewed Fellows, students, and visitors, and I chaired a number of College committees in the offices – the majority met in the Old Common Room underneath the Library. Nancy and I did most of our entertaining in the fine reception rooms, and if we had an evening engagement in College we slept in the Lodgings, the boys in the guest room.

We refurnished these rooms in a more traditional style than had been favoured by the Hills. From the Ashmolean we borrowed a Gilbert Spencer landscape and a Lawrence Gowing portrait to adorn the drawing room, where we also installed a walnut Broadwood grand piano, lent us by Jennifer Barnes. Opposite my study door hung a large and vivid contemporary portrait photograph of Benjamin Jowett. Coming upstairs after a difficult College meeting, I would look at the sardonic mouth and the heavily-lidded eyes, and could almost hear the old man saying, 'I would have handled that so much better than you did.'

A few years later I volunteered, if the Fellows so wished, to move back with my family into the Lodgings; but I was mightily relieved when the offer was turned down. This disappointed some of our old members, who had much resented Christopher's absenteeism and hoped that I would reverse it. Ted Heath, in particular, reproached me from time to time for failing to return. None the less, he greeted my Mastership with a great display of affection for the College, and in my first year established a Heath Junior Research Fellowship.

When I took up the Mastership, the old members of the College were very much on my mind. A Master of Balliol has to relate to the three different estates of Balliol: the junior members, the senior members, and the old members. It is one of his duties to try to make each of these groups understand and be ready to learn from the other: I spent much of my time trying to explain to undergraduates why dons think as they do, to dons why undergraduates behave as they do, and to alumni why the College today is not as it was when they were in the heyday of their youth. If I were asked to put the duties of a Master in a nutshell I would say that it is to be a peace-maker: to hold the ring between senior and junior members, to persuade one Fellow that he has not been impardonably insulted by another, and to reconcile old members to the College of the present day.

With his responsibility for binding together these three estates of the College, it is difficult for a Master to be equally *persona grata* with all three groups. Keir had been unpopular with the dons, and not taken very seriously by the undergraduates; but he was highly thought of by the alumni. Christopher was popular with the young, and always retained the affection of the dons; but he alienated many of the old members. I hoped that, as Master, I would remain on the same good terms with my colleagues I had enjoyed as a Fellow; but I set myself the task of winning back the old members whose loyalty had been tested during the 1970s. To do this would mean some reversal of the under-graduate ethos of those years, and this was bound to be repugnant to those junior members who regarded it as one of the attractive features of the College. I was prepared, therefore, to be unpopular with some of the junior members. I encouraged those among them, now becoming more numerous, who wished to restore some of the old customs of the College, such as a formal Hall. But on the first occasion when formal Hall was reintroduced, a masked figure appeared beneath the organ loft and shouted 'Long live the spirit of Christopher Hill'.

However, on one of the major issues of my first year as Master I concurred with the opinion of the left in the JCR. One of the earliest papers to arrive on my desk was a well-informed and well-presented report on 'Foreign Investment and Apartheid' prepared by a special JCR working party. At the height of apartheid the economic boycott of South Africa seemed (as indeed it later proved) the most effective non-violent method of bringing to an end that abhorrent regime. It was now some time since Balliol had held any direct investments in South Africa, but its portfolio, like that of similar institutions, contained shares in British companies which were active there. Like others of the dons, and many of the junior members, I felt that this gave ground for concern. But there were Fellows, including a succession of Bursars, who regarded as anathema any suggestion that the choice of the College's portfolio should be influenced by political or ethical considerations; purely economic considerations were, indeed, particularly pressing at this time. A financial commission of Fellows, under the new Investment Bursar Andrew Graham, had just reported that between 1967 and 1978 the real value of the College's endowments had fallen between 30 and 40 per cent.

In January I presented to Governing Body a long paper on the issue of South African investment. I set out the arguments of those who favoured British companies withdrawing from South Africa, and who urged Balliol to dispose of its shares in those companies who continued to operate there. I also put forward the counter-argument, that the sale of shares by Balliol would simply transfer ownership to different shareholders who might be totally unconcerned with company policy in South Africa, in which case it would surely be better for the College to use its position as a shareholder to ensure that companies in which it had a stake should pay decent wages in South Africa, adopt fair bargaining practices, and avoid racial discrimination at the work-place. In response to those Fellows who thought it was inappropriate for an educational institution to have regard to ethical or political considerations in the choice of its investments, I tried to evaluate the possibility of operating a 'clean hands' portfolio while fulfilling our responsibilities, as Trustees, for the prudent management of our funds. The College could not, I argued, remain totally indifferent to the sources of the dividends from which it derived its endowment income; it was only if we could be sure that our portfolio companies paid non-exploitation wages that we could avoid the charge that we were profiting from apartheid.

It was clear, as the history of other institutions showed, that South African divestment was a topic which could consume an amount of time in discussion, and generate a degree of heated disagreement, out of all proportion to the value of any action eventually resolved upon. Accordingly, I proposed that we should follow the example of some American institutions of higher education and become active share-holders, monitoring, and if necessary challenging at AGMs, the South African activities of the companies in which we held shares.

My proposals were accepted, and it was agreed that while investment decisions would continue to be taken on economic grounds, we should bring our weight to bear to ensure that any company in which we held shares played a constructive role with regard to South Africa. At my suggestion the College set up a Shareholder Action Committee, made up of four members of Governing Body, two junior members – who were often the best-informed members of the committee on particular issues – and two old members who would be able to assure the wider world that we were not forsaking our fiduciary duties. Tom Bingham, QC, and Michael Posner were the first alumni to accept appointment, and generously gave their time, authority, and experience to the work of the committee. The Governing Body devolved to it decisions about the appropriate action for the College to take as responsible shareholder; decisions about the purchase and sale of securities remained as before with the Investment Committee and its advisers. By this means the issue was defused and, for a time, Governing Body was spared divisive debates.

South Africa was not the only tyranny which had an impact on the College at this time. The members of the JCR imposed a levy on them-selves for the support of a refugee scholar. They were allowed to make their own choice, provided the Tutor for Admissions was satisfied that the successful candidate fulfilled the academic conditions for admis-sion. The scholar for 1978/9 was, unusually, an established academic, M.M. Kiwanuka, a refugee from Amin's Uganda.

Kiwanuka had been a Professor of History at Makerere University. He and the Professor of Geography had been summoned by President Amin and told to prepare a document setting out Uganda's historical and geographical claim to a portion of Kenya which the President had taken the whim to invade. They were devastated: the claim had no foundation, and to write in support of it would have violated the most basic academic integrity. On the other hand, Amin had already dis-played a penchant for shooting out-of-hand those who thwarted his wishes.

The two professors went to their Vice-Chancellor, Professor Lule, for advice. 'You must not refuse to do what the President asks', he shrewdly advised. 'Just emphasize that this document must be very thoroughly prepared if it is to convince the Organization of African Unity and the United Nations. Point out that, regrettably, because of Uganda's colonial past, the relevant archives are situated not in Kampala but in London.'

The professors took this advice, and were granted leave to travel to London to study the archives. Once outside Uganda, they took good care not to return while Amin was still in power; and that was how Kiwanuka came to be a refugee scholar at Balliol (he is now Uganda's Ambassador to the United Nations).

The most extraordinary, and time-consuming, issue of my first year as Master was the securing of work permits for Fellows. In addition to the professorial and tutorial Fellows who had teaching responsibility in College or University, Balliol, like other colleges, supported a number of Junior Research Fellowships. These provided young scholars or researchers with three years to establish a career in research, and imposed no teaching obligations. They were advertised widely, in very broad terms: history, or physics, or life sciences. The only criterion for election was intellectual promise, and on election a Fellow was given free range to pursue his or her own academic curiosity; accordingly, at any given time we had half a dozen Fellows researching on a variety of (possibly arcane) subjects. During one year of my Mastership, for example, we had researchers working on the text of Piers Plowman, Parmigianino's *Madonna of the Long Neck*, the history of Samos between 800 and 188 BC, the anthropology of Breton fishermen, the instabilities of tokamaks, and sex ratios, longevity and fecundity among mud-daubing wasps.

Early in 1979 the College elected to a Junior Research Fellowship in history Randall Rogers, an expert on the use of the mangonel in medieval warfare. Because he was an American citizen, we had to apply for a work permit from the Department of Employment. The permit was refused. We were told that in this time of scarce employment we should have appointed a native, and invited to re-advertise the fellowship. It was not sufficient, we were told, that Rogers was the *best* applicant; we were justified in electing him only if he was the *sole* qualified candidate.

We could not claim that Rogers was the only qualified candidate for a history fellowship: had he walked under a bus, there were several others we would have been delighted to elect. We could, I suppose, have re-advertised, restricting the fellowship to mangonel experts; Rogers would no doubt have emerged, to the satisfaction of the Department, as the sole qualified candidate.

I thought the matter serious enough to refer to the Conference of

Colleges, the assembly of Heads of Houses and their colleagues. I read out the most recent of the letters we had received refusing the permit. 'Whoever wrote that letter', boomed Lord Goodman, Master of University College, 'is a certifiable idiot.' 'I'm afraid it is not just a letter from a civil servant', I explained; 'this one is from the Minister himself.' 'I do not wish to alter either the noun or the adjective,' was the response.

With the encouragement of the Conference Balliol decided to fight the issue as a test case for academic freedom. I wrote many letters to the College's alumni in both Houses of Parliament. In correspondence with civil servants, I benefited from the guidance of Lord Trend, former Secretary to the Cabinet but now an ally, as Rector of Lincoln College. Knowing that once the College began to pay a stipend to the new Fellow it might find itself in a questionable legal position, in writing to the Department I tended to adopt a rather obsequious tone. Lord Trend went through my draft letters, striking out every expression of hesitation or conciliation. 'Don't concede a single jot or tittle until you are forced to,' was his advice. Acting upon it, we eventually secured Rogers a permit.

The problems in this case arose under a Labour Government very concerned about unemployment. In March, after a 'winter of discontent', Jim Callaghan's government fell, and in the general election that followed the Conservatives were returned to power under Mrs Thatcher. Many of us were worried that this might be bad news for universities, but in my annual letter to members of the College I put the best face on the results, pointing out that they showed a gratifying national swing to Balliol. The College now had twenty-one MPs (thirteen Conservative, five Labour, and two Liberal). Denis Healey's place as Balliol representative in Cabinet had been taken by Sir Ian Gilmour as Lord Privy Seal. Among Balliol members of the government outside the Cabinet were Patrick Mayhew, James Douglas-Hamilton, and the Earl of Gowrie.

Grey Gowrie became a junior minister in the Department of Employment, and played a significant part in the final resolution of the dispute about academic work permits. Other colleges faced the same problems as Balliol, and I was asked to write letters on their behalf, based on our experience with Randy Rogers. Gowrie drew our attention to the dictionary definitions of the word 'uniquely'. To say that someone was 'uniquely qualified' for a post could, with equal justice, mean that someone was the only qualified candidate – or that his qualifications were such that he surpassed all others.

We took the hint. We thenceforth certified our Junior Research

Fellows to be 'so far superior to the competition as to be effectively unique'. By this device, quickly circulated among the colleges, a number of deserving overseas scholars were enabled to take up their fellowships in Oxford during the early 1980s.

Within the College I revived the custom of Master's Essays, whereby freshmen had to read to the Master an essay on some general topic unrelated to their academic course. Since there were now far too many freshmen for one person to listen to them on an individual basis, as in Jowett's day, I invited the freshers in groups of four – a scholar and three commoners – and asked the scholar among them to read an eassy for discussion by the others. I also invited groups of freshmen to tea; but these invitations were not widely taken up, and the main beneficiary was Charles who, having been dropped in St Giles by the school bus, would pass through the Lodgings on his way home and eat up the left-over cakes. Nancy and I eventually settled for a pattern of entertaining first- and second-year undergraduates to Friday night drinks and finalists to Saturday lunches, in the Lodgings. My appointment as Master placed considerable extra burdens on Nancy, who had her own career as a singer and music teacher. Following an unrewarding period at a comprehensive school in Charlbury she continued to teach some sixteen hours a week at New College School.

I was glad to see the College's interest in rowing revive. Jonathan Barnes had returned to Balliol to succeed me as the Greats Philosophy Tutor, and brought from Oriel a great enthusiasm for the river, which he communicated to other SCR members. A group of alumni headed by Don Cadle provided a new eight, and a number of trophies. Though I had never before used an oar in anger, I took part in the 1989 Cadle Competition between coxless pairs. Thanks to imaginative handicapping, Jonathan and I survived until we were knocked out in the final – and thus fortunately escaped the traditional ducking. For the first time in living memory there was also a don's eight: gallant rather than speedy, it failed to qualify on the crucial day, in spite of making better time than some of the junior eights.

As Master I liked whenever I could to attend meetings of junior member societies. The most venerable of these was the Musical Society, founded by Benjamin Jowett, which has organized concerts of high quality in Balliol Hall every other Sunday in term-time since the 1880s. I chaired the committee which managed the Society's finances and chose the performers. To invite guests to dine on Sunday in Hall at 7.15, descend to dessert in the Senior Common Room at 8.15, and then bring them up to Hall again for the concert at 9, was a very pleasant way of entertaining. It was also a pleasing custom (dating, it seems, from a time when Jowett unexpectedly recovered from a life-threatening illness), if the Master dined on a Sunday night, for the junior members in Hall to express their pleasure by banging their spoons on the table. During the years of student trouble, however, it was essential to explain to nervous guests that the thumping was a sign not of hostility but of friendship.

There were less sedate societies of which I had been a member since my earliest years as a Fellow. The Arnold and Brackenbury, once a serious debating society, by the time I joined it resembled more Matthew Arnold the frivolous undergraduate than Matthew Arnold the sage of sweetness and light. It liked to debate motions, such as 'This house would prefer a double Napoleon to a pair of Wellingtons', which gave an opportunity for speakers to exhale ingenious and elegant nonsense on any topic they chose. The Victorian Society, which always met under the Union Jack and a portrait of the Queen-Empress, was devoted to community singsong. It was surprising that even an ironic survival of Victorian Values should have come unscathed through a decade of progressive Marxism in the JCR. The Society's major annual event was a steamer cruise from Folly Bridge to Iffley, which gave ample opportunity for vocalists to startle riverside dwellers with tuneless renditions of defunct music-hall ditties.

The year ended with two memorable events, one happy, the other not. The Dean and I felt obliged to suspend, *sine die*, the Balliol Players. Founded in the 1920s, the Players made annual tours of public schools to perform Aristophanes, and had included many undergraduates who later went on to distinction in public life. The plays had always been to some extent farced, but by the 1970s had come to have little connection with Aristophanes apart from the name, and numerous complaints had been received from hosts about the obscenity of the scripts and the misbehaviour of the actors. Attempts at reform had failed, and we decided the only solution was a surgical one.

The happy event was the award of an honorary degree to one of the College's best known alumni: Graham Greene was made a Doctor of Letters at the Encaenia. During his time as an undergraduate his attitude to the College, and the College's attitude to him, had been highly qualified, as he revealed in his autobiography. But in June 1979 he was happy to accept the hospitality of the Senior Common Room, and we were happy to bask in his reflected glory.

I I

Czechoslovakia

IN JANUARY 1979 the sub-faculty of philosophy in Oxford received a letter from a Dr Julius Tomin, inviting Oxford philosophers to visit an unofficial seminar which met regularly in his apartment in Prague. The sub-faculty was not entirely sure how seriously to take the letter – it was rather like picking up, from a liner, a floating bottle with a message from castaways. The secretary, Dr Kathy Wilkes, undertook to make on-the-spot inquiries.

We learnt that Julius Tomin had obtained a doctorate in philosophy at the Charles University in Prague in the mid 1960s under the internationally respected Jan Patocka. He had held a teaching and research post at the University, and through a group interested in Marxist–Christian dialogue was appointed to a visiting professorship at the University of Hawaii, shortly after the Soviet invasion put an end to the Prague Spring; he was offered a permanent post in Hawaii, but preferred to return home. Charles University was now closed to him and he had to work as a publisher's reader, a turbine operator, and a night-watchman. He and his wife had been among the original 242 signatories of Charter 77, the manifesto pressing for implementation of the human rights guarantees given at Helsinki in 1975.

In 1977 he had begun giving unofficial courses in philosophy, aimed principally at young people of university age who had had difficulty in getting places because their parents were Charter signatories or other dissidents. Almost from the beginning Tomin and his students were harassed by the authorities: students found it difficult to keep their jobs or get permission to travel, and an attempt – fortunately vain – was made to have Tomin medically certified as a paranoid psychopath. Zdena, a Charter spokesperson during 1979, was brutally attacked by a masked assailant; for several months the police kept a twenty-four-hour watch on the Tomins' apartment – allegedly to 'protect them', but in effect isolating them from all visitors.

In May 1978 Tomin wrote an open letter to Harvard, Heidelberg, the Free University of Berlin, and Oxford, describing his course, and something of the harassment it was subjected to; but the purpose of the letter was not to complain, but to invite visits. As it would be difficult to arrange meetings in the normal way, he wrote, 'Allow me to suggest a solution which I consider the most convenient: we meet to study philosophy in my flat every Wednesday at 6 p.m. from September to June. You will be most welcome whenever you choose to join us.'

No action was taken at the other three universities, and in Oxford the letter was mislaid; but after Kathy's inquiries it was agreed to make available a grant 'for two members of the sub-faculty of Philosophy to visit Czechoslovakia to meet dissident philosophers'. In fact, three philosophers visited, in April and June, and reported back enthusiastically. For 1979/80 the faculty board allocated £1,000 for visits to Prague, and there was quite a long waiting list. Philosophers from London, Norway, Canada, West Germany and Australia also paid visits, the arrangements being made by Kathy Wilkes.

At the beginning of the academic year 1979/80 I placed my own name on the list, and was told that I would have to wait until Easter. I had considered the possibility of combining a visit to Tomin's unofficial seminar with a formal visit to the Charles University in Prague under the auspices of the British Council. I could see advantages and disadvantages in this: it might afford a degree of protection to Tomin's group and its visitors – but it might merely create embarassment for the British authorities. I consulted Christopher Mallaby at the Foreign Office, who in turn consulted our Ambassador in Prague. The eventual answer was that it would be better to keep any such visits separate.

Until March 1980 there was comparatively little harassment of visiting philosophy lecturers: most were allowed to deliver their lectures, engage in discussion with Tomin and his students, and leave the country in the normal way. This was the experience of three successive visitors from Oxford during Hilary Term. But on Saturday 8 March Bill Newton-Smith, who had gone to Prague from his sabbatical leave base in the Netherlands, was reading a paper on the rationality of science when the meeting was broken up shortly after it had begun, by fourteen policemen. He was interrogated for two and a half hours at police headquarters, and ordered to tell all his colleagues that nobody must attempt to write, telephone, or meet Tomin, who was described as 'an enemy of the State'. In the middle of the night he was deported to West Germany by the secret police. Their Russian car broke down on the way to the border; he lent them his penknife to help mend it, and spend the time throwing snowballs to get rid of the written messages he was carrying.

None of the students attending the meeting was arrested, and after Newton-Smith had been removed Tomin took his own copy of the paper and finished translating it for the group. On 12 March about twenty-four people attended the next meeting to hear a lecture on the phenomenology of meaning by Radim Palous, who until he signed Charter 77 was a professor at Charles University. Again the police came and dispersed the meeting, and deported the one foreigner present.

As the head of Newton-Smith's College I sent a letter of protest at his deportation to the Czech Embassy in London. The letter remained unanswered, so I requested an interview with the Ambassador in person to seek an explanation of an episode which seemed to be in violation of a number of international agreements. At the Embassy in Kensington I was received by the Minister, Dr Telicka. The interview is described in the following letter, which I wrote immediately on returning home.

Balliol, 19 March 1980

Dear Dr Telicka,

I am grateful to you for the courteous way in which you received my representations of this morning on the subject of Dr Newton-Smith.

You and I both deplored the fact that Dr Newton-Smith had been harrassed and agreed that this could be seen as an impediment to normal cultural relations on academic matters. You spoke of the occasional possibility of police officers causing inconvenience to British tourists by over-zealous performance of their duties and said that in such cases in the past you had seen to it that the offenders were reprimanded. I said that I was not asking the Czech authorities to reprimand those who had arrested Dr Newton-Smith, but seeking to learn the legal justification for his deportation.

You replied that Dr Newton-Smith was not arrested but had merely had his visa terminated and had been escorted to the border. You said that you felt there were grounds for an apology on our side since Dr Newton-Smith had not behaved properly as a tourist.

I pointed out that the giving of unpaid philosophy lectures is a normal activity of philosophical tourists in most countries; on the last four holidays I have taken myself, I either gave or attended philosophical lectures. You said that Dr Newton-Smith should have stated his intention to lecture on his visa; I replied that no tourist can be expected to detail all his activities in advance, such as singing songs with his friends. Since, however, it seems that the Czech government has special views on the activities appropriate to tourists, it would be helpful if tourists were given in advance a list of permitted activities, and I pressed you again to say in what way Dr Newton-Smith's activities were illegal.

You agreed, of course, that the discussion of philosophy was not itself illegal in Czechoslovakia; there could be no objection, for instance, to somebody discussing philosophy with a group of people in a restaurant. But you suggested a number of specific reasons why Dr Newton-Smith's lecture was illegal . . .

I said that it would be important for Oxford philosophers intending to visit Prague to know under what law and in what respect Dr Tomin and his associates were regarded as forming an illegal society. We had been informed by Dr Tomin that there was nothing illegal about the holding of private seminars, etc.; you advised me that the Government had a different interpretation. I asked to know the precise terms of the law which was the subject of this disagreement of interpretation. You very reasonably replied that you did not carry it in your head. I repeat, however, as I said this morning, that I would very much appreciate your sending me a copy of the relevant law as its precise terms are obviously of great importance to any of my colleagues who may wish to visit Prague in the future.

You suggested that the visits of Oxford philosophers to Prague were motivated by a desire to embarrass the Czech Government. I replied that while my colleagues and I admire Dr Tomin for his continued devotion to philosophy under difficult circumstances, the purpose of our visits was not at all a political one but purely the exchange of philosophical ideas in a way that in most countries is regarded as totally normal and goes without remark.

I agreed with you that a tourist should in general respect the laws of any country he visits, and I assured you that my colleagues had no intention of breaking Czech law. However, there seems to me to be a clear and important distinction between activities which are illegal and those which are merely unpopular with a government. I am not sure how far I was able to persuade you of this distinction.

You suggested that there was an element of deception in Dr Newton-Smith's application to visit Prague as a tourist. I replied that there was no attempt to conceal the interest of Balliol College in the philosophy of Dr Tomin. I had myself sent to the Ambassador a copy of my letter inviting Tomin to lecture in the College.

You asked why my colleagues were not interested in visiting the Charles University. I replied that any of us would welcome an invitation to lecture there, provided that the lecture was open to the general public. You said that this went without saying because of the open nature of Czech society.

I am recapitulating our discussion at such length because I am anxious to communicate its contents accurately to any philosopher in Oxford who may wish to visit Prague. Please inform me if I have misrepresented your position in any way. As I said this morning, if you would prefer to give your advice in person to the members of the Philosophy Sub-Faculty I am sure you would be welcome in Oxford. I am sorry that the approaching end of your tour of duty makes this unlikely.

My interest in getting clear about the legal situation was particularly keen since it was my turn, in accordance with arrangements made several months earlier, to give the next lecture, in April. Though neither of us mentioned it, Dr Telicka must have known I was due to visit Prague: his own staff had but recently given me a visa. Moreover, the English Communist newspaper, the *Morning Star*, which was read in Prague, had actually published my name as the next visitor. Nancy and I had no wish to be arrested, but experts on Czech affairs in this country told us we were unlikely to be molested. In any case, if Tomin and his group wanted us to come as planned, it would have been hardly decent to call off a visit arranged long since.

However, it began to look very uncertain whether Tomin's group would be able to hold their normal meetings in April. Palous' next lecture, on March 19, was broken up roughly and eight people were detained for forty-eight hours; on the next Wednesday police observed, but did not interrupt, a lecture on Aristotle; on 3 and 10 April Tomin was taken off for interrogation, and on the second occasion detained for forty-eight hours.

My wife and I were due to arrive in Prague less than twenty-four hours after Tomin's release. We telephoned from Oxford to check that our visit would still be welcome. Of course, said Zdena; she would meet us herself at the airport; she was forty, she said, though she hoped she didn't look it; she would carry a copy of *Action, Emotion and Will* so that we would recognize her.

As we flew across Europe in the Tupolev airliner, Nancy and I wondered whether we would be turned back on arrival. But no, we were passed swiftly through Immigration and greeted Zdena according to plan. She helped us check in at the Park Hotel and then whisked us off in a taxi for a lightning tour of Prague. 'I hope you will have time to visit all these beautiful buildings at leisure on Sunday and Monday,' she said – we had indeed purchased a package tour which would enable us to sightsee once the seminar was safely over – 'However, one cannot be sure, and if you had to leave early it would be a great pity never to have seen them at all.'

So we joined the crowd of tourists to watch the fabulous clock strike the hour in the Old Town Square, and walked around the catheral and through the castle courts. We were moved by the monument to Jan Huss, the Czech patriot burned for heresy in 1415; Huss had been a disciple of an earlier Master of Balliol, John Wyclif. The Balliol–Bohemia connection, we told each other, was of long standing.

Over a snack of Moravian ham and Pilsner beer we gave messages to the Tomins from friends in Oxford, and passed over some money due to Julius as payment for an article he had written in the *New Statesman*. Then we went to the Tomins' flat, on the third floor of an apartment block up flights of stone stairs with metal bannisters (where the police had formerly encamped). All was now quiet; Zdena said we had brought luck, because often on the nights of seminars there were three police cars parked on the street outside. We were introduced to the Tomin family; their younger son had been sent to an aunt's home, in case of trouble. 'It isn't good for him to see his father arrested and pulled downstairs.'

The company was to assemble for our seminar at 7 o'clock. It was my first meeting with Tomin; I had ten minutes with him before the others arrived. He appeared tired, but was obviously looking forward to a long evening of philosophy. There was still no sign of the police; he thought they were unlikely to arrest anyone again so soon. But he seemed unwilling to talk about his recent imprisonment; what worried him was that I was going to quote some passages of the *Eudemian Ethics* that were unfamiliar to him: he wanted to make sure he understood how to translate them into Czech. He pored over the text with me, his face very grave. 'Why is that participle in the dative?' he asked. 'I do not see why.' 'It is in agreement', I said, 'with a first person plural pronoun which is understood.' He cheered up at once.

Twenty or so people filled the room. The topic of my lecture was the contrast between the ideals of the *Nicomachean* and the *Eudemian Ethics*. According to the former, the ideal life for a human being is the life of a philosopher; for the latter philosophy, though very important, is no more than a part of the good life. I intended to argue that the Eudemian ideal was more realistic: philosophy is indeed splendid and important, but it cannot be regarded as the sole essence of the happy life, as the Nicomachean treatise invites us to believe.

I began to expound Aristotle's theory. Tomin translated each passage with my commentary, sometimes adding comments of his own which he would then translate back into English. After a while, other members of the seminar joined in. Radim Palous objected to Aristotle's identification of philosophy with the good life. His argument was succinct: 'If the good life was the same thing as philosophy, then a better philosopher would be a better man. But Plato was a better philosopher than Socrates, but he was not a good man.'

No one in that room was going to challenge the moral ranking of Socrates, whose ideals and career had a special importance of them. We moved on to a passage where Aristotle argued that philosophy is the best of all lives, because it is the life which is hardest to take away. Other noble callings require wealth, power, and helpers; philosophy alone is something you can pursue even if you lose your money and your friends. The passage was heavily scored in Tomin's copy of the text. Just then a watcher in the windows said, 'They're here', and twenty uniformed and plainclothes policemen arrived and filled the apartment.

The Czech citizens were asked for their identity cards; a police interpreter came up to me and said, without asking for any identification, 'Mr Kenny, you must come with us.' My wife and I and a visiting French teacher, the only foreigners present, were escorted by the police to their headquarters in Bartolomejska Street. The Czechs followed shortly after, and were held in the same building for three hours before being taken to detention centres. Tomin used the time to give his students a further lecture on Aristotle, until the police lost patience and silenced him.

The Bartolomejska building, unexpectedly, resembled some convents I have known. There was the same drably austere style of decoration, and the same minimally comfortable furniture designed for people totally dedicated to their calling. At bends in corridors, where nuns might have placed a statue of St Joseph or St Theresa, there were little shrines to Lenin and to Czech socialist heroes, with busts, banners, flowers and texts.

I was interrogated for about an hour and a half by three detectives; I asked the chief interrogator his name, but was told, 'Just call me Inspector.' In many ways the interrogation was a replay of the interview I had had at the Czech Embassy in Kensington. In each case an insistence that it was illegal to talk to Tomin's group was combined with an unwillingness to specify what law had been broken.

'Who sent you to Prague?' 'No one *sent* me.' 'What was the content of your lecture?' That was an easy one: 'The relationship between the *Nicomachean* and *Eudemian Ethics* is one of the most interesting problems of classical philosophy. Most scholars rate the *Nicomachean Ethics* above the *Eudemian Ethics*, but on insufficient grounds. Moreover, there are interesting anomalies in the manuscript tradition . . .' They bore it politely for some minutes, and then rapped on the table. 'We are honoured that you should wish to come to Prague to present the results of your scholarly researches. But we wish you had done so at the Academy of Sciences and not before a group of criminals.'

From time to time I inquired whether I was under arrest, and asked that the British Embassy should be telephoned. They were evasive, and claimed to be having trouble with the telephone. (We discovered later that the Embassy had for some time been making energetic efforts to have us released.) Did I realize that my visit would do great harm to Anglo-Czech relations, and that the British Foreign Office would be very angry when they heard what I had done? 'I doubt if they will,' I said, 'but we can easily find out by telephoning the Embassy.'

A summary was typed of what I had said; when it was read over to me in English it seemed very garbled. The interpreter's English was imperfect, and sometimes broke down altogether (as when I referred to 'sabbatical leave'). She did not seem to relish her job, and tried to make things easier for me in various ways. When a question was simple (like 'What is your name?') she would translate straight off; if it was tricky (like 'Did you bring money to fund the Tomins?') she would put me on my guard by introducing it with, 'And now I have a very difficult question to put to you.' I was asked to sign the typed summary. Above my signature I wrote, 'I do not understand Czech; as translated to me it stands in need of correction.'

My wife was taken across a courtyard and into a different building for interrogation. This was the worst aspect of the situation for both of us: they could lie to each of us about what the other had said. Nancy in particular was worried that she might be released and expelled overnight, while I might be held much longer, as an obstinate offender in light of the warning given by Newton-Smith's expulsion.

After interrogation we were held, separately, for a while; I was returned to the waiting room beside the shrine to Lenin, where I found my briefcase. We both remembered a remark Tomin had made earlier: 'When you are in prison you must not wish for the time to pass more quickly: if you do, that means they have won.' In the briefcase was a Greek Testament, which I had brought to discuss with Tomin his theory that in the Gospel of John it is Jesus, not Pilate, who said 'Behold the man' after the crowning with thorns. We had not been able to pursue the point, but I was glad to have the New Testament to read instead of the only other thing on offer, the Communist newspaper *Rude Pravo*.

I had time to read most of the fourth Gospel before the police came to tell me I must go back to the hotel and pack. 'And then what?' I asked. 'Then you will come back here.' This was depressing: it sounded as if, rather than deporting us, they were considering holding us and making charges. I was driven through the deserted city to the hotel and we travelled up in the lift with a few late-returning revellers of various nationalities; I resisted the urge to shout 'These are Secret Policemen and I'm being wrongly detained.' I packed under their attentive eyes; they were able to point out that I had left behind two of Nancy's skirts.

Downstairs, at the hotel desk, I tried to reclaim the pre-paid voucher for a three-days' stay. 'You need not worry, sir,' the manager said, contriving to be obsequious both to me and to the Secret Police at the same time, 'there is nothing at all for you to pay.' 'But there is something for *you* to pay *me*', I insisted; the manager merely smiled in well-fortified incomprehension. He returned our passports; they were at once snatched by the senior police officer. 'Why do you want them?' I asked in German. 'I'm in your custody anyway.' 'They will be returned to you at the frontier,' he replied. This was very cheering; it was the first time the frontier had been mentioned. Driving back to the police station, I was in much better heart. They took me back to the waiting room. 'There is your wife: you may talk to each other, but you must not run away.'

Relief at our reunion was still mixed with uncertainty about our future. We were kept waiting while the French teacher was interrogated: he was given a much worse time, and his haversack was searched so thoroughly that he feared drugs might have been planted on him. But at two in the morning he joined us, with solid information that we were to be taken by car to the frontier.

The police car arrived about three, a limousine with three rows of seats; two male police sat in front, Nancy and a policewoman next, then the teacher and I in the rear. Two hundred kilometres of hard driving and imaginative braking on a winding road left us shaken up; but as the sky lightened we plunged into a Hansel and Gretel wood, with tall dense trees surrounding a border post. The driver handed our passports to the frontier guard, did a reckless three-point turn, and sped off towards Prague in a shower of pebbles. It was twenty to six.

The Czech frontier guards took their time. Our luggage was given a leisurely search, and our passports stamped to the effect that we had been expelled as undesirables and our visas terminated for violation of Article 202 of the Penal Code (the article forbidding hooliganism). Then we were free to go.

We carried our bags through the evergreens down to a rushing stream, and up the other side of the valley to the German post. At last out of the hands of the security police we expected, somehow, to be welcomed with open arms by the freedom-loving officials of the West. It wasn't quite like that. 'You have come from Czechoslovakia? On foot, with those bags?' 'I have been expelled for giving a philosophy lecture.' Not, perhaps, the most convincing story at seven o'clock on a frosty Sunday morning. We were told to wait, on a cold bench under photographs of the Baader-Meinhof terrorists.

Once a senior officer had arrived and convinced himself that I was indeed a philosopher, not a drug smuggler, the police treated us with great kindness, sending us in a private car to catch a small train which caught a large train which caught an aeroplane which took us back to England.

As we were chugging through the toy villages of Bavaria, Sunday newspapers were being delivered in England. Our arrest had been just in time to make the headlines. Our sons rushed down the street after their grandmother, on her way to church: 'Nana, Nana, Mummy and Daddy are in jail!' Luckily, only an hour or two later we were able to telephone from Munich, and by evening the family was reunited. The Czech members of the seminar were not so fortunate: they were held for forty-eight hours, then released without any charges being made.

The national press took a keen interest in our adventure, and on our return several days were spent dealing with their queries. The *Sunday Telegraph* printed a long interview, *The Times* wrote a sympathetic leader, defending my right to 'stretch the definition of tourism'; in a letter to the Editor I repeated the point I had made to Telicka, that there was nothing untoward in combining a holiday with giving an unpaid lecture. On the whole our visit to Prague, and those of the other Oxford philosophers, received warm approval right across the political spectrum. The *Oxford Times* on the right, the *Oxford Mail* on the left, both offered praise. The *New Statesman* published a series of articles on the Tomin seminars, and the Athenaeum invited me to become a member under a special rule in which the entrance fee for membership is waived. Many Balliol old members wrote letters of congratulation, most movingly Robert Birley. John Patten, the Conservative MP for Oxford, wrote a strong letter of protest about our treatment.

Only at home, in the University, were our activities frowned upon. Kathy Wilkes asked the Vice-Chancellor, Rex Richards, to protest about the treatment of the two senior members in Prague. On the advice of Hebdomadal Council he declined to do so. When I applied for my air fare to be reimbursed from the faculty funds earmarked for visits to Prague, I received the following letter from the Registrar:

> Dear Master,
> Your claim for costs . . . has come through . . . It is entirely in order and . . . will be paid shortly. At the same time I think I should record that this does involve us in a deliberate decision to discount the letter to *The Times* of 19 April which described the purpose of the visit (though we do of course understand the circumstances in which the visa application was completed) in terms which would have debarred us from clearing the payment, and even if we had been able to clear it would have involved us in declaring it for tax. For audit purposes I wanted this recorded on our file; that being so it should be on yours also.

I was summoned by the Vice-Chancellor and given what sounded very like a reprimand. Hebdomadal Council were worried about University money being used for what it regarded as political purposes. The Chairman of the Literae Humaniores board was instructed to earmark no more funds for philosophical visits to Prague.

The Foreign Office was more robust. Our Ambassador in Prague twice protested to the Czech Deputy Minister of Foreign Affairs. Peter Blaker, the Minister of State, summoned the Czech Ambassador in London. Christopher Mallaby reported to me the arguments used to claim that our visits were illegal. 'In our view,' he wrote, 'none of these arguments stands up to close examination, and the Czechoslovaks have been unable to quote any law or regulation in support.' He told me on the telephone that the Ambassador had expressed the hope that HMG would request Balliol to desist from future activities of the same kind. 'Like hell we will,' said Mallaby.

I wrote to the Vice-Chancellor aboutr Hebdomadal Council's wish that the Lit.Hum. board should cease to fund visits to Prague.

> It seems quite clear that it would be wrong to send people to Prague merely to be detained and deported as Newton-Smith and I were. I would not myself have gone unless I had thought – on the advice of people well placed to know, both in this country and in Czechoslovakia – that after the bad international publicity given to Newton-Smith's arrest it was unlikely that they would treat the next visit in a similar fashion. In my view it would be quite wrong to use University money to send people simply to make empty gestures in support of academic freedom. I expressed this view at the meeting of the Philosophy Sub-Faculty at the beginning of this term.
>
> On the other hand, I hope very much that the Philosophy Sub-Faculty will, as it has resolved to do, continue to support visits to Prague in order to conduct seminars and tutorials, and share ideas with Tomin and his studnets. I can assure you – as can any of the visitors to Prague – that the content of the seminar discussions is entirely philosophical and not at all political. The fact that the seminars have to be conducted in the face of difficulty and harassment seems to be a reason in favour of, rather than against, our lending our academic aid to them . . .

Some weeks after our expulsion, Kathy Wilkes became the third Oxford don to be deported. She had stayed with the Tomins, and given an impromptu talk to fifteen of Tomin's students while sheltering from the rain in a cave on a country walk. She was interrogated for three hours and then taken to the airport: three teenage Czech students braved the police to hand her a bunch of red roses. But Tomin had to suspend his seminars for a while, because the police began to beat up the students.

However, philosophers from Oxford and from several other countries continued to visit Prague and to take part in unofficial seminars with dissident philosophers, until the authorities who repressed them were swept away in Havel's revolution. On one well-publicized occasion Jacques Derrida was detained by the police, which brought upon the Czech authorities a personal rebuke from President Mitterand. But no further Oxford visitor, so far as I am aware, was molested in any way.

I2

The Dervorguilla Appeal

THE ACADEMIC YEAR 1979/80 was a significant one in the history of Balliol, marked by the arrival of women in the College. The first was Elena Ceva, from Ivrea near Turin. Like most of her compeers she settled in with aplomb and soon began to play a significant role in JCR politics; but some of the young women at first felt rather diffident in the still heavily male atmosphere. Nancy tried to smooth their way, as she recounted to her mother: 'I'm inviting the Balliol women 7 or 8 at a time for soup and cheese lunches here so that if they decide to have nervous breakdowns, illegitimate babies, or anorexia nervosa they know where to find me.' On the first such occasion, she recorded, one of the women was so shy that she spoke only to Stigger. But the Balliol women soon became a self-confident and powerful group, though for some years they were internally divided about whether they wanted to be recognized and represented as a group, with a women's tutor and a women's officer. Initially they preferred just to muck in with the men.

In my Master's Letter at the end of the first year of Balliol's life as a mixed college I wrote:

> Old members returning always ask anxiously, 'Does it make a lot of difference having women in the College?' The fact is that the presence of women has already come to seem so natural and such a matter of course that it is hard to know how to answer. The admission of women to Balliol reminds me of the introduction of decimal coinage into Britain. Before it happened, people were most apprehensive and there were those who said no good would come of it. Very soon after it happened it became quite hard to imagine how we had ever managed to do all those complicated calculations with shillings and pence.

What the old members did not realize was that ever since the relaxation of visiting rules and gate hours, women had been a familiar sight in the College at any hour of day or night; now they were student members of

Balliol, not camp-followers of male undergraduates. There was disappointment ahead, though, for those who thought the admission of
women would have the effect of making the mores of the JCR more
gentle and civilized. The women were anxious to show they could
compete in all male activities, good and bad. Ninety-two joined the boat
club, and female voices could be heard in the chanting of gordoulis (the
ritual jeers, hurled over the wall at neighbouring Trinity, at the end of a
party evening). In 1982 the JCR elected its first woman President,
Catherine Roe; her fresher's essay, read to me in 1981, was titled 'How
to be a feminist without being a lesbian'.

But if the College was happy to admit women, its more traditional
diversity was under threat. One of the first acts of Mrs Thatcher's
government was to force the universities to raise their fees to overseas
students. For 1980/81 fees for foreigners were increased from £940 a
year to some £2,000 for arts students, £3,000 for science students, and
£5,000 for medical students. These increases, added to College fees and
board-and-lodging charges, made Oxford at the time more expensive
than any of the Ivy League colleges in the US. The grant-in-aid to the
universities was to be reduced in proportion to the increased fee
income which would be forthcoming if as many overseas students as
before took up places; but as a consequence of the increase there was an
immediate drop of 20 per cent in the take-up of overseas places. It
seemed likely, therefore, that universities would suffer substantial
losses. But at Balliol we were more worried that the College would lose
the international character on which it had long prided itself, and I was
asked by the College to write to all its alumni in Parliament to protest
against the policy of 'full cost' fees.

In late November 1979 the JCR, unhelpfully, decided to hold a
'token occupation' in protest against the raising of overseas student
fees. I told the JCR President this was folly, but he and his colleagues
were quite undeterred by my explanation of how this was more likely to
hinder than help attempts to persuade the government to change its
mind.

I decided it was necessary to appeal directly to a JCR general meeting,
over the heads of the JCR Committee. I told them all that I, and other
dons, had done to protest against the full-cost fee policy. On 3
December, for instance, I had gone with other Heads of Houses,
including Daphne Park and Robert Blake, to protest to the Secretary of
State, Mark Carlisle. The JCR said they were merely hoping 'to demonstrate solidarity with the SCR' in its opposition to the policy. Their most
unhelpful move was an invitation to 'Red Robbo', a suspended British
Leyland shop-steward, to address the sit-in, in order 'to put the issue in

its wider context'. I explained that the government was trying to play down the concern of Vice-Chancellors and others by claiming they were just yielding to student pressure. I told the JCR, 'I'm not afraid of you, and you know that I'm not afraid of you, but the Secretary of State does not know that.' In the end, I persuaded them to call it off; but not before a hopeful organizer had sent off a full report to *Cherwell* describing a sit-in which never happened.

My letters to MPs drew many expressions of sympathy from both sides, but the longest and most helpful answer came from Peter Brooke, then a Conservative back-bencher. He told me there was no hope of persuading ministers to change their policy, while agreeing that Balliol's cosmopolitan membership was part of its essence. He suggested we should launch an appeal to our alumni, and volunteered his services as a fund-raiser.

Following a Financial Commission the previous year, the College had already concluded the time was ripe for a capital appeal to old members. It was not intended, as in 1963, to finance an ambitious programme of expansion; funds were now needed to consolidate our existing structure. Endowment income was becoming an ever more vital part of the College's total income.

College income derived from three sources: endowments, fees, and board-and-lodging charges made to junior members. At one time we had been at liberty to fix our own fees, which local authorities paid without question; now the fees reclaimable from local authorities were fixed each year by the government, while the ability of junior members to pay realistic charges had been diminished by a succession of years in which student grants had been raised by less than the increase in the cost of living.

The first object of the appeal was the endowment of specific existing Fellowships which would be under threat if they had to be funded from a diminishing general endowment. Balliol had maintained a teaching strength of one tutorial Fellow for every ten undergraduates and every four graduates; it was proud of its high tutor/pupil ratio, and had been more reluctant than some other colleges to farm out teaching to tutors who were not Fellows. Part of the stipend of College Fellows was paid by central University funds; but with the University itself facing cuts in income it could no longer be assumed that when the College had to replace a retiring Fellow, University funds would be available to contribute to the costs of a successor. The College also wished to fund the modernization of accommodation and facilities overdue for refurbishment. The only element of expansion in the appeal portfolio was to be a new building for undergraduate accommodation. Now it was decided to add to the goals of the appeal the establishment of a number of over-seas scholarships.

Plans took some time to mature. What should the appeal be called? Balliol had celebrated its septcentenary in 1963, but even at the time it had been admitted that the foundation date was based on legend rather than scholarship. The first statutes had been given to the College in 1282 by the Lady Dervorguilla of Galloway, widow of John de Balliol. She had, indeed, as good a claim as he to be the founder of the College as it was she who, after his death, put on a solid footing the paltry and reluctant foundation imposed upon him as a penance for kidnapping the Bishop of Durham. In 1979 the College had decided to celebrate Dervorguilla's centenary, and commissioned a set of historical essays in its honour. Why not attach the appeal to this solid centenary as The Dervorguilla Appeal? The name was approved, and the target fixed at £2 million.

In years of high inflation, the setting of student rents and charges – by the executive committee in Trinity Term for the following twelve months – was a painful process, involving long formal discussions between the senior and junior members, and informal bargaining between bursars and JCR officials, which it often fell to the Master to mediate. In most years we were able to settle on a figure which the JCR President, acting the role of Trades Union leader, would recommend to his members at a general meeting. When the increase was regarded as too swingeing, the JCR would call a rent strike. Those junior members who wished to strike paid their battels not to the College but into a strike fund, and when the strike ended – frequently on the terms originally fixed by the College – the money in the fund was paid over to the College, usually with the accumulated interest. Since strikers tended to pay their battels into the fund more promptly than the average indolent undergraduate settled his debts with the Bursar, the College was often better off as a result of a strike. And thus it was when the strike in Michaelmas Term 1980 was brought to an end in December.

In 1981 Jacko was due to retire as Domestic Bursar, and at the beginning of the year the College had to choose his successor. The selection committee was divided between those who wanted a candidate with similar service experience, and those who preferred someone who was explicitly a 'hotel' manager. The eventual run-off was between an admiral and a former NatWest Bank catering manager with service experience in the Catering Corps. In the event the College preferred the latter, Peter Roberts, who took over in the summer.

It was a busy spring for the Kennys. As well as teaching at New

College School, Nancy was now taking private pupils at home, fitting this in with the extensive (if silent) demands a College makes on the Master's wife and also giving a number of solo recitals as a mezzo-soprano. Luckily all our activities fell within a small area of the centre of Oxford, so we were able to see a good deal of the children. Charles rose to the top of his class at Josca's, and it was Robert's last term at New College school, full of ablative absolutes and quadratic equations; he won a scholarship to Magdalen College School; Charles was learning to play the guitar, Robert the flute; Charles grew tall enough to punt, and bridge took over from Dungeons and Dragons as Robert's favourite avocation – he commandeered the playroom in The King's Mound for a twelve-hour sponsored bridge tournament in aid of a muscular dystrophy charity.

In the Long Vacation we took things quietly, and travelled less than usual. In September I attended the Symposium Aristotelicum, an international gathering of classical philosophy scholars in Berlin. The city was still divided, and some of us decided to cross into East Berlin to visit the Opera. When we emerged from the *U-bahn* at the Friedrichstrasse checkpoint, my colleagues were waved through but I was marched off to have my passport inspected. When the police saw the record of my expulsion from Czechoslovakia, they refused to let me through and returned me to West Berlin. The following day I went to the British Consulate to ask for a new, clean passport so that I could try again. The officials were not encouraging. 'If you are in their computer as a trouble-maker, it won't help you having a new passport – maybe only make matters worse.' I said I was prepared to take the risk: I did have a right to have a new passport issued, didn't I? 'Sure – I suppose you have brought your birth certificate with you?' Never having travelled with one, I had to admit myself beaten. I took away an impression that once you got into trouble with *any* passport authority, *every* passport authority, East or West, regarded you as a nuisance.

The Master's Lodgings at Balliol are full of portraits of Balliol ecclesiastics. To those of three Archbishops of Canterbury, A.C. Tait and Frederick Temple in the nineteenth century and William Temple in the twentieth, I added that of Cardinal Heard. Between the end of the Second World War and the late 1970s, however, there had been a dearth of Balliol holders of senior prelacies. This gap was now filled: Dom Ambrose Griffiths had become Abbot of Ampleforth, and Graham Leonard was appointed Bishop of London – I attended his enthronement at St Paul's in September 1981.

In November of 1979, King Olav of Norway had paid a twenty-four-hour visit to Balliol, taking in a rugger match at his own request.

Fortuitously, this was another period when I was attempting to keep a diary:

3 November

King arrived 10.30, a little later than planned and embarassingly by back door. Spent morning showing him round the newish Balliol buildings and the tatty JCR (posters for Mugabe clearly interested him). Lunch at King's Mound much easier; he was very Santa Claus-like with children and answered their questions, such as 'Do you wear a crown?', 'What is your second name?' Charles, pointing to his Vincent's tie: 'I say, I do like the crowns on your tie.' He turns out to be grandson of Edward VII, and told us his cousin, George VI, had to wear the heavy crown two hours a day for two weeks in preparation for coronation. After lunch to watch Balliol defeat Exeter 16–6 at Rugby in gloom and drizzle.

At 6 p.m. sherry in hall for JCR to meet King: gratifyingly large, enthusiastic, and well-dressed turn-out. We then changed for dinner – pushy *Cherwell* reporter burst in and had to be bundled out. We were joined at 7.20 by Nancy and the Scotts who were staying at King's Mound while the King and I stayed in the Lodgings. Agreeable dinner in the SCR. During port the K. began to doze off, having been up early this a.m. to fly over; so I took him straight to Lodgings for bed, thus regrettably preventing many Fellows from meeting him.

Reviving in the night air in the quad, he didn't wish to go to bed, but called for his pipe and his bowl and we got through quite a lot of Bell's before retiring about 1 a.m. Security guard, who had attended K. all day, came in around midnight to warn of a telephone call saying 'Balliol: you have the King of Norway: beware'. I could recognize the voice of Trinity even if the detective could not, and told him there was no need to sleep beside the K. as he wished; I would answer for his safety.

I asked the King what was the part of his job which kept him busiest. 'I've all those things to sign,' he said. So Christopher Robin's Alice was right after all.

4 November

N. made breakfast for Scotts and Andersons while Mrs Roberts [the Lodgings butler] did so for K. and me in Balliol. I invited Jasper round to meet K. since he hadn't seen him much the night before in spite of hard work with seating plans etc. He arrived about 10 after K. and I had sat together reading newspapers for an hour. Altogether K. is very cheerful and relaxed and seemed to enjoy himself. He left about 11.15.

In December of 1980 I had paid my first visit to Norway since Arthur Prior's death, to lecture at Oslo University under the auspices of a philosopher friend, Dagfinn Follesdal, who commuted between Stanford and Oslo. King Olav kindly invited Nancy and me to lunch. He was clearly a popular monarch, and his subjects spoke with bated breath of his energy, despite his age, as a skier.

King Olav paid another visit to the College in November 1981. The oil company BP, who enjoyed substantial revenue from Norwegian oil-fields, had agreed to pay for a portrait of the King, by a Norwegian artist of his choice, to hang in Hall, and King Olav came to unveil it. The new Bursar, worried lest someone might paint a false moustache on it, slept with it in his room until the day of the ceremony. But in the end one hundred undergraduates in collars stood respectfully silent, and the ceremony passed off with dignity, if not with ease. 'He is such a nice King,' Nancy wrote to her mother. 'He really is shy, so you chatter away to set him at his ease, and then suddenly think "This is a *king*", and shut up. How grim, especially if you're shy, to have that effect on people.'

In the same month we received the devastating news that Robert Ogilvie, now Professor of Latin at St Andrew's, had taken his own life; only a few weeks earlier I had entertained him, apparently in excellent spirits, in the Lodgings. It was incredible that so much life, talent, and energy had been prematurely quenched. We understood he had been involved in a bad car crash earlier in the year, and had come to believe he was suffering from cancer. His son Alexander had just come into residence at Balliol to read mathematics, and I had to break the news to him that his father had shot himself. It was the unhappiest duty of my entire Mastership.

By statute, a Master of Balliol is only required to live in Oxford for six months of the year, including sixteen weeks in term. In theory, therefore, a Master could absent himself for one term in three, but I followed Christopher Hill in taking sabbaticals with the same frequency as the Fellows, one term in seven. My first as Master was due in Trinity Term 1982; I was a visiting Professor at the University of Minnesota. On the way there we spent a delightful week in the British Virgin Islands.

The term at Minnesota was pleasant. The department was full of congenial colleagues, and I had a light teaching load. Our house backed onto the university golf course, and for the first and last time in my life I played regularly. The boys accompanied us, and they too relaxed: their high school had a magnificent swimming pool, and did not impose homework. From time to time I flew to New York for a series of American Bampton Lectures I had been invited to give at Columbia University. Arriving for my first lecture, the first thing I saw was a sweatshirt saying 'Balliol College Rugby Tour' – worn by a member of a Columbia team defeated by the Balliol XV a few days previously.

I took the opportunity to renew links with American Balliol alumni, and prepare the ground for the Dervorguilla Appeal. Nancy and I spent Easter week at Topsfield near Boston with the most important American Balliol man of all, Bill Coolidge.

Coolidge had been a commoner of the College in 1924–27. With wealth inherited and enhanced he had built up an exceptional collection of paintings and become a substantial benefactor to many religious and educational causes. In particular, he had won the affection of many generations of Balliol men through his foundation in 1955 of The Atlantic Crossing Trust, familiarly known as The Pathfinder Scheme. This provided a travel grant and pocket money for eight chosen final-year students to enjoy the hospitality of a network of hosts around the US built up among Bill's friends and returning Balliol Americans. He had also been one of the most generous benefactors of the centenary appeal, and had been made an Honorary Fellow of the College in 1963.

Shortly after I became Master we had invited Bill to the College for a reunion of all Balliol men who had been Pathfinders. He enjoyed this visit greatly, and on his return initiated steps to perpetuate the Pathfinder Scheme after his death. However, the admission of women to Balliol had now created a problem; in 1982 for the first time there were women as well as men among the candidates for Pathfinder awards; and one of the purposes of our visit to him that Easter was to persuade him to accept this development. His response was so full of alarm that it was decided not to send any female Pathfinders that year; instead, the women who had been elected were given grants by the College from its own funds, and arrangements for hospitality were made instead by Nancy's parents.

The other purpose of our visit to Bill was to solicit help for the Dervorguilla Appeal. We had been advised that it would be injudicious to launch the appeal and announce our target of £2 million until we had secured advance pledges of some thirty per cent. Bill was very sympathetic, and promised a generous contribution.

Staying at Topsfield was always a delight. One dined beneath a Rubens and an El Greco, while the guest-room bed had a Turner at the head and a Renoir at the foot. Bill would show one lovingly round his main picture gallery. But his sight had now begun to fail, and it was heart-rending to see him point out particular delights on canvases which he could no longer see but whose features were graven on his memory. At one time I tried to persuade him to bequeath to Balliol his El Greco of St Catherine, the College's patron saint. But the collection was destined for the Boston Art Institute, and he did not want to break it up.

Balliol is fortunate in its alumni, and another who had used his wealth in imaginative ways, both aesthetically and educationally, was Irwin Miller, chairman and longtime chief executive of Cummins Engine. In the company town of Columbus, Indiana, he had offered to pay the architectural fees for every public building, provided the architect was chosen by a panel headed by Saarinen. In this way he had turned the town into an exhibition of specimens of the finest modern architecture. Irwin was a most comfortable benefactor. If I went to stay with him, he would say immediately, 'Tell me what I can do for the College.' All would be settled on the Friday night, and for the rest of the weekend one could relax and enjoy his and Xenia's lively company without one's begging duties hanging over one.

From Minneapolis I went round to beg for Balliol in San Francisco, Washington, Princeton, and New York; in each place regional fund-raising committees were set up, under the national chairmanship of Irwin Miller. My father-in-law Hank, with his experience of fund-raising for Cornell, was full of helpful advice, and sometimes accompanied me; he told me college deans and presidents often needed to be kicked under the table by their development officers, to make sure they actually got around to asking for money.

I returned from America, in time for the June Gaudy, with sufficient advance pledges for the launching of the Dervorguilla Appeal. The book of essays on Balliol history comissioned for the centenary was brought to publication in good time; my own contribution was a piece about Elizabethan Catholics in Balliol, and in particular the career of Robert Persons, who after being Bursar of the College went on to become the best-hated Jesuit of the English Counter-Reformation.

In July Bristol University awarded me an Honorary Doctorate, a courtesy the University often extended to Masters of Balliol, in memory of the role Benjamin Jowett had played in the foundation of Bristol College. Among my fellow honorands I was glad to meet Anthony Powell, who had been an Honorary Fellow of Balliol since 1974. Another new acquaintance made that summer, who soon became a firm friend, was Norman St John Stevas, lately expelled from the Cabinet because of his undue levity about the Blessed Margaret Thatcher. He and I shared a common background, having both been students at the English College in Rome; but he had gone on to a distinguished political career, and our only previous contact had been a controversy between us in the Catholic newspapers in the 1960s, about the justification for the nuclear deterrent. Now, in July 1982, he invited Nancy and me to celebrate the Feast of St Pambo with him at his house in Preston Capes – a delightful luncheon which culminated, rather improbably, with Benediction of the Blessed Sacrament in honour of the Speaker of the House of Commons, George Thomas, MP.

The actual date of the Dervorguilla centenary was 22 August but the College, feeling that to be an unpropitious time of year for a celebratory banquet, fixed the Dervorguilla Dinner for Saturday, 18 September. It has been eloquently described in Anthony Powell's *Journals: 1982–1986*.

To Oxford for the Dervorguilla Dinner at Balliol. On arrival I looked in for tea at the (old) Senior Common Room, where six or eight Strullbrugs of fearsome aspect were sitting in gloomy silence facing each other, giving grimmest portents of what was likely to be in store. Sherry party in Master's Lodgings now vacated by Anthony Kenny, with whom I had evaded staying, tho' at Bristol I had found him & his American wife agreeable . . .

At dinner I was seated at the High Table, backing on the undergraduate tables, now filled with Dervorguilla guests. On my right was Stanley Wells, of the Oxford University Press, Shakespearian specialist, married to the writer Susan Hill (never met), who sometimes reviews for the D[aily] T[elegraph]. On my left was Richard Cobb, who arrived only just in time for dinner. He looked very thin, crimson in the face. He was hard to hear as acoustics were bad, and there was a fearful row of chattering . . .

Beyond Cobb sat a ninety-year-old, eminently spry, white-bearded Balliol man called Myers, some musical affiliation, probably there as the oldest member of the College still on his feet. Opposite me at the High Table, Bill Williams . . . on Williams's right, Denis Healey, MP; the Master, Tony Kenny; next to him the Chancellor, Harold Macmillan, eighty-eight, looking every day of it, tho' he began to do that years ago.

Cobb told me he had reviewed Graham Greene's book *J'accuse* for the *Sunday Times* at proof stage, then was told it could not go in owing to fear of libel. I had wondered why there were no reviews, having thought what had already appeared of the book in serial form to be poor stuff . . . Cobb said he thought Graham wanted to end his life by being murdered at the hands of a Nice Mafioso. I certainly think Graham has always felt, from his earliest days, that somehow his life is not glamorous enough in the eyes of the public, although he is always doing things to make it sound exciting.

A similar conversation about Graham Greene was taking place between the Master and Denis Healey opposite, Tony Kenny saying that obviously Greene ought to write about the Ambrosiano money scandal at the Vatican, now going strong, a subject no doubt particularly attractive to Kenny, as a former priest. If such a book were to be any good (not sort of Peyrefitte stuff) I think it would take a cooler, better informed, better organized, grasp of public affairs than Graham possesses. Healey, immediately addressing me as Anthony, turned out to be a fan . . .

Healey brought up alleged resemblance of Widmerpool to Ted Heath, something that [had] never occurred to me, although the Tory group called The Monday Club wrote asking me to address them on 'Heath as Widmerpool', which I declined. Healey said a friend of his in the CID had been investigating suicide (possible murder) of the financier Calvi (concerned with above Vatican money scandals) in London. CID man's first act had been to go to sex shop in Soho, buy a rubber woman, that legendary piece of equipment, now easily procurable (more appropriate word than purchased). I asked if the CID man had carried her away in his arms. Healey said she is packed in a box and inflated when you got home (presumably with a bicycle pump; otherwise it would leave one with little breath to obtain sexual satisfaction), in this particular case possibly done on the spot, where she was to be used to reconstruct Calvi's death . . .

I turned to Cobb to discuss this ingenious expedient (worthy of Sherlock Holmes) to find he was, in fact, sleeping like a child, with his head on the shoulder of his ninety-year-old white-bearded neighbour, who looked across at me, raising his eyebrows in appeal for sympathy, whether for Cobb or himself I was uncertain. I had missed the moment of Cobb's sudden collapse. He equally suddenly revived during the Master's speech. This subsequent recovery was sufficient for him to clap loudly after the Chancellor's speech, and express great enthusiasm to me. It was indeed a good speech, in the characteristic Macmillan manner.

Later we adjourned to the (new) Senior Common Room, a somewhat grim addition to the College. Kenny was talking to Macmillan. By this time feeling like retiring to bed, I touched him on the shoulder, and said goodnight. By an exceedingly adroit movement, Kenny managed to flit off in a flash, leaving Macmillan on my hands, in fact placing bed further off than ever. Macmillan is perfectly coherent when talking, if fairly heavy going *vis-à-vis*. In his speech he had remarked how difficult it was to know what people were like in 1282, the year the Lady Dervorguilla Balliol (perhaps more correctly Dervorguilla, Lady Balliol, tho' she was a considerable heiress in her own right) confirmed the establishment of Balliol as a College, compared with what he, Macmillan, felt about Classical times.

To bat the ball back, I said I felt reasonably at ease in the Middle Ages (far from the truth), a claim in any case completely ignored by Macmillan, who went pressing on, enlarging his own thesis. He remarked that one would have no difficulty in talking to Cicero, 'if he came into Pratt's'. I allowed that Cicero might well have been a member of Pratt's, otherwise full of young Praetorian Guardsmen. Macmillan then lost interest in the subject, beginning long diatribe against the iniquity of pulling down churches and monasteries. 'Now it's the Inland Revenue,' he said. I expressed hearty agreement. At that moment the Master appeared with another human offering. I escaped swiftly, leaving Macmillan with his new victim. Healey was at the bar. I waved good-night. Healey replied with a reasonably steady mock military salute.

A second Dervorguilla Dinner was held in October, and the academic year 1982/3 was largely taken up with the Appeal. Knowing it was going to be a busy one, I set myself at its beginning to accomplish a long overdue task: the simplification of the College's committee structure. There were now twenty-seven committees, some reporting directly to Governing Body, but most of them sub-committees reporting to the Tutorial Board or the executive committee. I proposed that the business of these sub-committees should be conducted by the committees they reported to, and that the sub-committees themselves should only be called together in specially difficult cases, and in effect be allowed to whither away. The proposals were approved in principle by a straw vote of 26 to 4 when presented to a College meeting in October. Foolishly, however, I suggested that the reforms should be approved in detail by a Consilium a week later – by which time conservative instincts had reasserted themselves, and the proposals were voted down decisively in favour of the *status quo*.

Brochures setting out the objectives of the Appeal were circulated to all UK old members in the autumn of 1982, and worldwide in 1983. Old members volunteered to act as regional organizers and as class secretaries. I stumped the country to meet local gatherings, as did Maurice Keen, now Vice-Master. A committee of old members, headed by Rodney Leach, met regularly in London to solicit gifts from corporations, foundations, and potential individual benefactors. One of the most devoted members of this group was Peter Brooke, until he had to resign on his appointment as Minister with responsibility for higher education. The Permanent Secretary in the Department of Education and Science at this time was David Hancock, Peter's Balliol contemporary of 1954, a situation which seemed to us so reminiscent of the TV series *Yes, Minister* that in January 1984 we invited Peter and David to a celebratory lunch in the Lodgings with Paul Eddington, who played the Minister.

The Appeal aimed to raise the £2 million from three sources: £1 million from old members at home, £500,000 from alumni overseas, and £500,000 from non-Balliol sources. By June 1983 we were half-way to our goal, with more than £500,000 from home alumni, £200,000-plus from alumni overseas (mainly in the US), and nearly £300,000 from other sources. I ended my own round of overseas visits in July with a two-week trip to Australia where, having given philosophical lectures in eight universities to pay my fare, I made an almost completely unsuccessful plea for funds to alumni in four major cities. Sir Warwick Fairfax, Balliol 1921–25 and publisher of the *Sydney Morning Herald*, and his wife Mary had spent some time in Oxford in autumn 1979 to see their son – also Warwick – settled in at Balliol, and Nancy and I had become acquainted with them then. Sir Warwick entertained me handsomely in Sydney, and at his country house, where a handle at the bedside could roll away the ceiling above and reveal the night stars. But he regretted that he was currently short of cash, and unable to contribute to the Appeal until planning permission had been given for the disposal of one of his farms for development.

Graham Greene, when approached for a benefaction, suggested the

College should hold an auction at Christie's of items donated by old members, and promised to set the ball rolling by giving some of his own MSS. Sadly, they proved disappointing – typescripts of four-page introductions to reprints of his works, and the like. Other alumni were more generous. In November I gave a luncheon at the Oxford and Cambridge Club for King Olav's eightieth birthday; Prince Harald was there, too. ('Food and drink were good', Powell recorded in his diary. 'Kenny is obviously determined to put Balliol on the map again, after a dynasty of dreary Masters, either dull or actively harmful to the College. One must applaud his attitude.') The King presented for the auction a gold watch given him by his grandfather, King Edward VII; when the catalogue was drawn up by Christie's the watch, because it bore no English hallmark, was listed as being 'of yellow metal'.

In the end, not enough items were received for a special auction, and the donations had to be sold as individual lots in normal sales. Another unsuccessful project was a Balliol tour, aimed at the upper end of the US tourist market: an expedition around historical sites, under expert guidance by Balliol dons, and including visits to the homes of Balliol noblemen. This, to be charged at $10,000 a head, of which $3,000 represented a gift to the Dervorguilla Appeal, was undersubscribed and had to be cancelled – to the relief of a number of Fellows who considered the whole project *infra dig*.

In a manner that was very timely for the College's ambitions, the Rhodes Trustees had arranged to hold a reunion in Oxford in June 1983 of all Rhodes Scholars, to mark the eightieth anniversary of the foundation of the scholarships. The highlight was a garden party at Rhodes House at which HM The Queen and the Duke of Edinburgh were the guests of honour; part of the wall between Rhodes House and Wadham had to be knocked down to accommodate the throng of guests. I had been told off to introduce to Prince Philip John Templeton, a Balliol alumnus who had just made a most generous gift of £3 million to turn the Oxford Centre for Management Studies into Templeton College. As John had been one of my own major hopes as a benefactor of Balliol, I viewed this munificence with mixed feelings. The Prince congratulated him warmly but, mindful of his duties as Chancellor of Cambridge University, remarked jokingly, 'I can think of another place where the money could have been better spent.' I could not help murmuring, 'That makes two of us.'

As the final celebration of the three-day reunion, the Rhodes Scholars from each College were entertained to a dinner by their own *alma mater*. Balliol, long the most popular college among Rhodes Scholars, provided a banquet which filled the Hall to capacity, at which

Harold Macmillan made a magnificent speech, despite having had to speak to the assembled scholars on behalf of the whole University in a marquee in Trinity the previous night.

It was perhaps no coincidence that the American alumni were the first of the Balliol old members to reach their target: at the beginning of 1984 Chuck Barber, the energetic Vice-Chairman of the National Committee, telephoned to say that £500,000 had been raised. The College now felt confident enough of success to anticipate the completion of the Appeal by founding a number of overseas scholarships, and by starting a rolling programme of staircase modernization. There was a moment of discouragement in February, when the inflow of funds seemed to have dried up, and a scaling-down of objectives was considered; but when the total sum passed the £1.5 million mark we felt justified in going ahead with a new building. The architects Barnett, Briscoe and Gotch offered to design and build accommodation for 40 undergraduates on the Master's Field for £500,000. Architect friends had reservations, but the plans were found acceptable by the Fellows in June 1984, and work went ahead with a view to occupation in Michaelmas 1985. It was embarrassing, therefore, that at the end of the academic year 1983/4 we were still some way from our two-year target. The person who finally came to our rescue was Robert Maxwell.

The Maxwell I knew best was Elizabeth, whom I had assisted in the preparation of her doctoral dissertation. Three Maxwell sons had been at Balliol – Philip (1966), Ian (1975) and Kevin (1977) – and in 1981 the younger daughter, Ghislaine, had applied to the college to read modern languages but had been rejected because her A-levels were not good enough. Under heavy pressure from her father, she re-took them and improved her grades sufficiently to be accepted in 1982. She did not have an easy time in Balliol: a kidnapping threat in her second year had to be taken seriously, for it was not long since a son of Paul Getty had had his ear cut off by kidnappers.

From time to time I had visited Headington Hill Hall to solicit funds from Robert Maxwell for various good causes unconnected with the College. Commonly I left empty-handed, after half an hour of the grilling and hectoring for which he was famous; yet in the early 1960s he had helped fund a Fellowship in Politics in the College.

In June 1983 Nancy and I had been invited to Maxwell's sixtieth birthday party, a lavish occasion. Guests, greeted with champagne at the door, were shown to their places in a marquee; there was a present for everyone. Asparagus, lobster, *boeuf* Wellington and grapefruit mousse were accommpanied by fine wines. But there was a price to be paid: at the end of the dinner came a long series of speeches in praise of the birthday boy – from his wife, from the Russian Ambassador, the Czech Ambassador, the East German Ambassador, the editor of a scientific journal, a member of the Harvard Faculty, the Bulgarian Ambassador, and Harold Wilson. Remarkably, Wilson's speech stood out for its wit and brevity. Each speaker was followed by a response from Maxwell himself. Thanking the Bulgarian Ambassador for an honorary degree just conferred on him, Maxwell said, 'In the heart of every English man and woman there beats a note of friendship for Bulgaria.' This was too much for a lady at my table, who said, very audibly, 'Not in mine there doesn't.' She slipped off her chair, and was escorted away by her husband; but she spoke for all of us.

But now, a year later, Maxwell became suddenly helpful, and the final stages of the appeal were remarkably painless. He persuaded a Japanese friend to give £200,000 towards our new building. There remained £300,000 needed to complete the appeal. I lunched with Jack Dellal, who offered £200,000, provided the building was named after him. I telephoned an American alumnus; he promised £50,000. Then I got back to Maxwell, and told him the situation. Would he make a further contribution, and would he mind the building being named after someone else, even though in effect he had been the major facilitator? He promised to take us over the top, and made no difficulty about the naming. By the second anniversary of the Dervorguilla Dinner I was confident of the success of the Appeal, and Harold Macmillan formally announced it at the dinner on St Catherine's Night, 1984.

13

Past Masters

A MASTER OF BALLIOL is, by statute, obliged to take part in the educational work of the College. I did so by listening to freshers' essays and giving occasional undergraduate tutorials in philosophy, providing cover, perhaps, for a colleague on leave. But most of my teaching was done for the University rather than the College, supervising graduate students who were writing dissertations, and giving general University lectures.

Most of my lectures were on topics of medieval philosophy – Aquinas, Duns Scotus, or the problem of freewill in the Middle Ages.It was not that the medieval period was the one which most interested me: it was the one most neglected by other Oxford philosophers. When I first arrived in Oxford there was a Reader in Medieval Philosophy, Lorenzo Minio-Paluello, a scholarly man who placed the international Aristotelian community in his debt, but not one to catch and keep the interest of contemporary analytic philosophers. The vacancy left by his retirement in 1975 was not filled, and there was no one in the Philosophy Faculty with any responsibility for teaching medieval philosophy. As I thought it a scandal that a university which had been one of the main centres of scholasticism in the Middle Ages should so lack interest in its own philosophical past, I lectured most years, to keep the subject alive, even though I have never been a professional medievalist. Perhaps it was a mistake to do so. The Medieval Readership remained in abeyance, and when the refilling of other posts was given priority I suspect one argument used was, 'No need to worry about medieval philosophy; Kenny will take care of the few oddballs who are interested in it.'

Though I did more teaching of University graduates than of Balliol undergraduates, I did take a keen interest in the College's academic performance. One way in which a Master was supposed to protect tutorial standards within the College was assigned by tradition: the last week of every eight-week term is taken up by 'handshaking'. Undergraduates, unless they have been writing examinations, come one by one to sit at the dining room table in the Lodgings, and listen to their subject tutors, sitting across the table, as they report to the Master on the term's work. Some alumni recall the event with a degree of terror – Graham Greene, in his autobiography, recounts being propped up, drunk, by his tutors as he appeared before the Master. Most undergraduates nowadays take it in their stride. As a tutor, of course, I had been familiar with this exercise for thirteen years. As Master, I found the experience exhausting but fascinating.

First, it gave one a sober overall view of what was happening in the College. After a term in which a domestic crisis or some outrageous JCR demand had loomed large, it was reassuring to realize, as the interviewees came and went for their three-minute report, that most members of the College were quietly getting on with their academic work and keeping their tutors reasonably happy.

Next, it was pleasant to savour the variety of relationships between tutors and pupils: some rather stiff and formal, others relaxed and laid-back. Tutors' methods of reporting often reflected the ethos of their subject: a maths tutor might simply reel off a list of numerical marks for each week's problems solved; an English or Classics don would articulate a term's progress in an elegant encomium or diatribe.

Finally, handshaking gave the Master an opportunity to check up on the tutors as well as the undergraduates. Most pupils were taught personally by the Balliol Fellows, and only rarely – either as Senior Tutor or as Master – did I have to complain that too much teaching was being farmed out to surrogates from elsewhere. It was not difficult to tell, at handshaking, how well a tutor knew a pupil for whom he was responsible. If a tutor made an unfavourable report, a pupil was always given a chance to respond on the spot. A few would seize the opportunity to shift the blame onto a tutor; those who appeared reluctant to do so I would later invite to see me privately, to discover whether they had any genuine grievance. Even so, I always found a great reluctance in junior members to complain about their tutors. Partly this was due to the camaraderie which, even in the days of student power, grew up between pupil and tutor; but mainly, I believe, it was because there was very little ground for complaint. All my probing left me with the impression that the Balliol tutors were in general a conscientious lot, and that on the rare occasions where pupils were short-changed by a particular tutor, the slack was taken up by other tutors in the same subject.

However, in the mid 1980s the tutorial system was under some strain. I did feel that tutors in certain subjects encouraged too relaxed an attitude to College and University examinations. I was not altogether gratified when the student *Alternative Prospectus* for 1985 said that 'Balliol has a very strong academic tradition, despite an apparent lack of pressure from the SCR', and I was horrified to learn from some junior members that they felt three or four hours of academic work a day to be quite adequate. When I queried tutors about this, each would tell me that in *their* subject such indolence would be unthinkable: the lawyers, medics and engineers felt this particularly strongly.

In the 1980s the decline in Balliol's academic performance was halted, but not reversed, and there were some disappointing years, such as 1984, when I had to write to old members to reassure them. 'In the last five years', I wrote, 'Balliol has achieved 115 Firsts, this being 22.2 per cent of all candidates ... a percentage higher than any other college during the period. The College continues, however, to have an unduly high number of Thirds, which means that we do not perform as well in the Norrington Table as we do in the table of First Class degrees.'

Balliol continued to attract high-calibre applicants. At one time the A-level results of university applicants were quantified in such a way that the maximum score of a candidate with three As was 15; the entry average of Balliol was 14, compared with an Oxford average of 13.5 and a national average of 10.1. In some subjects the average score of entrants was even higher: Classics, English, Engineering and Mathematics, for instance, all scored 14.8. On the one hand this was flattering, and showed that Balliol was preserving its reputation as an institution of academic excellence; on the other hand, it clearly meant we could not afford to be complacent about examination results, as even without any 'value added' by the College they could be expected to be impressive.

In one way Balliol had become a victim of its own success. The college's century-old reputation for effortless superiority was a terrible curse: it was so much easier for a pupil to imitate the effortlessness than the superiority. Equally, many Fellows had reached a level of academic distinction which meant that they were awarded University or British Academy Readerships, Royal Society or Research Council posts, or Radcliffe Fellowships such as I had held while Senior Tutor. The College took a pride in these promotions, but the cumulative effect of such secondments was that there were often several tutorial Fellows whose main term-time effort was devoted not to College tuition, but elsewhere.

Nationwide, external pressure was brought to bear on academics to publish research results. Shortly after I became Master the College itself introduced a scheme – strongly opposed by some traditional tutors such as Maurice Keen and Colin Lucas – allowing a number of tutors in each year to take a remission from the normal full teaching load, to enable them to pursue research. Administration also took its toll. Among the ageing Fellowship there were now many former College officers. This provided a welcome weight of experience on the Governing Body; but it also meant that a Fellow, having served the College with devotion for several years in an administrative capacity, might feel on retiring from office that he should turn his surplus energy to good causes outside the College.

Tutors in their forties or fifties were likely to be much less involved informally in the lives of junior members than they had once been; it was not natural for them to share the sports, recreations, and enthusiasms of the young as they had twenty years earlier, and the College had to rely largely on Junior Research Fellows to provide sporting links between JCR and SCR. It had become rare for tutorial Fellows to live in College, and the provision in the College statutes that two persons engaged in the educational work of the College must reside within the walls was usually fulfilled by lecturers and short-term tutors, rather than by official Fellows. Changes world-wide in relations between the sexes and in matrimonial mores meant that male Fellows took a greater share in domestic tasks which kept them out of College, and could no longer expect their wives to devote themselves to the entertainment of pupils at home.

From time to time I encouraged Governing Body to address and remedy these problems. However, I was not myself in any position to complain if Fellows wished to devote a large part of their time to scholarly publishing. The statutes place no obligation on a Master to pursue research, but historically the Fellows have preferred, rather than inviting in a grandee from public life, to elect as their head an academic scholar. I wanted to follow in the footsteps of Christopher Hill and keep up my academic writing. Like Christopher, I decided to submit my work for the degree of D.Litt. This, like the doctorates in divinity, civil law, music and medicine, is what is known as a 'historic doctorate', one which antedates the introduction of the D.Phil. from America early in this century. The D.Litt is not an honorary degree, but awarded on merit, although there is no examination; instead, one submits a selection of one's published work to date for evaluation by a pair of examiners. In 1980, when my work had been read and approved, I went to the Sheldonian to receive the degree.

Now that I was no longer employed to teach philosophy I felt free to follow my academic curiosity into other fields of scholarly endeavour. One of the first books which appeared while I was Master was *The Computation of Style*, the textbook on stylostatistics which had grown out of my work on the Aristotelian ethics. As the decade wore on, I broadened my interests and published on literary, political and legal topics. In the early 1980s most of my writing was still philosophical, but it was philosophy of a popular rather than a professional kind.

In 1978 Oxford University Press launched a series of small books on great thinkers of the past, with the title 'Past Masters'. Each book was to present its subject's major ideas in a popular form within some 30,000 words; I was commissioned for the volume on Aquinas.

Aquinas' works must be more voluminous than those of almost any other writer of comparable stature. In his short life of fifty years he wrote at least eight million words; if works dubiously attributed are genuine, the total rises to about eleven million. Obviously any popular account of his work would have to be highly selective, and in my *Aquinas* I made no attempt at systematic coverage of his ideas. First, I treated him as a philosopher, not a theologian: that is to say, I wrote for readers who did not necessarily share his theological interests and beliefs. But of course I drew on his theological works, since it is in them that one finds many of his most important philosophical insights.

The 30,000-word limit invited a structure of three ten-thousand word chapters. The first was an account of Aquinas' life and works and an assessment of his significance for contemporary philosophy. Now he had been freed from his distorting niche as official philosopher of the Roman Catholic Church, I argued, he could be seen as worthy to rank on equal terms with the greatest philosophers of all time.

The second chapter was a synopsis of Aquinas' metaphysics, treating of his systematic concepts such as matter, form, substance, accident, actuality and potentiality. I claimed that many of these were of abiding interest, but also maintained that some of the most celebrated were enmeshed in confusion. The theory of the real distinction between essence and existence, and the thesis that God is self-subsistent being, are often presented as among the most profound and original contributions made by him to philosophy. I argued that, on the contrary, even the most sympathetic treatment of these doctrines could not wholly absolve them of the charge of sophistry and illusion.

Aquinas' philosophy of mind, on other hand, as I went on to argue in the third chapter, has an interest at the present time which is as great as that of any other system on offer. In spite of confusions in detail and substantial lacunae of which later philosophers have made us aware, St Thomas's philosophy in this area contains a structure which is fundamentally sounder than its modern rivals such as Cartesian dualism or scientistic materialism. In my view, it is a structure on which future philosophers would do well to build.

The book proved popular, and was reprinted three months after publication; according to the OUP editor, it was being outsold only by Jesus, Marx and Hume (in that order).

Between 1979 and 1981 I gave a set of endowed lectures in the Theology Faculty at Oxford, the Speaker's Lectures on Biblical Studies. In these I made use of the stylometric techniques I had used on Aristotle, to build up a statistical picture of the stylistic regularities to be to found in the New Testament, and then used these features to throw light on some traditional problems of authorship.

The first two concerned relationships between individual gospels and certain other books in the New Testament. According to a strong ancient tradition, the Acts of the Apostles were written by the evangelist Luke, author of the third Gospel, but not everyone now agrees with this attribution. According to a majority of ancient authorities, the Book of Revelation or Apocalypse was written by the Apostle John who wrote the fourth Gospel, but this attribution was questioned even in ancient times, and is no longer widely accepted. The statistics I collected provided clear evidence relevant to these two issues: in respect of style, Acts is closer to Luke than to any other book of the New Testament, while the Apocalypse is further away from the fourth Gospel than from any other book.

The work on my third problem, that of the Pauline corpus, did not present such clean results. On the basis of my statistics I felt able to reject the hypothesis defended by A.Q. Morton, following the nineteenth-century Tübingen school, that only four Epistles were the work of Paul; but I could not put forward with confidence any sharp alternative hypothesis. The Epistle to Titus stood out as different from all the others; otherwise, I saw no reason on the basis of the evidence I had assembled to reject the hypothesis that twelve of the Pauline Epistles were the work of a single, unusually versatile author.

My statistical work on the New Testament was transformed when, two-thirds of the way through the lecture series, I spent my sabbatical leave in Minneapolis. At the computer centre there I learnt of the machine-readable parsed New Testament prepared by the Wycliffe Bible translators, Barbara and Timothy Friberg; I brought back with me a set of microfiche concordances based on the Fribergs' text. These concordances, which formed henceforth the basis of my work, enabled one to study not just word-usage, but various levels of grammatical and syntactic structure; so that my eventual study was based on ninety-nine different quantifiable features of style. Because of this precious new material the lectures took some time to write up for publication, were not sent to OUP until October 1983, and not published until 1986, under the title *A Stylometric Study of the New Testament.*

While giving my Speaker's Lectures I was also, during the years 1980 to 1983, giving the Stanton Lectures at Cambridge. These were endowed lectures on the philosophy of religion, similar to the Wilde Lectures I had given in Oxford in the 1970s. I was allowed to pack the lectures into four visits a term, Friday evenings and Saturday mornings, so that I did not have too much commuting to Cambridge. In the first year I lectured on the relationship between faith and reason; in the second, I presented what I regarded as the strongest argument for the existence of God, namely the argument from design; in the third year, I balanced that with the strongest argument against the existence of God, namely the difficulty of conceiving a truly disembodied mind.

I have never completed writing up the second two series of lectures into book form, though I have not given up hope of doing so, and I have published some of the material in short articles. The first series was published, but not until the lectures had been substantially rewritten when I was asked to give the American Bampton Lectures at Columbia University, New York, in April 1982.

On this occasion, the eight lectures were distilled into four. The first analysed the virtue of reason, which stands midway between the vices of credulity and scepticism. The second treated of the general question of the justification of beliefs: under what conditions is it rational to hold a given belief? The third concentrated on the particular issue of theism, belief in the existence of God: does this belief fulfil the conditions for rational belief? Individuals, I responded, may reasonably believe in God without proof or grounds, but only if it is in general possible to offer sound arguments for his existence – in other words, if traditional natural theology is a possible discipline. Whether the existence of a God was something provable was something I did not claim to know.

In the final lecture I turned to the question of faith in the strict sense: the faith which is a belief in particular propositions on the alleged word of God, a belief in divine revelation. Such faith is often presented as a virtue, but I argued that it is not a virtue, but a vice, unless certain conditions can be fulfilled. One condition is that the existence of God can be rationally justified without appeal to faith. Another is that the historical events which are claimed to constitute the divine revelation must be independently established as having the same kind of historical certainty as that Hitler existed, or that Charles I was beheaded in London, or that Cicero was once consul in Rome. I doubted whether the events which are pointed to as founding charters for the world's great religions could rationally be believed with this degree of commitment.

The lectures must have seemed to many of my audience maddeningly non-commital. I concluded:

When I, from my agnostic standpoint, look at my theist and atheist colleagues, I do not know whether to envy them or pity them. Should I envy them for having a firm belief on a topic on which it is important to have a firm belief, and on which I myself have none? Should I pity them because of the flimsiness of the arguments and considerations which they use to justify their theism or atheism? From my viewpoint, they appear as credulous; from their viewpoint, I appear as sceptical. Which of us is rational, I do not know. Whether this is my own tragedy, or part of the human condition, I do not know.

Faith and Reason was published by Columbia in 1983, and was reissued by OUP in 1992, with additional essays, under the title *What is Faith?* After this, I published no more original philosophical writing during my Mastership; my eleven books of this period were all reprints of earlier papers, books on non-philosophical topics, or popular presentations of the work of long-dead philosophers.

Finding the 30,000-word format of the 'Past Masters' congenial, I volunteered to contribute a second volume, on Thomas More. I was no expert on Tudor history and literature, but had been fascinated by More ever since being given, as a child, a copy of Chambers' Life of him. I regarded More as an incarnation of the peculiarly English ideal that a good man meets adversity and crisis, not with silent resignation, nor with a sublime statement of principle, but with a joke.

My admiration had survived my departure from the Catholic church, and Robert Bolt, in his play and film *A Man for all Seasons*, had shown that More could be made attractive to a contemporary and secular public. But I thought Bolt's portrayal was unfaithful to the historical figure; and I wanted to show that the real More, with his virtues and his vices, could be seen as a coherent and mainly admirable character.

The problem is that there seem to be three different Mores: the witty, light-hearted, humanist scholar, friend of Erasmus, promoter of Renaissance learning, author of the liberal satire *Utopia*; the upright public figure, a loyal servant to his King so far as conscience allowed, but then a martyr prepared to die for a point of principle; and the hammer of the heretics, the crude polemicist of the unrelenting attacks on Luther and Tyndale. In my book I tried to show that the scholar, the martyred public servant and the controversial prose writer were not three different, conflicting personalities, but a single, consistent human being.

I did not attempt to defend the invective of More's controversial writings; on the contrary, I emphasized the painful contrast between such vituperation and the care with which a scholastic like Aquinas tried to put the best possible interpretation on the theses of those he disagreed with. More's scurrility has its roots in the humanism of his youth and the contempt for medieval academic practice which was the darker side of Renaissance scholarship.

There is no ultimate conflict, I argued, between the ideals of *Utopia* and More's final constancy to Catholic belief:

> If only More's fellow Catholics can fully enter into what More died *for*, all too many people in the present age have had experience of what he died *against*. The imposition of a novel ideology by fear and force is hateful in itself, whether its consequences be good or evil; few can refuse to admire the courage of those who, like More, die rather than submit to such an imposition. The ideal of a supranational community to which the individual can appeal from the oppression of local tyranny is one which in both its religious and its secular forms has a pressing appeal to the present age.

More stands in contrast to many of the martyrs of the Reformation and Counter-Reformation who seem almost to have cultivated martyrdom as a profession, people who would have been misfits even in the most tolerant society.

> More is that rare figure, an Establishment martyr: a man to whom the world and all its promises were open, who had riches and power to hand, which he could have kept if he had been willing to bend to the wind, and who went to his death without bitterness, and with a jest. The Utopians would have been proud of him: when a good man dies, 'No part of his life is so oft or gladly talked of, as his merry death.'

In 1984 my attention, and that of the College, began to focus on a past Master of Balliol. John Wyclif died on the last day of the year 1384; he had been – by one count – the thirteenth Master of Balliol, in 1360 and a year or two thereafter. The College was anxious that his sexcentenary should be appropriately celebrated in Oxford. So the faculties of Theology, History, and English sponsored a series of commemorative lectures in Michaelmas Term 1984.

In my introduction to the lectures – as Master of Balliol and a successor of Wyclif – I remarked that when I was young there were two facts about Wyclif which every schoolchild was supposed to know: that he was the first to translate the Bible into English, and that he was the theorist responsible for the Peasants' Revolt. Learned spoil-sports had now called both into question; none the less, it seemed to me, Wyclif was a genius who could interest scholars of very varied backgrounds and expertise.

The success of these lectures bore out this judgement; but it was one I had only very recently reached myself in respect of my own subject. Like most historians of philosophy I had hitherto regarded Wyclif as a very minor figure of decadent scholasticism. Then, out of the blue, an exiled Czech scholar, Ivan Mueller, who had prepared an edition of Wyclif's unpublished treatise *De Universalibus*, asked me to help him get it published by OUP. The Press was willing to do so only if it could be accompanied by a translation by myself. Partly out of sympathy for the exile, partly out of piety to my predecessor, I agreed; but with a heavy heart, as I expected the work to be dull, difficult, and pettifogging. Difficult it was, but I soon found it anything but boring: the treatise proved to be a highly ingenious contribution to the age-long debate between realists and nominalists about the nature of universals, stoutly realist, and deserving of quite as much respect as the nominalist tracts on the other side by better-known authors like William of Ockham.

The translation was a long, slow business; however, as I learned more about Wyclif, I began to want to make him known to an audience wider than the Evangelical Protestants who were nowadays almost his sole admirers. Having made contact with the power of his intellect I wondered at first why his philosophy had been so neglected. But the explanation was not far to seek. The Catholics who were interested in his kind of philosophy disowned him as a heretic, while the Protestants who hailed him as a forerunner looked on scholasticism as one of the corruptions from which the Reformation had liberated them. In fact, I came to believe, Wyclif was the Evening Star of Scholasticism no less than the Morning Star of the Reformation. I wanted to convince people that he was the last of the great Oxford schoolmen, worthy to form a third with Scotus and Ockham.

Early in 1984 I wrote to the series editor Keith Thomas to ask whether he would accept yet a third 'Past Master'. I was delighted, and rather surprised, when he agreed. I had lately read that Hilaire Belloc, to meet a deadline, had given up alcohol from Palm Sunday to Easter Sunday and written a whole book during Holy Week: I decided to see if I could do the same. I failed in the project of total abstinence, but I did get *Wyclif* written within the week. Of course, five thousand words a day for six days would not be regarded by any journalist as a particularly large output, and all the scholarly reading for the book had been done over many previous months.

I also edited the series of centenary lectures for publication, under the title *Wyclif in his Times*. Attached to the lectures was a number of other original essays, including two by myself, one a philosophical treatment of Wyclif's theory of universals, the other a historical account of his reputation in the Counter-Reformation. This book appeared in 1985, as did the two volumes of the text and translation of the *De Universalibus* – the latter was a hideous publication, typical of the days when academic publishers insisted on the delivery of camera-ready copy produced on pre-word-processor typewriters.

Another book of mine was published in 1985, not at all academic. In 1980 Lord Longford, impressed by my *Aquinas*, had asked me to sign a contract with Sidgwick and Jackson for an autobiography: he was particularly interested in my time as a priest and my reasons for leaving the priesthood. I was reluctant to accept the commission because I was doubtful about the possibility of telling the story at all accurately without causing widespread pain and embarrassment to past and present friends; however, I allowed myself to be persuaded, and for four years, during my spare time, I wrote down memories, checked them against what records I had preserved, and went on to cut and paste and polish.

I told the story of my childhood in Liverpool and in the diocesan junior seminary at Upholland where I studied until I was eighteen. I described in detail the life of an English student at the Venerable English College in Rome, for which I retained a keen affection. I told of my time at Oxford as a doctoral student, my four years as a curate in Liverpool, my recurrent doubts about the authority of the Church and my eventual laicization, and ended the story with my arrival at Balliol in 1964. The finished text I sent to Marigold Johnson, then working as an editor for Sidgwick and Jackson. She went through the manuscript carefully, and improved it greatly.

The book appeared in late 1985 under a title suggested by Paul Johnson, *A Path from Rome*. For a brief period it caused a flurry of press interest. Reviews in general were kind, even from some reviewers who were notorious axemen. I received many letters, from old friends and from perfect strangers. One or two Catholics quite unknown to me wrote to denounce the book: 'You have obviously no interest in anything but money', said one. But most wrote warmly, and my old classmates and colleagues seemed to think I had given a fair and not unfriendly account of the institutions of the Church I had left. Some wrote to point out tricks which memory had played: I had, for instance, misdated by four years the Pope's definition of the dogma of the Assumption of the Blessed Virgin. Many Catholics and ex-Catholics whom I had never met wrote to say that they had been through similar experiences of doubt and disillusionment. The most unexpected of all the congratulatory letters I received came from Dr A.L. Rowse of All Souls: I had never imagined that he was a writer of fan-mail.

14

Hebdomadal Council: Urgent

IN THE EIGHTEENTH and early nineteenth century, the government of Oxford University was a simple matter. Convocation, the assembly of all living Masters of Arts, was the theoretical sovereign body of the institution; but it did not concern itself with its day-to-day affairs. The heads of the colleges formed a Hebdomadal Board, presided over by a Vice-Chancellor – an office held in rotation by the heads of colleges – assisted by two Proctors who were elected year by year by the members of two colleges according to a rota. This simple machinery sufficed when most academic business was carried out within colleges, with only the University Church, the Bodleian Library and the University Press as substantial federal institutions. It was even adequate when the University introduced such new-fangled things as classified examinations. It became far too simple a structure after the expansion of professorships on the model of German universities, and the growth of the sciences, with their demands for facilities and laboratories which no single college could afford. By the 1980s Oxford was governed in a much more complicated fashion.

The ghost of the Hebdomadal Board survived, however. When nineteenth-century reforms stripped Heads of Houses of most of their powers in University affairs, they clung to one which then seemed of paramount importance: the annual choice of a Bampton Lecturer to give an endowed series of sermons in the University Church. In the 1980s the only occasion when Heads of Houses met formally together to conduct University business was when they assembled as electors to the Bampton Lectureship. These meetings could be richly evocative of a departed age. Once, when the name of a distinguished divine had been proposed and widely supported, the head of a woman's college rose: 'May I draw to your attention that one of the duties of a Bampton Lecturer is to refute heresy. How can Professor X carry out that duty, being himself an heretic?' She proceeded to illustrate, with quotes from

X's recent publications, that he was very unsound on Chalcedonian doctrine.

The rest of the business which was once the province of Hebdomadal Board is nowadays divided between Hebdomadal Council and the General Board. The old Convocation of all MAs now has only two duties: the election of a Chancellor, and the election of a Professor of Poetry. The sovereign body is now Congregation, an assembly of all the MAs who have jobs in the collegiate University. The presentation of policy to Congregation, and the general management of the University, is the task of Hebdomadal Council, an elected body of some two dozen members presided over by the Vice-Chancellor which, in the 1980s, met weekly in term time and at least once in each vacation. Major academic issues are determined by the General Board of the Faculties, composed of representatives of different academic disciplines, a body theoretically inferior to Council, but with much greater practical decision-making power. General Board elects its own Chairman, who is the only full-time academic University officer other than the Vice-Chancellor.

The powerful position of the General Board dates from the reforms of the 1960s instituted after the report of Lord Franks. The history of the University over the centuries can be seen as a series of swings of power between the colleges and the central University, with the University powerful in the early medieval period, the colleges supreme in the later Middle Ages, the University reinforced by Tudor reforms, the colleges back in the saddle in the eighteenth century, and so on. The Franks reforms aimed to make the central University more efficient, and therefore more powerful. Franks himself had wished also to make the colleges into a more coherent group. Instead of an anarchical collection of equipollent self-governing corporations, incapable of collective action if even a single college opposes, Franks wished to set up a senate of colleges which could bind each of its members by majority vote. This was too much for conservative Oxford, and the Conference of Colleges which was eventually set up had no power to bind its members. It was little more than a talking shop, to which each college would send its head, plus one other Fellow (commonly a bursar) to keep an eye on the head to make sure that he or she did not speak out of turn.

As Master of Balliol I was a regular attender at the Conference, was soon elected to its standing committee, and in due course became chairman. I quickly discovered that the one effective organ of the Conference was the committee of bursars which annually negotiated the level of college fees with officials in the Department of Education, and which proved itself remarkably skilful at presenting the colleges' case for increases which at least kept pace with inflation.

In 1980 I was elected to membership of Hebomadal Council, and remained a member during the rest of my time at Balliol. The members of Council, wearing their black gowns, met on Monday afternoons around a ring of glossy tables in the van Houten room in the University offices in Wellington Square. Proceedings always began with prayers: 'Prevent us, O Lord, in all our doings . . .' the Vice-Chancellor would intone. When first I joined Council I was told, and for a while believed, that if you had not arrived in time for prayers, you were not allowed to vote.

The agenda for the Monday meetings were delivered by messenger to members' colleges on Friday evenings. A heavy envelope which might contain up to a hundred pages of paper would thud through the letter box, heavily stamped in red 'Hebdomadal Council: Urgent'. This caused some merriment in my family since, given the stately pace with which Oxford conducts its business, it was hard to believe any very high degree of urgency about, say, a decision to set up a Bapsybanoo, Marchioness of Winchester Prize in International Relations.

Much of the business of Council was, indeed, largely formal. Important matters on the agenda reached Council only after extensive discussion by lower bodies such as the University Chest or the Curators of libraries and museums and other institutions, so it was rare for Council to reach a decision which differed from that recommended at a lower level. In particular, it was almost unheard-of for Council to disagree with a recommendation of the General Board. If such a conflict should arise, the Franks statutes contained elaborate, if rarely invoked, procedures for Congregation to resolve the dispute.

One issue on which Council acted quite on its own was the presentation to Congregation of candidates for honorary degrees. These degrees were conferred at Encaenia, the formal ceremony marking the end of the academic year in June. The choice of candidates for the following Encaenia was always a substantial item of business for Council each Michaelmas Term.

Major policy decisions, and many issues of detailed implementation, have to be presented by Council for approval by Congregation. Congregation meets, in theory, several times a term; but unless there is a controversial item on the agenda, very few dons exercise their right to come and vote. If every member of Congregation turned up to a meeting, no building in the University would be large enough to hold the assembly. However, on a normal Tuesday attendance is so small that business can be carried out in the tiny Congregation House, a sleepy, blackened Jacobean hall which only comes to life for one or two annual ceremonial occasions, or when being used as a mock-up for the eighteenth-century Parliament House in films such as *The Madness of King George.*

Some issues came repeatedly before Council. The University Theatre in Beaumont Street, for instance, always seemed to be in a state of financial crisis, and a package would have to be put together, with central University funding, to bail it out. No sooner had one rescue scheme been devised than the health and safety authorities would impose new regulations which called for yet another whip-round. Single-sex colleges, too, provided a perennial topic for discussion. Most of Oxford's academic staff hold joint University–College appointments, and it was no simple matter to draw up advertisements and contracts which preserved the autonomy of one employer, the single-sex college, while ensuring that the other employer, the bisexual University, complied with the legislation prohibiting sex discrimination.

When I joined Council, it was attended only by senior members of the University. There had, however, long been pressure to include junior member observers from the student unions. On the basis of my Balliol experience, I voted against this when it was proposed; but I found myself in a minority, and experience proved that the majority was in the right. The junior members who attended Hebdomadal Council during my remaining years on that body were almost without exception a helpful presence. There was never any attempt to disrupt or distort the business of Council, or to waste its time; and very often the junior members were able to point out to us unforeseen and undesirable consequences of proposed measures which would otherwise have escaped our notice.

Members of Council are expected to serve on the committees which prepare its business. In 1983 I was appointed to chair the committee which managed the St Cross building. Its duties were to look after the fabric of the handsome ziggurat erected by Sir Leslie Martin, and to keep the peace between the three diverse entities which occupy it: the Bodleian Law Library, the Institute of Economics and Statistics, and the English Faculty Library.

Much more time was taken by the Staff Committee, which I joined in 1984. This acted as the management side in negotiations with representatives of the University's employees. It dealt with four groups, each with different unions. Janitorial staff were represented by NUPE, the public employees' union, technicians by ASTMS. No single union was recognized to negotiate on behalf of clerical and library staff – CLNC, the Clerical and Library Negotiating Committee, was a mixture of union and non-union representatives. Academic and academic-related staff were represented by the AUT.

The style of the employees' committees was very different. The local branch of NUPE appeared torpid, and gave no difficulty. ASTMS fielded a highly skilful team, always well-briefed on the relevant facts and contractual agreements. CLNC could be fractious, but was not usually difficult to match in argument. Negotiations between the University and the AUT had a certain air of farce, as both sides of the table consisted largely of dons who worked together every day in other contexts; moreover, dons who were college Fellows were in any case largely responsible for fixing their own salaries and terms of employment.

The real value of the Staff Committee was in holding the ring between the professors in large scientific departments ('the science barons') and the academic-related research workers and technicians who were employed by them. We had to see that the barons, some of whom were tempted to cut corners, abided by terms which had been agreed between different departments in Oxford, or which the University as a whole had agreed with the relevant unions. Individual members of the committee spent a lot of time, in panels of two or three, adjudicating disputes about grading or appeals against discipline or dismissal procedures.

Negotiations with Balliol JCRs over the years had prepared me for the tedium and irritation inevitable in meetings of this kind, and it was even a relief to be dealing with real trades unions rather than with an imaginary one. I formulated Kenny's Law: what managers would be doing if they were not at a union meeting is more interesting than continuing the meeting, but continuing the meeting is more interesting than what employees would be doing if they were not at the meeting. This is an important factor in determining the outcome of negotiations between employees and management: managers are more likely to make concessions because they are more anxious to get the meeting over.

Whether because of this or, as I prefer to believe, because of an innate sense of fair play and sympathy for the underdog, I quite often found myself taking the side of the technicians against the professors, and was sometimes the only member of the management side to vote with the union representatives. Off-duty, one union representative told me I was acquiring a reputation as the Workers' Friend.

My own union was the AUT, which I had joined in the 1960s when it was largely a professional organization, devoted to securing for its members cheap motor insurance and discount carpets. Now, though I did not at first fully appreciate this, it had become, at a national level, quite a militant body; at the local level it was mild, rational, and even conservative. In Oxford it spoke on behalf of those academic-related staff, without college Fellowships or tenured posts, who were not full members of the University's democracy. Rather to my surprise, I was invited onto the committee of the Union, and then elected its chairman.

The strangest duty I had to perform in this role was that of waiting on the Queen at Buckingham Palace. When in 1981 the Prince of Wales became engaged to Lady Diana Spencer, we learned that Oxford University was one of half a dozen so-called Privileged Bodies which had the right to present a Loyal Address to the sovereign on the occasion of the marriage of the heir to the throne. The Chancellor, the Vice-Chancellor and several members of Hebdomadal Council were deputed to do so, in July; I was among those chosen to attend, not as a member of Council but as chairman of the AUT.

We left Oxford in a fleet of cars and minibuses at 6.30 a.m., bearing full academic dress with robes and bands, for a rehearsal at Buckingham Palace at 9.30. When the real ceremony took place an hour later, I was the last to be presented to Her Majesty by the Chancellor, Harold Macmillan. He treated with contempt any briefing that I was there as a trades unionist. 'And now, Ma'am, I have the honour to present the head of the finest college in Oxford, my own college of Balliol.' The Queen gave what, coming from anyone else, would be described as a giggle. I reported this back to my Balliol colleagues as the Royal Assent to the Chancellor's description of the College.

The delegation from the University to the Palace had not included any junior members; not all of them might have wished to be associated with the Loyal Address. At the end of Trinity Term I discovered that the Keble Tyrrels, that College's dramatic society, were intending to put on, in the theatre in Balliol's Lindsay Rooms, an extravaganza called 'Don't Do It, Di'. After consultation with the Warden of Keble, the Lord Mayor of Oxford and concerned citizens I took pains to ensure that permission was refused. On this occasion at least, the young proved themselves wiser than their elders.

The duties of the chairman of the AUT were not normally so purely ceremonial; I had to attend national council meetings, which opened my eyes to the nature of the AUT's national representatives at the time. The AUT had indeed plenty to be angry about, at a time when universities were being systematically under-funded and government spokesmen frequently denigrated the academic profession. But the union's unrealistic demands, and still more the class-struggle rhetoric in which they were couched, did nothing to increase respect for the profession, and hampered the efforts of the University Grants Committee to win from government a decent deal for the universities.

What finally made me leave the AUT, however, was its maintenance of an academic boycott of South Africa – this, though I was in favour of economic sanctions against the apartheid regime. As Master of Balliol I had worked to ensure that the College, as investor and purchaser, played its part in the economic boycott. In particular Balliol had made use of its position as a customer of Barclays to try to influence the Bank's policies in South Africa.

In 1980 I and the members of our Shareholder Action Committee had a number of meetings with directors of Barclays to protest against advertising material the Bank had produced to encourage foreign investment in the Transkei and other homelands. We complained that the documents were worded in conformity with South African government policy and concealed the fact that the homelands were mere instruments of apartheid. As shareholders we raised the same issue at the AGM, without receiving any very satisfactory answers. Instructed by Governing Body, I wrote to say that unless Barclays ceased circulating these documents by 31 August we would move our account elsewhere. Shortly before the deadline, Sir Anthony Tuke informed us that the leaflets had been withdrawn. So the College's account remained with Barclays – for the time being.

Initially I viewed the academic boycott in the same terms as the economic boycott. My eyes were opened, however, by Francis and Lindy Wilson, from the University of Cape Town, who were in Oxford in 1980/81 while Francis held a Visiting Fellowship at Balliol. An economist, he had worked untiringly to expose the economic consequences and cruel exploitation of the poor which apartheid involved. The Wilson's anti-apartheid credentials were impeccable, and they were close friends of many black and coloured leaders in the struggle. They convinced us that the academic boycott did most damage to people in the universities who were seeking to overturn apartheid, none to the authorities who upheld it.

Each year Balliol offered a Visiting Fellowship which enabled one of its Fellows to spend the Long Vacation in the University of the Witwatersrand in Johannesburg. The Fellowship was named after the Balliol Rhodes scholar Jan Hofmeyr who had been the first Vice-Chancellor of Wits and who, taking to a political career, would have succeeded Jan Smuts as Prime Minister of South Africa in 1948 had he not been regarded by many of the electors as too much of a 'kaffir-lover'. In summer 1984 I decided to take this Fellowship, and travelled out with my family. It was one of the most important educational experiences in all our lives.

We flew to East London and hired a car there to drive to the Wilsons' house at Hogsback. We drove through the 'homeland' of Ciskei, a valley of parched earth and centreless villages, inhabited by women and children whose menfolk were working 'away' in Port Elizabeth or Johannesburg, and got home perhaps once a year. Women in bright shawls, with woolly caps, carried firewood on their heads as they walked along the superhighway while cars sped past. We climbed up out of the dusty Ciskei into a forest which had been planted, before the First World War, by Francis Wilson's missionary grandfather. His mother, the historian Monica Wilson, had made a formal garden with ponds, and built a house with a library in the centre of the compound, around which were rondavels for members of the Wilson clan and the three black families who worked on the land, all high on a spur of cliff over-looking the valley. There was an alpine nip in the air and we were glad to take warm baths and gather round a wood fire.

We spent three days at Hogsback exploring paths, planting trees, gaping at the southern stars, and learning the politics of South Africa. Francis's brother Tim, a medical doctor, was there with his wife Ilse, daughter of Braam Fischer, the Communist Rhodes Scholar who had died in prison. They had just been allowed passports after twenty years' refusal, and were going to London so that Tim could take a course in community medicine. We got the impression that Ilse did not approve of our coming to South Africa, but believed in a total boycott. Francis was more anxious to tell us about the ventilated pit latrine, a snail-shaped concrete structure simply but cunningly designed to be fly-proof. He had seen its effectiveness in refugee camps, and was keen to encourage its use in parts of Africa which lacked plumbing.

We left Hogsback to drive in pouring rain (for the inhabitants, a welcome end to a long drought) through Fort Beaufort, past the black university of Fort Hare, and on to Grahamstown, the site of Rhodes University, which looked like a Pennsylvania campus town, surrounded by three townships. Looming over it was the monument to the English settlers who had come inland from the coast in 1820. After an excessively quiet weekend in Grahamstown we returned our car to East London before flying to Cape Town (on the way we admired the enormous breakers of the Indian Ocean and saw our first 'this beach is for the use of whites only' sign).

While Nancy and the boys explored the beautiful city and its surrounding mountains, I prepared the lecture I was to give at the University on academic freedom. I discovered that some of the books I wanted were on the banned list and had to be summoned by special call numbers. Some of Christopher Hill's works fell into this category, and while most of the volumes of Harold Macmillan's autobiography were on the open shelves, the one which contained his 'winds of change' speech was kept under lock and key.

The Wilsons took extraordinary pains to help us get a feeling for the political situation. The Nationalist government had just established a new tri-cameral legislature with separate chambers for whites, Indians, and coloureds, and the United Democratic Front was urging Cape Coloureds to boycott the coming elections. At dinner at the Wilsons' we listed to Alan Boesak (then a leading light in the black Dutch Reformed Church as well as in the UDF) arguing the pros and cons of the election boycott with the journalist Helen Ziller. I wondered why Coloureds did not follow the Irish tradition of voting in the elections, winning seats, and then refusing to take them up so that the empty chamber was a permanent protest. Alan thought this was too complicated for his supporters; instead, he was trying to collect a million signatures denouncing the constitution.

Lindy Wilson showed us two films she had made, one about the destruction of District 6, a mixed-race community in an area which had been redesignated for whites only, the other about Crossroads, the illegal black shanty town near the airport. Blacks who had lived for years in Cape Town had moved to Crossroads so that families could stay together rather than be separated by the Group Areas Act, which put the men in town hostels while the women and children were deported to the Ciskei. The government had made repeated attempts to clear Crossroads, sending in bulldozers at three in the morning to sweep up the flimsy houses. Besides making films, Lindy was working with SACHED, an organization that provided bridging tuition to enable the victims of the Bantu education system to qualify for university by taking a proper matriculation examination, in place of the worthless one they had been fobbed off with. Shortage of appropriate textbooks was one problem, and Lindy was writing a history of black Africa, with videos in support.

On 25 July I gave two lectures in the university – one on moral luck to a philosophy seminar, and one on 'Enemies of Academic Freedom' to a general audience. I distinguished between external and internal enemies. The external threats came from ideologies and governments, most of all from governments in the service of ideologies. I quoted recent infringements of academic freedom by government departments in the UK, while recognizing that any problems we had were insignificant compared to those suffered by academics in South Africa, where books were banned and lecture audiences contained police informers. Internal enemies of academic freedom were to be found among both teachers and students: teachers who abused academic freedom in ways which damaged their students, and students who persecuted unpopular teachers and used force and threats to determine academic decisions.

At one point I ventured into local politics. In the face of student demonstrations against unwelcome visitors, the Senate and Council of the university had recently affirmed support for freedom of speech and asserted the right of academics to invite any person to take part in any academic programme. I argued that the right was too broadly defined: one should distinguish between invitations to academics, and invitations to politicians. There could be invitations to those who expounded views so evil, or represented regimes so obnoxious, that the invitations themselves amounted to an abuse of academic freedom. In order to control this, the academic body as a whole, rather than individual academics, should have the oversight of non-academic invitations.

> If a colleague of mine invited an academic from a South African university to report on the operation of the race laws, I would regard that as a legitimate use of his academic freedom, and extend the College's protection to the lecturer, even if there were violent demonstrations by students. But if he invited the South African Ambassador, I would regard that as an abuse of academic freedom. Since the invitation involved a non-academic visitor, I would regard it as one which required the approval of the appropriate governing body, and in the governing body I would endeavour to have the visit forbidden on two grounds; first, that any academic purpose to be served by such a visit could be served by other means; and secondly, that an ambassador is not an academic but a representative of a government; so that offering him a platform is a measure of support of that government's policies.

These words, and indeed my own presence in Cape Town, implied that I did not agree with the academic boycott of South Africa; and I concluded the lecture by explaining why, while supporting the economic boycott, I made a distinction between academic links and sporting, cultural and economic ones. Those who were affected by the academic boycott were not the South African government or the supporters of its policies, but rather 'those who have fought those policies bravely and provided a focus of opposition for them in difficult times – namely, you, who have devoted yourselves to the idea of a university whose character is determined by scholarship and not by ethnicity.' The University of Cape Town, under its Vice-Chancellor Stuart Saunders, was indeed working hard to re-open its courses and facilities to all races, and did not shrink from breaking unjust laws in order to do so.

On the next evening we went to Athlone in the Cape Flats to hear Francis Wilson lecture on the inquiry into South African poverty which he and Mampela Ramphele had just completed. This set out, coolly and factually, the fearsome economic consequences of apartheid. Paternalistic nationalists had always argued that though blacks had no political rights in South Africa, in terms of education, health and living conditions they were better off than the inhabitants of independent sub-Saharan states. The Carnegie study showed that in fact, in respect of such indicators as infant mortality and expectation of life, South Africa's black population came near the bottom of the league table.

The lecture was given in an unheated hall by the light of Calor gas lanterns; the audience was largely professional people whose views, from their questioning, seemed to resemble those of British left-wing intellectuals of the 1930s. Questioners tried to get Francis to say whether and how the system should be changed; but he refused to be drawn. The impact of the Carnegie Report was in fact all the greater because of its objectivity and lack of rhetoric.

Our most memorable day in Cape Town was our last. Francis drove us into Crossroads to visit a childhood friend of his from the Ciskei. The friend had a permit to work in Cape Town, but according to the law he should have been living in a male hostel (for which he was indeed paying rent) and his wife should have been a thousand kilometres away in the Ciskei. His house was a wooden frame topped with corrugated iron; some of his neighbours had only plastic sheets as roofs. Inside, the single room contained two beds, crockery, a table, and a television set (run on what electricity?); every item of furniture was spotless, and there was clean linen on the table. An astonishing thing about Crossroads was that there was no smell detectable, although there were 30,000 people living in shacks with water only in standpipes and sanitation on the 'bucket system'. At one time we passed a man carrying his home – the timber and corrugated iron that made a house – on his head. So in spite of the threats of demolition, people were still moving into Crossroads.

The purpose of our visit was to retrieve some rabbits belonging to Francis, which his friend had been looking after while the Wilsons were at Hogsback. (The rabbits were part of an experimental breeding scheme designed to produce cheap protein for urban blacks.) The most extraordinary feature of our visit was the complete absence of bitterness among the people we met. As Nancy recorded in her diary:

> The real miracle of Crossroads is the spirit of the place which is happy and positive and not at all resentful. There we were, a big white VW bus with four whites in it, bumping . . . through groups of these shacks which are always under threat of being bulldozed by the white government, and we were greeted with not so much as a rude gesture. And when we stopped the bus to collect the rabbits we were surrounded by heaps of smiling, curious children, and greeted warmly by Francis's friend, his wife, and her brother, and invited into their house with great dignity.

On the next day we set off for Johannesburg on the Transkaroo train; mostly a rather dull journey through scrubby red earth. Even in the middle of the night we were reminded of apartheid. In order to make sure that the white carriages, which had been at the near end of the tracks in Cape Town Station, arrived in Johannesburg at the front end of the train, there was a very noisy shunting operation at midnight in Kimberley, waking everyone up to preserve the proper order of things. As we approached Johannesburg the train passed through Soweto; after Crossroads, it appeared substantial and prosperous.

The Philosophy Department at Wits had assigned us a flat in a compound for visiting faculty – pleasant, but small for a family of four. However, Jonathan Suzman, the chairman of the department, had to go to London with his family for six weeks, and he invited us to house-sit for him. His house was an ample one, with a billiard room and a swimming pool, both very popular with the boys, though the weather was still a little cool for adult swimming.

My first academic duty was to give a public lecture on the ethics of nuclear deterrence; about a hundred people turned up to listen. My regular classes were not due to begin until 8 August, and before that the department had arranged visits for us to the Blyde River in the Eastern Transvaal, and the Kruger National Park, with the department's other academic guests, David and Stephanie Lewis. We drove to a chalet above the gorges of the Blyde River Canyon, on to God's Window for a view of the canyon and the veld, and then into the Kruger Park to see impalas, zebra, wildebeeste, giraffes, warthogs, and a single elephant, huge and dramatic as it lurched across the road in front of us. Stephanie delighted us all with her expert knowledge of birds, and David gave the boys a crash course in logic – only partially successfully, it has to be admitted.

Without the Wilsons as guides, we found it less easy to assess the political situation in Johannesburg, but our hosts continued to educate us. The brother and sister-in-law of one of my Balliol colleagues took us to the Vortrekker Monument to give us a sense of Afrikaner history and Afrikaner grievances. We went on to Pretoria to visit the park surrounding the Union Building, seat of the government for part of the year, and saw another of the paradoxes of South Africa – these gardens, dominated by a massive symbol of apartheid, were a favourite venue for black weddings, and two lively parties, brides in white with pink and blue bridesmaids, were gathered in celebration on either side of us as we picnicked on the lawn.

In Johannesburg as in Cape Town we met many people, especially among colleagues at the University, who were doing their best to chip away at the fabric of apartheid, among them the formidable female activists of the Black Sash movement. Professor John Dugard, a community lawyer, was in the news for having detected and denounced the way in which political trials, when they came before the bench, were always assigned to a small minority of right-wing judges. While we were there he was arrested and fined for reading out at seminar a paper by a colleague who had just been banned. I renewed acquaintance with Eddie Webster, once a PPE pupil at Balliol, who had been imprisoned for a year for making a speech in favour of trades unions and for saying that blacks outnumber whites in South Africa.

At *Amampondo*, a concert of African music at the Market Theatre, and at a Sunday service in the Anglican cathedral, we could sense what South Africa might be like without apartheid. Most surprisingly, we had a similar feeling when we descended the Cullinan diamond mine: the cleanliness, neatness and strict safety regime made it seem as if, for once, all employees were being treated with equal concern. But we were brought back to reality when, trying to take a short-cut home through Orlando township, we were quickly turned around by plain-clothes policemen.

It was not, indeed, at all easy to meet blacks. Nancy was able to get to know the maids who lived in the house, and learnt much about their sorrows and those of their families. The one black member of the Wits Philosophy Department, Dr Vincent Maphai, had to leave departmental gatherings or parties early if he was to get home to Soweto (where he was warden of a somewhat explosive student hostel) without breaking the curfew. When we invited his family to a braai with us in Craighall, the children of both families enjoyed splashing together in our chilly pool, but when Robert and Charles suggested that they should all go across the road to play in the communal playground, Vincent told us sadly that that would be quite impossible.

Our last weekend was spent in the Royal Natal Park, a small but exciting section of the Drakensberg escarpment, with steep cliffs dropping to green pasture land. It was pleasant to be able to hike and scramble everywhere rather than driving, but of course the wildlife did not compare with that in the Kruger, and we saw nothing more exotic than baboons.

We left at the end of August, just before the elections. The Vice-Chancellor of Wits, when I went to take my leave of him, had been up since four to prevent the police coming onto the campus to arrest students who, in violation of the law forbidding the assembly of more than three persons, had been demonstrating against the new constitution. Vincent, driving us to the airport, said we were leaving just in time.

Apartheid South Africa was both much worse and much better than we had imagined it at a distance. It was much worse, because only on the spot could one really appreciate the oppression involved by the Group Areas Act. Blacks might have to make a four-hour journey from a distant township to work in the centre of a white city; labourers whose official residence was in the homelands saw their families, a thousand miles away, only once or twice a year. On the other hand, I had imagined South Africa to be like an Iron Curtain country, in which even verbal dissent was impossible; I was astonished to read the violent attacks on apartheid in the English-language newspapers, and to discover how many comfortably-placed whites devoted a great part of their lives to working with blacks to overthrow the system. Most of all I was moved by the apparent lack of bitterness on the part of blacks. It was encouraging that, even at this late stage, the extra-parliamentary opposition to the government's policies should come from a group, the UDF, which was both multiracial and non-violent.

1 5

The Ivory Tower

PHILOSOPHERS ARE OFTEN accused of living in an ivory tower, remote from the practical concerns of real life. This is a rash judgement. The methods of philosophy are, indeed, highly intellectual, but the clarification of thought the philosopher seeks is no less precious to the decision-maker than to the theoretician. My own studies in the area of philosophy of mind have concerned the concepts we use in describing and understanding mental states, processes, and activities, and the framework by which we make intelligible human action and conduct, ideas which are the fundamental prerequisites of moral, legal, and political thinking. Philosophy of this kind does not stand at a distance from practical life: human activity is its very subject matter.

Throughout my philosophical career, but especially in the 1980s, I tried to bring this out by relating abstract philosophical inquiries to issues which were, literally, matters of life and death. In 1978 I had published a short book with the title *Freewill and Responsibility*, based on the Ryle Lectures I gave in 1976 at Trent University in Ontario. This contained a popular presentation of the account of human action and volition in *Action, Emotion and Will*, and related it to a whole set of legal notions. I explored the meaning of *mens rea*, the state of mind necessary for criminal responsibility; I discussed necessity and duress as defences to a charge of murder; and I examined the M'Naghten Rules which governed the defence of insanity in English law. In particular I focused on two recent House of Lords cases, the murder case of *Hyam* and the rape case of *Morgan*.

In the 1980s I returned to these issues many times, in particular to the definition of murder and the scope of the defences which may be offered to it. But before doing so, I decided I ought to place my understanding of the legal issues on a rather more systematic basis than the selective reading I had undertaken when writing *Freewill and Responsibility*. Accordingly, I joined Lincoln's Inn, and enrolled for the

167

Bar Examinations. I was lucky enough to be permitted to take advantage of the old system by which, for the academic part of the qualification, it was sufficient to pass the examinations, without having to attend any courses.

My only duties to the Inn were to eat dinners there at the students' tables, which I did with pleasure on the too-rare occasions when I had time to do so. My fellow students, a very international group, were friendly and helpful, quite oblivious of any gap in age. As I stood in the queue on my first night, wearing my short student's gown, a neighbour advised me, 'Make sure you sit at a vegetarian table.' 'But I'm not a vegetarian', I said. 'No matter – they will always serve you meat if you want. But most vegetarians are also teetotalers, so you will be able to hog the whole carafe of wine.' My status also meant that I received the circulars of the National Union of Students, and thus became privy to whatever mischief was brewing against Vice-Chancellors and heads of Oxbridge houses.

Throughout the academic year of 1979/80 I swotted up textbooks and casebooks, on Criminal Law, Tort, Trusts, Land Law, Constitutional and Administrative Law, and finally presented myself for the examinations at the City University in the summers of 1980 and 1981. In the end I passed all the papers, though I had to get permission to postpone one of them to a second session because it clashed with a meeting with an important Balliol benefactor.

Preparation for most of these examinations I found instructive and enjoyable: the cases to be found in the courts are so much more interesting, and incredible, than any examples invented by even the most imaginative philosopher. But there was one exception: I could never find any pleasure in the mysteries of land law, and could barely remember the difference between gavelkind and impeachment of waste. Immediately after writing my land law examination I wandered disconsolate for several hours in Hyde Park, convinced I had failed and feeling I would look pretty foolish if a gossip columnist got hold of the story: 'MASTER OF BALLIOL FLUNKS ELEMENTARY EXAM'.

I have now totally forgotten what little I knew of land law, but the reading in Criminal Law and Tort has been of constant use to me in the relevant areas of philosophy, and a knowledge of where to find things in textbooks on Equity has stood me in good stead while presiding over an exempt charity and being a trustee or secretary of several Trusts. Since I had no intention of practising I have never taken the professional examinations to become a barrister. I felt I had done enough to make myself, if not an honest lawyer, an honest philosopher of law.

Murder is killing with malice aforethought; and murder has been with us so long that one might expect the courts to have worked out exactly how it is to be defined. But in the years which followed the Homicide Act of 1957 the exact meaning which the courts attached to 'malice aforethought' went through astonishing variations. A series of cases extended it beyond intentional killing, and beyond killing foreseen as an unintended consequence of a person's actions, to deaths resulting from an act which the accused should have foreseen (not necessarily *did* foresee) as very likely to cause serious bodily harm (not necessarily death).

This was widely, and justly, regarded as an unacceptably broad definition of murder, and the case of *Hyam* in 1974 gave the House of Lords an opportunity to rectify matters. In that case the appellant Hyam, out of jealousy of another woman B who had supplanted her in the affections of her paramour, went to B's house in the early hours of the morning, poured petrol through the letter box, stuffed newspaper through it, lit it, and then went home leaving the house burning, with the result that B's two daughters were suffocated. Hyam's defence was that she had set fire to the house only in order to frighten B into leaving the neighbourhood.

By a majority of three to two, the House of Lords dismissed Hyam's appeal against conviction, but the exact effect of their ruling was unclear. The three judges of the majority – Lord Hailsham (then Lord Chancellor), Lord Dilhorne, and Lord Cross of Chelsea – dismissed the appeal on the basis of three quite different, and incompatible, theories of malice aforethought.

In a series of papers beginning in 1976, some of which were republished in the 1980s, I analysed the ambiguities of the decision, and proposed a new and, I believed, clearer and juster definition of murder. This drew on Jeremy Bentham's distinction between direct intention (something sought as an end in itself or a means to a chosen end) and indirect intention (something not sought as an end or a means, but a foreseen consequence of a directly intended action), and built on elements in Lord Hailsham's judgment in *Hyam*. It ran as follows: Murder is the performance of an act which causes death, with the intent either to kill or to create a serious risk of death: the intent in each case to be direct. The intent to kill should be taken to include the (direct) intent to bring about a state of affairs from which one knows death will certainly follow.

I sent a copy of one of my papers to Lord Hailsham. Knowing from experience what a chore it can be to reply to unsolicited comments on one's published work, I expected no more than a brief formal acknowledgement. I was surprised and grateful when four foolscap sheets of longhand comment came almost by return of post. Several other philosophers, in subsequent years, wrote articles in a similar vein to my own. I do not know how far judges in general take note of comments by non-legal academics; but since *Hyam* a series of decisions has narrowed the excessively broad definition of murder and brought it much closer to the definition my colleagues and I argued for.

It was not only the definition of the crime of murder which in the 1970s had been too broadly drawn: so too, and perhaps not by coincidence, had the defences to a charge of murder: in particular, duress and diminished responsibility.

In 1979 I took part in an interdisciplinary symposium on the defence of duress, my role being to reply to a paper by the Law Lord, Lord Kilbrandon. In the 1975 case of *Lynch*, the victim of an IRA gunman, the Law Lords decided by three to two that duress was available as a defence to an accessory to murder. In the case of *Abbott* the Privy Council decided, again by three to two, that duress was no defence if pleaded by an actual killer. Lord Kilbrandon, who had been in the minority in *Lynch* and the majority in *Abbott*, argued that these decisions had left the law in an unsatisfactory state; that the solution lay in abolishing the crime of murder and merging it with manslaughter into a new crime of unlawful homicide; and that duress should be available, not as a complete defence to this charge, but as a factor in mitigation. I agreed that the present state of the law was indefensible, but argued that the solution was not to extend *Abbot* but to overrule *Lynch*. Duress should be neither a defence nor a mitigation to a charge of murder, whether as principal or accessory. The reform which I suggested corresponds to the line which has been traced by a number of legal decisions in the years since 1980.

The definition of murder was not the only defect of the Homicide Act of 1957. The Act provided for a defence of diminished responsibility which allowed the accused in a murder case to be convicted of the lesser crime of manslaughter if the jury found that he was 'suffering from such abnormality of mind . . . as substantially impaired his mental responsibility for his acts'. I believed that the wording of this defence rested on philosophical confusion between matters of fact, morality, and law, and forced psychiatrists who were called as expert witnesses to go well beyond their professional competence. An invitation to give the Blackstone Lecture in 1982 provided an opportunity to expound this thesis to an audience of lawyers in Oxford. I did so within the broader context of the role of the expert witness in the English system, an issue in which, as I have already mentioned, I had become personally involved through invitations to act as an expert witness in stylometry cases.

I argued that there were two fundamental things wrong with the current practice:

> The first is that the adversary system does not fit well with the use of experts to assist the courts. It leads to dangers that the experts will be more concerned to assist one or other party to win their case than to assist the court to arrive at the truth. Secondly, the present practice runs counter to the profound truth of moral philosophy, which is that there are no experts on morality. Neither judges nor bishops nor doctors are such experts; it is because there is no expertise that we have juries. Juries are chosen precisely because they are not and know they are not experts; they are living witness to the fact that in matters of morality no man is in possession of information denied to others. I am not saying that one man's moral judgement is as good as another's; that would be folly. But what makes one man's judgement better than another's is not that he possesses information that the other lacks; it is not knowledge, but wisdom. And whether somebody possesses wisdom is something which calls for a tribunal higher than any human court can claim to be. All we can do is to empanel twelve 'good men and true' on the optimistic assumption that everyone has an equal *chance* of being wise.

To remedy the abuses of the expert evidence system, I made three proposals: repeal the provision in the Homicide Act which forced expert witnesses to usurp the function of the jury; remove from the courts the decision whether a nascent discipline (such as stylometry) is a genuine scientific expertise; take the provision of expert evidence out of the adversarial structure. The issues which I raised were addressed, in a different context, by the Royal Commission presided over by Viscount Runciman in the 1990s; the report of the Commission went some way, but in my view not far enough, in proposing reforms of the abuses of which I complained.

I had expected my lecture, 'The Expert in Court', to be ill-received by psychiatrists, since I had accused them of going beyond their professional competence in testifying before the courts. On the contrary, I found myself invited to a forensic psychiatric conference to repeat my lecture, and a revised version appeared in the *Journal of Medical Ethics*. Several psychiatrists told me they found that the Homicide Act placed on them an impossible burden, and they welcomed me as an ally in trying to convince the public of the unworkable nature of the Act.

My interest in homicide has long extended beyond individual murder to mass murder, and the issue of the legitimacy of nuclear warfare was one of the elements which brought me into conflict with my ecclesiastical superiors in the days when I was a priest in Liverpool. I returned to the topic in the 1980s and, with Michael Dummett, Bernard Williams and other philosophers, was a contributor to a Routledge anthology, *Objections to Nuclear Defence*.

My contribution, entitled 'Better Dead than Red', began by spelling out some senses in which I agreed with the then-popular slogan. For instance, not being a pacifist, and not being a Marxist, I believed that a citizen of a country like the UK should be prepared to risk his life to prevent that country being overcome by a Communist power. If that was all 'Better dead than red' meant, it was fine with me.

But of course, in the context of the debate about nuclear warfare the slogan was commonly used, in quite a different sense, to mean that in order to prevent the evil of having Communism imposed upon us we would be justified not only in going to war but in waging a war of mass destruction and indiscriminate killing. Better for everyone – both on our side and theirs – to be dead, than for us to be made red; that is, to have Communist rule forced on us.

In this sense, the slogan was a monstrous falsehood. Nothing – neither the material nor the moral advantages which the West enjoyed by comparison with the East – could justify the use of nuclear weapons to destroy large centres of population, and to bring an enemy society to an end.

Of course, 'Better dead than red' might not be the expression of a moral judgement, but merely of a personal preference. If someone told me that he would prefer to be killed in a nuclear attack than to be subject to Soviet hegemony, who was I to disbelieve him? But the inhabitants of Warsaw in 1984 already suffered what we would have had to suffer if we surrendered to Soviet nuclear blackmail. Could anyone really believe, I asked, that what the Polish dissidents wanted, even in the worst days of martial law, was for the West to put them out of their agony by dropping a nuclear device on the centre of Warsaw?

In the mid 1980s I developed the ideas of 'Better Dead than Red', and worked with various groups aiming to change the deterrence policy which the Ministry of Defence had set out in its White Paper of 1981. I was wary of CND, though I arranged meetings in the Master's Lodgings for protagonists on both sides of the nuclear debate, including Bruce Kent. I found more sympathetic a group organized by Stand Windass and Frank Barnaby, with the name 'Just Defence', which sought to develop realistic non-pacifist, non-nuclear alternatives to the current defence policies. A particularly impressive member of this group was General Sir Hugh Beach.

Our activities seemed to cause some concern to the Ministry of Defence. A senior civil servant, David Fisher, was seconded to Oxford for a year to study, and counter, academic objections to the deterrence policy. I invited Fisher to join me in giving a series of seminars in Balliol in Hilary Term 1984 on the ethics of nuclear deterrence; we were to take it in turns to argue the opposing views. The seminars were very well attended; of about 150 in February, about 40 per cent were from CND and about 20 per cent from the US military. (One of these, a woman astronaut, then an undergraduate at Balliol, was also an occasional squash partner of mine; she usually let me win, not wanting, as she put it, to be insubordinate to a three-star general.)

Both Fisher and I learnt a lot, and the audience followed with keen interest. I wrote to a friend, half way through the series:

> One of our Chilean students said he did not know whether to be more surprised at the moral concern and philosophical skill of the man from the M.o.D., or the respectful attention given him by the largely unilateralist audience who might instead be expected to throw eggs. I do not know whether either of us will convince the other, but it is proving to be a most interesting class.

I also came to be on friendly terms with Fisher's superior, Michael Quinlan, the Permanent Secretary of the M.o.D., a devout Catholic and the author of the policy statement I was attacking. The friendship and obvious good-will of these senior policymakers did nothing to convince me that their policy was justified, however; I developed the ideas I had set forth in the seminar into a book, *The Logic of Deterrence*.

Here I first propounded the traditional theory of the ethics of the just war and concluded, as I had done in many previous writings, that the waging of nuclear war could not be justified. But this was no very startling conclusion: even President Reagan had recently gone on record as saying that a nuclear war could not be won, and must not be fought. In the central portion of the book I addressed the much more difficult question: notwithstanding the wickedness of waging nuclear war, may it not be reasonable to pursue a policy of nuclear deterrence which has as its goal the prevention of such a war? I argued that the existing deterrent policies of both East and West were unacceptable on three grounds: they were extravagant, dangerous, and in the last analysis murderous. In argument with defenders of the deterrent, I wrote, there always comes a point where one wishes to put this question to one's interlocutor:

> Suppose that deterrence breaks down: suppose, that is, that you are faced with a choice of carrying out the deterrent threat, or of forfeiting the good things which the deterrent was meant to protect. What do you do then? I accept that the whole point of having a deterrent is to prevent being faced with the choice of using it or surrendering; but one can have no certainty that

this choice will never have to be faced. Suppose that it fails, and you are faced with the choice: what, in your heart, do you think you should do?

If my friend says that if, God forbid, it ever did come to such a point, then obviously the only thing to do is to surrender – if he says that, then I know that fundamentally we are morally at one, and we can settle down in a comparatively relaxed way to discuss questions of risk and danger and expense. But if he says, 'Well, I hate to have to say it, but if you are committed to the deterrent, you have to stick to what you believe in and you must go right on and use it if it ever comes to the crunch' – if he says that and means it, then I can only tell him, quite soberly, that he is a man with murder in his heart.

Those lines, I discovered, had an effect on a number of readers, including serving officers in the US Air Force, one of whom asked to be moved to a branch of the service where he would never have to execute a command to operate the deterrent. Another came to Oxford to write a dissertation under my supervision on the topic of nuclear deterrence. With service friends such as these I discussed the issues addressed in the third part of my book: what policies, in the concrete, should be pursued by a society that resolves to forgo reliance on the murderous threat implicit in our current strategies? I set out a series of steps for a staged and prudent disarmament, free, as I believed, from the taint of murder which disfigured our present policies, but treading a middle way between the illusory hopes of the multilateralists who sought disarmament by negotiation, and the impractical idealism of those who called for the immediate and total unilateral disarmament of the West.

David Fisher wrote up his side of our seminar debates, and our two books were published almost simultaneously. I set them as the text for the 1985 Balliol reading party on Mont Blanc, and amid unseasonable August snow we discussed, in the spirit of David Urquhart, the morality of war and the possibilities of peace. That reading party was also memorable for the record set by Jonathan Brooke (the son of Peter), who ran down the 4,000 feet to St-Gervais and back up again in 45 minutes to bring us fresh croissants for breakfast.

I, too, set a personal record in 1985. The *Logic of Deterrence* was published in July, just in time for the chalet. In the same month Blackwell's, who were bringing out my collected papers in four volumes, produced the one entitled *The Ivory Tower*, which comprised my shorter pieces on murder and nuclear warfare, rounded off with the lecture on academic freedom I had given at the University of Cape Town during the previous year's South Africa visit. My 'Past Master' *Wyclif* had appeared in March, and the translation of *De Universalibus* and the autobiography

The Path from Rome in April. The local newspaper ran a story under the headline 'Top Oxford don's five-book year'.

Ronald Reagan, in his later years as President, came to believe that nuclear war could be avoided if the United States put in place a super-terrestrial shield which could destroy any incoming missiles. No expert whom I was able to consult, including some senior figures in NATO, believed that this strategic defence initiative was a realistic possibility. For a time, however, it was an important item of US foreign policy, and in February 1986 I was invited to oppose at the Oxford Union a motion to be proposed by the US Assistant Secretary of Defense, Richard Perle, 'That the Strategic Defence Initiative may make the world safer'. Perle was to be supported by Lord Chalfont, I was to support the Rt Hon. Enoch Powell and the Shadow Defence Secretary, Denzil Davies. Among the junior member speakers there stood out the president-elect of the Union, Boris Johnson, a brilliant but only spasmodically industrious Balliol undergraduate whom I was used to seeing at handshaking hiding from the censures of his tutors beneath his substantial fringe.

It was odd to find myself on the same side as Enoch Powell, but I already knew him to be rather different from the crude racist of popular perception. I had first met him at a dinner at Westminster College, where he made a speech in Ancient Greek and challenged me to reply in a Classical tongue: I had to get by with an impromptu piece of stammering Church Latin. In *The Logic of Deterrence*, I had quoted a brilliant speech he made against the British independent deterrent. We did not make as good a showing in the debate as we should have; however, it is not the debate, but the dinner which preceded it, which stands out in my memory.

The officers of the Union had assembled a glittering group which included Benazir Bhutto, then in exile, and Caspar Weinberger, the US Secretary of Defense. I found myself seated next to Weinberger, and seized the opportunity to tell him what I thought of US nuclear strategy. As I became heated, my wife nudged me under the table to bring me back to the conventions of the dinner table. I took the hint: 'I'm sorry, Mr Weinberger, if I have been too heated: but if you have the power to destroy the world, you must expect people to get excited when talking to you.' 'But perhaps,' he purred in response, 'I have the power to save it, too.' Not since the Last Supper, I thought, had such a claim been made over the dinner table.

16

Towards a New Ireland

THOUGH I HAVE Irish ancestors on both sides, for the first forty years of my life I paid no attention to Irish affairs and never set foot in Ireland, North or South. In the 1970s, however, I began to take an interest in the course of the troubles in Northern Ireland. This was not because I had strong feelings in support of either the Nationalist or the Unionist cause; rather, I was concerned, as other British citizens were, at some of the things being done by the security forces in our name.

At the of the 1970s and in the 1980s I accepted a number of invitations to visit Belfast, as lecturer or external examiner. Queen's University had both a department of scholastic philosophy and a department of analytical philosophy. There seemed to be little real difference of philosophical theory between the two – one could lecture on Wittgenstein in the scholastic department or on Aquinas in the analytical – and I suspected that the distinction was, or had originally been, merely a euphemism for a division between Catholics and Protestants. In any event, both departments gave me a warm welcome, and I became fond of Belfast.

When first I went, security was tight; lecture rooms were searched for bombs and on entering a room people would look to see where glass might fall if a window was blown out, and choose their seats accordingly. Academic visitors from Great Britain found their hosts in the Northern Ireland universities embarrassingly grateful: they had difficulty getting visiting lecturers and external examiners. It seemed to me indecent that people should refuse to accept for 24 hours risks which those inviting them endured every day of the year.

Early in the 1980s my interest in Northern Ireland became more explicitly political. Working on my autobiography for Sidgwick and Jackson I came to know Frank Longford and Marigold Johnson, one of their editors. At the same time, I became friends with David Astor in the course of organizing a set of lectures to be held at Balliol in 1984 to commemorate the fortieth anniversary of the death of Adam von Trott, the Balliol Rhodes Scholar who was executed for plotting against Hitler. All three of these people were active in the British Irish Association, a charity devoted to political education; at the time David was Chairman and Marigold Secretary. The Association brought together in conferences on neutral ground, usually in Oxford or Cambridge, representatives of different factions in Northern Ireland, and politicians and civil servants from the British and Irish governments. The aim was to enable the different groups to learn about each other and personal friendships to be formed between people on the two sides of the confessional divide who, at home, would have to maintain a political distance. From 1983 David and Marigold drew me into the affairs of the Association, and I offered Balliol as a venue for some of its meetings.

The Taoiseach, or Prime Minister, of Ireland in 1983 was Garret Fitzgerald; the son of a Protestant mother and Catholic father, he devoted himself to working for reconciliation between North and South. From the beginning of his premiership he emphasized that the free consent of the people of Northern Ireland was an essential prerequisite for any reunification of Ireland. In 1983, at the suggestion of John Hume, the leader of the SDLP, the constitutional Nationalist party in Northern Ireland, he set up a New Ireland Forum in Dublin. This was a meeting of representatives of all Catholic and Nationalist parties, North and South, to spell out the way in which they hoped to achieve the unity of Ireland by consent. The Forum was attended by members of the SDLP, of Fianna Fáil, the largest party in the Republic, then in opposition under Charles Haughey, and of Dick Spring's Labour Party, then in government in coalition with Fitzgerald's own Fine Gael party.

The New Ireland Forum did not fulfil Fitzgerald's hopes that it would present a radically new version of Nationalism and thus pave the way for a reconciliation with Unionism. Haughey and his allies exacted, as the price of their participation, that in the final Report the Unitary State – the United Ireland of tradition – be given prominence as the Forum's preferred option for the future. A system of joint authority (which had been carefully analysed in an unpublished report of a sub-committee of the Forum which included Senator Mary Robinson), along with a very rudimentary sketch of a federal/confederal state, were also presented in the Report, but described simply as proposals received as to 'how Unionist and Nationalist identities and interests could be accommodated in different ways and in varying degrees in a new Ireland'.

The Forum Report was published in May 1984. Garret Fitzgerald emphasized the open-endedness of the report, summed up in its statement that 'the parties in the Forum remain open to discuss other views which may contribute to political development'. The Forum, he insisted, was not a blueprint but an agenda. The fifth chapter of the Forum Report set out what it called the necessary elements of 'a framework within which a new Ireland could emerge'. As elsewhere in the Report, there was a clear condemnation of attempts to impose solutions by violence; other requirements listed appeared, on the face of it, obscure or platitudinous. The initial reaction of the British government was dismissive: the Secretary of State, James Prior, predictably ruled out as unrealistic the proposals for a United or Federal Ireland. But even the more moderate proposal for joint authority, he said in Parliament, was against the spirit, if not necessarily the letter, of the 1973 Northern Ireland Constitution Act, intended to guarantee 'The Unionists' right . . . not only to belong to the United Kingdom *but to be apart from the Republic.*'

However, close attention to the detailed wording of the Forum Report, and perhaps also to the spaces between the lines, suggested to some, in Britain as well as in Ireland, that Fitzgerald's initiative deserved a carefully thought-out response from the British side. The British Irish Association decided to sponsor an independent inquiry into the merits of the Forum proposals. It asked Lord Kilbrandon – the author of a widely respected report on devolution in Scotland – to assemble an all-party group to examine the practicability of the Forum Report and of the alternative proposals which had been made, in its wake, by the Unionist parties. The committee contained several academics, a solicitor, a businesswoman, a journalist and several politicians. Among its members were a former Conservative Cabinet Minister, David Howell, and the Deputy Leader of the Opposition in the Lords, Lord Underhill. Lord Kilbrandon asked me to join the committee and act as its vice-chairman, and because at the time his health was failing a lot of the work of chairing meetings and preparing texts fell to me. Simon Jenkins was marvellously skilful at drafting the most difficult paragraphs; the secretary of the committee was the indefatigable John Little.

The Kilbrandon Report was a completely unofficial study of the New Ireland Forum Report. The members of the committee saw it as their task, by spelling out possible British responses, to help ensure that the Report was taken seriously in official circles in the United Kingdom as an expression of the willingness of Irish Nationalists, and in particular of Fitzgerald's government, to assist in achieving a peaceful settlement in Northern Ireland. The eventual response of the British government showed that the Irish initiative had been, in the end, taken very seriously indeed.

Our deliberations began in May 1984. We had a series of plenary meetings, between which two or three of us would go off to interview some of the main players. I interviewed Garret Fitzgerald, which was a great pleasure, and led to a continuing friendship. I also interviewed Charles Haughey, a disagreeable task. I have never heard anyone make, with a perfectly straight face, so many statements which he cannot possible have expected me to believe. Once the British government agreed to everyone sitting round the table together, he maintained, it would be a trivial task to persuade the Unionists of the merits of a United Ireland. Other members of the committee visited representatives of the different parties in the North, including Sinn Fein councillors. I visited Belfast as the guest of Sir John Hermon, the Chief Constable of the RUC, and interviewed him and his colleagues. Jim Prior, now no longer Secretary of State, gave a friendly interview and let us have sight of his parting Memorandum to Mrs Thatcher. Throughout the work of the committee I received help and friendship from the widely respected Irish Ambassador in London, Noel Dorr.

At the end of the summer the British Irish Association was due to meet in Balliol. The College was crawled over by police sniffer dogs; Hermon, as the most likely target for any attack, was given a room in the Lodgings, while politicians and others took their chances in the student rooms. We also arranged a plenary meeting of the Kilbrandon Committee, at which it became clear we were not going to reach a unanimous set of recommendations. Eight members were willing to go some way towards the Forum's (unpublished but leaked) model of joint authority; others were afraid of the effect any such proposals would have on Unionist opinion. Simon Jenkins (for the minority) and I (for the majority) sat together writing and rewriting drafts and running them off on the Balliol photocopier. But our efforts to reach consensus were unavailing.

While we were unsuccessfully striving to reach agreement, the urgency of a solution to the Northern Ireland problem was brought home to everyone in Britain: the Provisional IRA exploded a bomb in the Grand Hotel, Brighton during the Conservative Party's annual conference. The Prime Minister and other members of the Government narrowly escaped death, five people were killed in their beds, others were seriously injured.

In the end the Kilbrandon Committee's Report was in two parts, one unanimous, the other divided. In the unanimous part we criticized the one-sided history in the Forum Report, while broadly agreeing with the Forum's assessment of the contemporary realities and requirements in Northern Ireland. We declared impracticable each of the three frameworks – unitary state, federation, and joint authority – put forward in the Report but stated that the joint authority proposals contained ideas which provided scope for progress.

The Kilbrandon Committee unanimously recommended several specific reforms: a Bill of Rights should be enacted, entrenching minority freedoms, and the Republic should be given a carefully defined role in its enforcement. The Flags and Emblems Act (which prohibited the display of the Irish Tricolour in the North) should be repealed; the RUC should be made accountable to a strengthened police authority, which might consult representatives from the Republic. Trials by Diplock courts (in which a single judge sat without a jury) might be replaced by trial by jury in Great Britain, or two-judge courts with one British and one Irish judge.

Beyond that point, there were disagreements within the Committee about the appropriate degree of Dublin involvement, both in law enforcement and in the internal administration of the province. The final chapter of the Report, therefore, presented two different models of possible co-operation between the Republic and the UK. A minority favoured a small number of detailed measures, which they called 'Functional Co-Operation'. The majority, to which Kilbrandon and I belonged, favoured what we called 'Co-operative Devolution'. We wanted the new strengthened police authority to include membership from the Republic; it might consist of one Northern Ireland Office minister, the Minister of Justice in the Republic, and three members from Northern Ireland, two from the majority community and one from the minority. Co-operation with law enforcement must go hand in hand, we believed, with political co-operation, and we aimed to combine a degree of involvement of the Republic in the affairs of the province with a substantial return of control to locally elected politicians.

To be effective in Northern Ireland a devolved executive must be representative, it must have an effective decision procedure, and it must be made proof against boycott. The Kilbrandon majority proposed that, under overall British sovereignty, the top tier of government within the province should be a five-man Executive, consisting of the Secretary of State or his deputy, the Minister of Foreign Affairs of the Irish Republic, and three members elected by the voters of Northern Ireland, in such a way that two of them were representative of the majority community, one of them of the minority. (The three European Members of Parliament from Northern Ireland, Paisley, Taylor and Hume, might fill this role: they had been democratically elected and already had experience of working together to promote the interests of the province within the EEC.) Such an Executive would be fairly representative: the majority would be represented two-to-one among the local members, and the minority plus their patron would be two-fifths of the body, approximately the proportion among the population.

Within the Executive, a simple majority of those present and voting should be decisive. The Executive was so constituted that its voting pattern would not necessarily be predictable. No doubt there would be occasions when the British and Unionists would unite to outvote the Nationalist and Irish vote, but as Nationalists have consistently preferred rule from Westminster to Stormont majority rule, this implies that there were likely to be matters in which Westminster would favour Nationalists against Unionists. The Secretary of State (or his representative) would, in effect, be holding the balance between the Orange and Green votes: this would reflect the underlying reality of British sovereignty over a divided province, while allowing the fullest practical sharing of power among local representatives. To cover all eventualities, the UK government would no doubt wish to reserve a power of veto, in certain matters, to its own representative.

Such an Executive would be comparatively boycott-proof because if all the local representatives adopted a boycott, the default position would effectively be joint rule by the Westminster and Dublin members. There would be little incentive for a single local faction to boycott, since that would involve forfeiting its own share of power and leaving local power in the hands of its opponents.

The extent of the powers to be given to the political Executive was not specified in detail by Kilbrandon: it was suggested that they should be initially modest, then increased in the light of experience. At the full extent of devolution, the Executive could decide on the allocation of resources to particular departments, within an overall budget to be determined by the UK government. It should be concerned with the matters administered through the six Northern Ireland departments of Finance and Personnel, Economic Development, Environment, Agriculture, Education, and Health and Social Services; ministers for these departments should be appointed by the Executive.

The relation between the devolved Executive and the existing Northern Ireland Assembly was left vague by the Kilbrandon proposals. It was suggested that the Assembly should 'scrutinise' the conduct of the Executive and its ministers; but it was not explained how this was to be reconciled with the responsibility of the Secretary of State to the Westminster Parliament, nor that of the Irish Minister of Foreign Affairs to the Dáil.

Like the Forum sub-committee, the Kilbrandon majority believed that if any form of joint authority was to be successful, it must fulfil three conditions. First, it must be accepted as a durable solution, not as a method of coercing Unionists into a United Ireland. Second, it should be enshrined in a form which was solemn, transparent, and definitive: a treaty between the two governments, deposited with the United Nations. Third, it should have the possibility of continuing even if, as a result of population changes, there were to be a majority in Northern Ireland who favoured union with the Irish Republic.

Unlike the Forum sub-committee, the Kilbrandon Committee believed that throughout the duration of the treaty sovereignty should remain with the United Kingdom. Moreover, should the treaty be revoked, all powers conferred under it on representatives of the Irish government should revert to the United Kingdom government. If a majority of the population of Northern Ireland came to wish it, sovereignty should be transferred to Ireland and the treaty terminated; but a new and symmetrical joint authority treaty should then be made between the two sovereign states.

The Kilbrandon Report was launched in a room in the Palace of Westminster on the same day in November as Mrs Gandhi was assassinated; accordingly it received comparatively little press coverage in Britain. However, it was denounced by both sides in Ireland. The Republican *Irish Press* said it pointed back in the direction of Stormont Rule; a Unionist speaker, in a debate condemning it in the Northern Ireland Assembly, dismissed its proposals as 'fantasy and green dreams'. Even the non-denominational Alliance Party was highly critical. Only a debate in the House of Lords, later in the year, gave the proposals a more sympathetic consideration. Several peers associated themselves with its main lines, and Lord Lyell, for the government, took a stance between the Kilbrandon majority and the Kilbrandon minority.

Four days after the Assembly debate Fitzgerald and Thatcher met at a Chequers summit. In a press conference Mrs Thatcher was asked for her opinion of the three main options in the Forum.

> I have made it quite clear – and so did Mr Prior when he was Secretary of State for Northern Ireland – that a unified Ireland was one solution that is out. A second solution was a confederation of two states. That is out. A third solution was joint authority. That is out.

Mrs Thatcher's 'out . . . out . . . out' speech gave comfort to Unionists and caused outrage in the Republic. But at the very summit which she had just left, important steps were taken which were to lead to an agreement between the two governments which in some way went beyond our 'green dreams'.

In September 1985 the British Irish Association was once again, by my invitation, to meet in Balliol. A week before it was due to assemble, David Astor, Marigold Johnson and I were summoned to the Cabinet Office. Robert Armstrong and Christopher Mallaby asked us to postpone the meeting: discussions between the two governments were going well, they said, but had reached a critical point, and informal public discussions between politicians and officials, such as took place at BIA, might prove a hindrance to an agreement.

We agreed to the postponement – but at considerable inconvenience to Balliol. This was the first such sensitive conference since the Brighton bombing, and the security forces were determined to introduce new and more rigorous procedures. It did not matter that the conference had been called off; the entire College had to be searched and sniffed, because of the IRA practice of concealing bombs weeks before they were primed to explode. Moreover, the same procedure would have to be undertaken all over again when the conference was eventually held. Some of the Fellows made it clear to me they were thoroughly disenchanted with my involvement in Irish affairs.

For days the police crawled over the college, destroying suspicious objects in controlled explosions and taking up floorboards, their dogs sniffing every piece of furniture. At one point a sniffer-dog barked in the middle of the rare books in the fifteenth-century Library. 'Oh, my God!' I thought. 'Will they blow up all our treasures?' But no. A senior dog was summoned from Windsor Palace. It trotted through the library, nose in air, without a sound. The junior sniffer was over-ruled, and our books were safe.

On 15 November all was revealed. The Prime Minister and the Taoiseach were to meet to sign an agreement by which, for the first time, the British Government was to allow the Government of the Republic a formal role in the provisions for the administration of Northern Ireland. Earlier in the day Mallaby telephoned from Downing Street and read out to me the main heads of agreement. The second article established an Intergovernmental Conference concerned with Northern Ireland and with relations between the two parts of Ireland, to deal on a regular basis with political matters, security and related matters, legal matters including the administration of justice, and the promotion of cross-border co-operation. The basis of the Conference was set out thus:

> The United Kingdom Government accept that the Irish Government will put forward views and proposals on matters relating to Northern Ireland within the field of activity of the Conference in so far as those matters are not the responsibility of a devolved administration in Northern Ireland. In the

interests of promoting peace and stability, determined efforts shall be made through the Conference to resolve any differences . . . There is no derogation from the sovereignty of either the United Kingdom Government or the Irish Government, and each retains responsibility for the decisions and administration of government within its own jurisdiction.

Both governments declared their support for a policy of devolution: if a devolved administration should be established, the devolved matters would be taken out of the purview of the Conference. In the meantime, the remaining articles of the agreement spelt out the areas of concern: article 5 spoke of the rights and identities of the two traditions, and the protection of human rights and the avoidance of discrimination; article 6 spoke of the role and composition of the bodies existing in Northern Ireland to safeguard rights and eliminate discrimination; article 7 spoke of security policy within the province, article 8 of the enforcement of criminal law and the administration of justice, article 9 of cross-border co-operation in security, article 10 of co-operation in economic and social development. I listened to Mallaby's list with keen interest and excitement, and then waited. 'That's all fine for the Nationalists', I said, 'and what are you giving to the Unionists?'

The Hillsborough Agreement marked an epoch in Anglo-Irish relations; but there is no doubt that it was very one-sided, and in that respect even 'greener' than our Kilbrandon proposals. I was unsurprised by the reaction of even moderate Unionist friends like Harold McCusker, MP.

> I went to Hillsborough on the Friday morning . . . I stood outside Hillsborough, not waving a Union flag – I doubt whether I will ever wave one again – not singing hymns, saying prayers or protesting, but like a dog, and asked the Government to put in my hand the document that sold my birthright. A senior police officer went into Hillsborough Castle, asked for the document and brought it out to me.
>
> I felt desolate because as I stood in the cold outside Hillsborough Castle everything that I held dear turned to ashes in my mouth.

I was in Belfast very shortly after, to lecture to a group of civil servants. I visited Mary Robinson, whom I knew through the BIA, and joined her in lamenting the one-sidedness of the agreement. In protest at its terms, she resigned her membership of the Labour Party in the Irish Senate. It was a generous gesture, one which she may well have believed would end her career in public life.

Despite its defects, the Anglo-Irish Agreement was a milestone on the long, desperate, uphill road to peace and stability in Northern Ireland. Later Prime Ministers and Secretaries of State moved forward from it until peace came and a permanent agreement seemed, at least for a while, tantalisingly close. I like to think that in a modest measure the Kilbrandon Committee helped on the process.

I told the story of the Forum, the Independent Inquiry, and the Anglo-Irish Agreement in a small book entitled *The Road to Hillsborough*. It was offered to Pergamon Press, and Robert Maxwell agreed to publish it in 1986. But it was not the book on Ireland he wanted me to write: he had tried to persuade me to write a short book, to be distributed free with copies of the *Daily Mirror*, calling for a British withdrawal and a United Ireland.

17

Oxford vs *Thatcher*

IN HER LIFE of her father, Lord Lindsay, Drusilla Scott reminds her readers that the Master's Lodgings in Balliol has two doors, one leading into the College quadrangle, the other into the Broad and the world outside. As Lindsay grew older, she suggests, the door into the College was opened less, that into the world more.

My own Mastership followed the same pattern. Some of my political activity was my own choice. But in the 1980s political action – at least in the form of protest, canvassing and lobbying – was forced on the Master and his fellow officers, to secure Balliol's conception of its nature as a College and its role as part of a collegiate university against attack. Unlike Lindsay's offensive to carry Balliol ideals to the nation, the political activities of the 1980s were essentially defensive.

The raising of fees to overseas students made the Conservative government unpopular at the beginning of its term of office. This was followed by drastic cuts in the allocation to the University Grants Committee for the funding of universities: in 1981 it was announced that over the next three years there would be a cut in real terms of 8.5 per cent. This was in addition to the 2.5 per cent cut in block grant which the universities were supposed to recoup by charging in fees the full cost of the education of overseas students. Council and the General Board thought costs could be fully recouped only if overseas fees were set at a rate even higher than that recommended by the Secretary of State. Congregation, however, already angry at the massive increases imposed by government, voted against placing any further burden on overseas students. As a result of the UGC cuts and of Congregation's principled stand, professorships and lectureships had to be left unfilled and placed on a Register of Suspended Posts; others were earmarked for abolition – including a number associated with Balliol Fellowships.

In the early 1980s, settlements agreed nationally for academic salaries were consistently underfunded – in some years, up to the level of 1½ per cent of turnover. The number of funded places for home students was reduced, and a series of cuts, year by year, reduced the real value of student maintenance grants to below subsistence level. The Secretary of State for Education, Sir Keith Joseph, added to the troubles of the universities a crusade of his own against sociologists and economists, insisting that the word 'science' be dropped from the title of the Social Science Research Council. The government began to be seen as the enemy of the universities, not only by radical and left-wing students, but even by dons whose general political sympathies were Conservative.

In 1981 three Balliol Fellows invited Sir Keith to address a University seminar they were giving in the College. I foresaw trouble which might be difficult to control: if there was a demonstration by non-members of the College, we would have no jurisdiction over them; on the other hand, we could not exclude non-Balliol people from the College since all members of the University were entitled to attend. The Dean and I decided that it should be moved from College to University premises, where the Proctors and their police would have jurisdiction over all who attended. I was glad to have done so, for there was indeed a noisy demonstration which broke up the meeting. We were then able to offer Sir Keith shelter in our Senior Common Room, where the seminar was completed in the presence of a well-behaved rump. But long debates followed among the Balliol dons about whether and how to discipline the one Balliol student who had been an obnoxious heckler.

It was a remarkable fact that during the three Thatcher administrations, whose policies were consistently unpopular with the current senior and junior members of Balliol, there was almost always a significant presence of the College's alumni in the Cabinet and among junior ministers. There was one brief gap when, after the departure of Sir Ian Gilmour in 1981, the Cabinet for the first time since 1951 lacked a Balliol member. As I pointed out to a dinner of Balliol parliamentarians shortly afterwards, this Cabinet reshuffle was followed by an immediate fall in the stock market. By the time I ceased to be Master, the government contained no fewer than three Balliol Secretaries of State. But of course, during these years the most distinguished Balliol member of the House of Commons, Sir Edward Heath, gave powerful voice to many of the misgivings felt in the College. And whenever the Prime Minister was greeted in Oxford by rowdy demonstrations to the theme of 'Maggie, Maggie, Maggie, Out, Out, Out', one might see, from time to time, the Balliol offspring of ministers joining in.

At the same time, the Labour Party had become unpopular among many who previously supported it – not least because of its inability to present itself as a credible alternative government. Many people in

Oxford were relieved by the foundation of the Social Democrat Party. At Balliol there was particular excitement when Roy Jenkins, an Honorary Fellow of the College since 1969, became the first leader of the Party, in 1982. Nancy and I gave a party in the Lodgings to celebrate his appointment. Like other disillusioned Labour supporters, I paid my subscription to the SDP: the first and only time in my life that I have been a paid-up member of a political party.

Mrs Thatcher may have been unpopular in the unversities, but the election of 1983 showed that she was popular elsewhere, including Oxford's own constituency, which elected a Tory candidate, John Patten, then geography tutor at Hertford. In mockery of 'Vote Conservative for a better future', some geography students scrawled on the department wall, 'Vote Patten for a better tutor'.

Now that Mrs Thatcher had been returned to power for the second time it became, in the eyes of many people, more and more of a scandal that she had not yet been offered an honorary degree by her own University. Naturally, as soon as a Somerville graduate first became Prime Minister, the question was raised in Council whether she should be proposed for an honour at Encaenia. It was not easy to decide between the reasons for and against. The raising of overseas fees, so early in her administration, had made her very unpopular in the University. It would be dangerous for Council to put her name forward at a time when it might be rejected in Congregation: that would be the worst of all possible worlds. Council decided to wait until she became more popular with the average voter in Congregation.

We waited, and we waited, and the years went by. In February 1984 a glittering banquet, attended by the Heads of Houses and all the most senior figures in the University, was held in Balliol to mark the ninetieth birthday of the Chancellor, Harold Macmillan, Lord Stockton. The Vice-Chancellor and I sat either side of him in the middle of High Table. At one end was Ted Heath, at the other Roy Jenkins. There could hardly have been a more visible symbol of the contrast between the warmth of the University's feelings for its past graduate Prime Ministers and the coolness with which it had treated the present holder of the office.

At last, the time seemed ripe to put Mrs Thatcher's name forward for an honorary degree. During 1983/4 there was a slackening in the pace of retrenchment. Some Foreign Office money was made available for overseas student scholarships; funds were provided for the appointment of some younger academics to 'new blood' posts. When Council considered honorary degrees in Michaelmas Term 1984, Mrs Thatcher had just survived the IRA's attempt to assassinate her at Brighton. At my suggestion, Hebdomadal Council asked the Vice-Chancellor to write congratulating her on her escape. We all admired the physical courage she had shown on that occasion, and the moral courage with which she had resisted pressure to adopt a hostile stance towards Ireland. Now, we thought, was the appropriate time to recognize her virtues without appearing to endorse her policies. So we voted for her to be given an honorary degree.

In accordance with the ancient procedures of the University, a long period elapsed between this vote by Hebdomadal Council and the decisive vote being taken in Congregation. During that period Mrs Thatcher proposed the abolition of free tuition for undergraduates; when the measure was withdrawn because of pressure from Conservative back-benchers with children at universities, the loss to the Treasury was made up by reducing funds budgeted for the support of science. Between October 1984 and January 1985 two new constituencies of anti-Thatcherites had been recruited.

During Hilary Term 1985 I was on sabbatical leave as a Visiting Professor at Oberlin College, Ohio during January, and the Balliol Governing Body was chaired by Jasper Griffin as Vice-Gerent. From the second to the seventh week of term I was in Oxford, working on *The Logic of Deterrence* and *A Stylometric Study of the New Testament*; I also lectured to the Royal College of Psychiatrists on the defects of the Homicide Act 1957, and the lecture was printed in the *Journal of Medical Ethics*. At the end of term I went to Leuven as Cardinal Mercier lecturer, and addressed a series of seminars at Leiden and Nijmegen in Holland. But in between times, the second half of the term was swamped with the backwash of Congregation's vote to refuse to offer Mrs Thatcher the honorary degree.

On the day the vote was taken I was out of town, recording a television commentary which had been contracted many months before. I could not avoid discussing the Thatcher degree: I did my best to carry out the impossible task of explaining both why Council had proposed the honour, and why so many of my colleagues had voted against it. The whole affair was a source of universal embarrassment. Those who thought Mrs Thatcher should have been honoured have never forgiven Congregation for its rejection; those who thought it hypocritical to flatter such a foe of the universities could never understand why Hebdomadal Council put her name forward in the first place.

I returned to College to a deluge of letters from old members. Of the two hundred who wrote to the Vice-Master or myself, just over half expressed themselves in favour of Congregation's rejection of the degree; but those who took the opposite view were considerably more vehement in their disapproval. The Vice-Master at the time was Denis Noble, founder of the Save British Science Campaign. We divided the labour of replying: I, who had voted on Council in favour of the degree, replied to the pro-Thatcher correspondents while he, who had been active in the campaign for a negative vote, replied to the rest. In the middle of the ferment Ian Gilmour told me that public reaction to the refusal had made him think Oxford had, after all, been right – it had been like the response to an insult to the Führer.

Roy Jenkins tells the story of how Harold Macmillan bore down upon him in the lobby of the House of Commons. 'Terrible business, Roy, this insult to the Prime Minister by our old University, terrible.' After much shaking of the head, a certain light came into the old man's eyes. 'You know, it's all really a matter of class. The dons are mainly upper-middle class, and they can never forgive Mrs Thatcher for being so lower-middle class. But you and I, Roy, with out working-class ancestry, are above that kind of thing.'

Among the other names proposed for honorary degrees on the same day as Mrs Thatcher's was that of President Pertini of Italy. (Council had fondly hoped that by coupling the name of a British Conservative head of government with that of an Italian Socialist head of state it would avoid any appearance of political partisanship.) At Encaenia in the summer I sat next to Pertini at the celebratory lunch in All Souls. He lamented the absence of Mrs Thatcher. 'Si chiama dama di ferro,' he said gallantly, 'ma dentro quel forte petto batte un cuore dolce e gentile.'

The scars of those days remain with us. But in 1985 many of the most significant government interventions in the management of universities were yet to come. In its early years the administration had concerned itself with the overall sums to be given to universities, but had left it to the universities to decide how best to spend their grants; as the decade wore on the government's funding councils took more and more interest in how the money was spent. Universities, once totally free to determine their own priorities between academic disciplines, were steered towards those which the government regarded as being relevant to the needs of the economy. The proportion of 'new blood' posts had to be nine in science and engineering for every one in non-science subjects. A division between teaching and research was introduced into the calculation of grants; and the size of the research-based grant was tailored to the University Grants Commission's evaluation of the quality of each institution's research. The government began to take an interest even in the content of individual courses: the Department of Education and Science complained to the Vice-Chancellor of the Open University that a course offered in his social studies department used an excessively Marxist approach. Interventionism on this scale was widely seen as an affront to academic autonomy.

The filling-in of forms and the answering of questionnaires began to be time-consuming for both institutions and individuals. Most important, and also most irritating to many, was the business of responding to the UGC's inquisitions into research productivity. Vice-Chancellor Warnock spoke for many when he said in 1985, 'It is a pity that academics, instead of just getting on with their work, should have to take time out to describe what work they are doing, in terms that they hope will look appetizing when set out on the market-stall.'

In Trinity Term 1986 the UGC published the first list of annual grants based on the new system of comparative evaluation of universities' research records. Oxford appeared near the bottom of the list, with a zero increase in money terms for 1986/7. This was reported in the press as if it meant Oxford had been rated thirty-first among the nation's universities in respect of research. In fact, when the actual research gradings were published, a week later than the grants, it was found that Oxford's record was second to none in the country. Every one of its major departments was rated outstanding by international criteria, with the single exception of law. A few weeks later, after much head-scratching and breast-beating in the law faculty, it transpired that law, too, had been rated outstanding, but the asterisk to indicate this on the chart had been omitted in error by a typist in the UGC.

The zero-increase in the funding of Oxford University was a consequence of the interest the government had begun to take in the relationship between University and college finances. In a reasonable desire to avoid any double funding, the UGC had asked the University to spell out in detail the contribution made by colleges and paid for by college fees, which in a non-collegiate University would have had to come out of central funds; the University made the calculation, and its block grant was then reduced by that sum.

Many of us suspected this was a clever, almost Machiavellian, move to reduce overall Oxford funding. It was obviously in the interest of the University officers to put the value of the colleges' contributions as low as they honestly could, since the bottom line they produced would determine the size of the cut to be made in University funding. Once the size of the cut had been agreed, it would have been open to the DES, the next year, to write to Oxford on the following lines: 'Now you've told us how much the colleges' contributions is worth, we will restore the cut we made last year, but instead we will abolish the payment of college fees from public funds. We will leave it to the central

University to pass on to each college a sum appropriate to the value it places on its services.'

This would have been a disaster for Oxford, since – to take just the most important item – the real cost to the colleges of the labour-intensive tutorial system is far greater than the money the University saves by not having to provide the centralized undergraduate courses found in non-collegiate institutions. But though it was clear there continued to be a feeling in Whitehall that a collegiate university was an expensive luxury, the second part of the UGC's Morton's Fork was never applied. College fees remained, as before, the subject of separate negotiation between the Conference of Colleges and the DES. At one time the Research Council threatened to cease payment to colleges of fees for graduate students; but even this threat was removed once the colleges spelt out in detail the services they provided to graduates in return for the fees.

The crudest intervention by government came in 1988. This was the result of its determination to ensure that universities introduced a scheme of performance-related pay. It had long been a principle in Oxford, as in Cambridge, that – leaving aside clinical staff as a special case – all academic staff at a given level, no matter what discipline they belonged to, should be paid at the same, publicly fixed, rate. This system contrasted sharply with that prevalent in American universities, where each professor's salary was the subject of private bargaining. The government thought the Oxbridge practice insufficiently competitive, and believed there should be salary differentiation on the basis of either subject or merit.

In January 1987 Secretary of State Kenneth Baker announced the provision of funds for academic pay restructuring. The money needed to pay for any salary increase for the next year would be forthcoming only if 'a satisfactory new pay structure is assured, providing management with more flexibility to take account of the quality of lecturers' performance and recruitment and retention problems.' The Secretary of State's requirements were incorporated in the twenty-third Report of the Committee on Academic Salaries, published in February.

A statute of Oxford University provided that all professors should be paid the same salary. Accordingly, the lengthy procedures of University legislation would be necessary if the University was to fulfil the conditions laid down for the salary award. Convinced that staff would be unwilling to forgo the overdue increase of 23 per cent, the administration proclaimed its acceptance in principle of the requirement to provide for management flexibility, but that the particular form the differentials would take was to be announced. Congregation was informed of this in Hilary Term 1987 and no objection was raised. On this basis the University Chest began to pay the increased salaries, attaching to each academic employee's payslip a note explaining the understanding on which this was being done.

Throughout the academic year 1987/8 there was much deliberation and consultation about the new salary scales and the principle of merit awards for professors. Some, particularly among scientists, were in favour of differential pay; but majority opinion was probably hostile, and news was brought that Cambridge intended to make a special case to the UGC for exemption from the requirements of the twenty-third Report. Council, however, took the view that if Oxford and Cambridge stood out, the UGC would be unable to inform the DES that universities accepted the principles of the report, and this would jeopardize for all universities the salary increases granted on the basis of those principles. Council's position was reinforced, in the most unwelcome way, when the UGC, impatient of the delay, began to withhold from the monthly grant cheque to the University the additional money provided for by the Report. Over a year, this would amount to £2.5 million.

However reluctantly, therefore, Council asked Congregation to repeal the statute providing for equal pay, so that it could institute a merit scheme for rewarding distinction among professors. John Lucas, the Merton philosopher, proposed a wrecking amendment to Council's motion. I was one of the hapless pair appointed by Council to introduce and defend the obnoxious legislation.

> Let me say at the outset that my heart is with those who have proposed the motion today. We used to have a statute which obliged our University to give equal pay to all its professors. That was an admirable statute. It was something to be proud of. We used to quote it to support our claim that Oxford, beyond all other universities, was a republic of scholars.
>
> Like the signatories of the motion, I am under no illusions about the motives of those who urge universities to adopt merit schemes. The principle of awarding merit is surely admirable. What the words suggest is a system in which a few persons of eminent distinction are paid a surplus – a surplus on top of a decent salary which compares fairly with other professions in this country and with our own profession overseas. The merit scheme that we are offered is something quite different. It is a device to enable our paymasters to underpay the great majority of academics . . .
>
> Our paymasters' insistence on differential salaries was both misguided and cynical. But the government's advocacy of merit schemes was not limited to contemplation, or advice, or encouragement. The DES threatened to withhold, from universities which refused to adopt their advice, a substantial proportion of the funding of their salaries. Council and the General Board believed that members of Congregation would not wish to forego their long

overdue salary increase of 23 per cent in order to preserve professorial equality. The acceptance of differential salaries was one of the many disagreeable prices the University has had to pay, in these difficult days, for survival.

I went on to say that, distasteful though it was, the introduction of differential salaries was not a measure which would wreck academic standards: the experience of the best American universities was sufficient proof. Above all, the time for argument on the substantive issue was over: the matter had been settled by Congregation a year earlier.

> The proposers of the motion tell us that they do not wish to press for the repeal of the amendment to the statute. They merely wish the system of merit awards to be implemented in a different way.
>
> . . . Of the improvements suggested the most carefully thought out is the proposal that the new funds made available might be distributed to professors as a reward for serving on Council and the General Board. May I invite members of Congregation to take out their University diaries to see what such a suggestion would mean in practice?
>
> It would clearly be invidious to make a distinction between the funds made available for service on each of these august bodies. So, of the two hundred thousand pounds made available for the professoriate, half must go to the professors on the General Board, and half to the professors on Council. At present on the General Board there are three professors: Sir Peter Hirsch, Professor Llewellyn Smith, and Sir Richard Southwood. On Mr Lucas's proposals they would each receive £33,000. Honorable men, all of them, and worth every penny. On Council, there are only two professors, each of whom will receive £50,000 under the Lucas scheme. They are Professor Patrick Sandars and, need I say, Sir Richard Southwood. I understand that Sir Richard has announced his intention of addressing the House, later this afternoon, in opposition to Mr Lucas's motion. In the light of the figures I have quoted he may well wish to reconsider his position.

I stressed how unlikely it was that Cambridge would succeed in resisting the UGC pressure, and calculated that if the Lucas motion succeeded, Oxford would be likely to lose in the long run £3.5 million per annum.

> But the proposers of the motion suggest that Oxford should rise above such mundane financial considerations. Let me therefore try to meet them on their own austerely moral ground . . .
>
> All our professors have now been led to believe that if they apply they have a chance of a merit award. Those who have applied have named referees who have taken the trouble to supply the University with testimonials to their remarkable distinction. Appointments have been made and posts accepted on the basis that the appointees would be eligible, in due course, for distinction awards. If the scheme is now abolished, or substantially modified, the

University will be guilty of bad faith to all these people, and very possibly of breach of contract to incoming professors . . .

If Congregation accepts the motion today, what signal will Oxford give to the world? Will the vote show that Oxford values its proud democratic traditions above financial considerations? That might be the message if the motion proposed that all those who had accepted money under the twenty-third award should return it to the University for repayment to the Exchequer. But that is not what the motion proposes . . .

The important distinction is between whether it was wise to enter into an agreement, and whether it is right to welsh on the agreement once it has been made. Many members of Congregation will have had the experience of selling a house. When you receive an offer from a purchaser, it is often difficult to decide whether it is wise to accept it. Once you have accepted it, you may find, to your chagrin, that you would have got a better offer if you had waited. But you don't, if you are decent, renege on your original offer. I don't myself believe that, in this case, any better offer is on the market; but whether that is true or not, I hope that Congregation will not, in the name of the honourable traditions of the University, adopt the morals of the gazumper.

Congregation accepted the lead of Council and the General Board by a substantial majority; but I would prefer to have been victorious in a better cause.

The financial cuts imposed on the universities for a large part of the 1980s necessitated considerable reductions in staff levels. Many universities, including Oxford, introduced premature retirement schemes which held out substantial financial inducements to dons to quit their posts. But voluntary retirement schemes alone had a limited effect, and it was discovered that in most cases academic tenure prevented axe-wielding Vice-Chancellors from making all the cuts they wished.

At the end of 1987 the Government published an Education Reform Bill which had as one of its purposes the ending of tenure in academic appointments. Strictly speaking, the Fellows of Balliol did not have, and never have had, tenure: their appointments were renewable at intervals of no longer than seven years. But under the Bill Commissioners were to be set up to examine the statutes of all Oxbridge colleges, and satisfy themselves that they were not in conflict with the new legislation. They were to insist, for instance, that the definition of 'good cause' as a reason for removal from office included inefficiency as well as gross misconduct. The Visitor's jurisdiction over the Statutes would no longer be exclusive, so that provision would have to be made for appeal. Balliol, perfectly content with its existing, recently reformed statutes, had been happy to submit to the exclusive jurisdiction of the Visitor. The elaborate provision for termination of employment contained in the Bill made it, in fact, for better or worse, harder rather than easier for a college to get rid of a Fellow whose performance was less than satis-factory.

Other features of the Bill were more sinister. It gave unprecedented powers to the Secretary of State to determine in detail the ways in which universities were to spend the public moneys voted to them by Parliament. It abolished the arms-length University Grants Committee which hitherto had had the duty to advise the government on the needs of the university system and to distribute, independently of the govern-ment, the funds entrusted to it by grant-in-aid. Henceforth there was to be a University Funding Council, which had no duty to advise and which was to distribute funds subject to any conditions which the Secretary of State might determine.

Hebdomadal Council resolved 'that the clauses of the Bill relating to the universities are unacceptable as they stand. They should never have been put forward in their present form, and their enactment without amendment would be contrary to the best interests of the nation'. Sir Patrick Neill prepared a stinging attack on the Bill's defects which was distributed by Council with the *University Gazette*. Along with other Heads of House I was asked to send the statement to my College's members of both Houses of Parliament, urging them to seek amend-ment of the more objectionable features of the Bill. Most, from various parties, replied sympathetically, and there was particularly heartening support from Ted Heath, Denis Healey and Lord Grimond; predict-ably, there was a rather more waspish response from Nicholas Ridley, on the theme of 'he who pays the piper will always call the tune'. In the end, thanks especially to the efforts of academic peers, and among them our own Honorary Fellows Lord Jenkins and the Bishop of London, the Act as passed was, in several significant respects, less obnoxious than the Bill in its original form.

At a late stage, the government tacked on to the Education Reform Bill a clause laying a duty on institutions of higher education to ensure that freedom of speech within the law be secured for members, stu-dents and employees of the establishment, and for visiting speakers. The clause imposed a duty to ensure that the use of any premises of the establishment was not denied to any individual or body on the grounds of their policies or objectives.

The addition of the clause was provoked by a number of disgrace-ful incidents in which visiting politicians had been insulted and ill-treated in several universities and colleges. But as usual with over-hasty legislation, the remedy proposed was out of all proportion to the mis-chief to be prevented. In an article in *The Times* I pointed out that the government appeared to be confusing academic freedom with freedom of speech, and also to be twisting the significance of the latter.

Academic freedom – the freedom to conduct teaching, research and administration free from force or fear, internal or external – was fundamental to the nature of a university. It was protected, in Oxford, by a statute which made it an offence punishable by expulsion to 'disrupt or attempt to disrupt teaching or study or research or the administration of the University'.

Freedom of speech 'for visiting speakers' was a different matter. Freedom of speech is a most precious civil liberty. Traditionally, it is the right of citizens to say what they like without interference from government. What the new clause stove to entrench, under this venerable cloak, was the right of members of the government to say what they liked without interruption by citizens. Certainly, university authorities had a duty to protect those whom they invited to speak on their premises; but the proposed Act took away from them any right to decide who should be invited. If the Moonies had asked to use Balliol Chapel for a missionary service, if Provisional Sinn Fein had asked to use the Senior Common Room to promote the cause of the IRA, I would, under the terms of the Act, have been in violation of the law in refusing them permission.

Any Head of House in the 1980s found himself called on to protest against government removal of liberties previously enjoyed by College and University. In Oxford we have now, I suppose, come to take it for granted that the University is no longer allowed to pay all its professors equally, as befits equal citizens in the Republic of Letters; we have acquiesced in the removal from college governing bodies of the right to decide who shall, and who shall not, hold political meetings on college premises. But I do not regret that my files are full of letters, articles and speeches against these innovations.

No doubt some of our fears were exaggerated, some of our protests over-strident. For instance, the number – if not uncontrovertibly the calibre – of overseas students in Oxford is now greater than it was before the imposition of full-cost fees. But there remains the fascinating irony that unparalleled intrusions on academic autonomy were made by an administration which prided itself on its commitment to the reduction of government control over the life of the citizen. With hindsight, the immediate anger long past, academics are justified in believing that the government's successive intrusions on university autonomy damaged the country's higher education system.

The damage was done not by the cuts in university funding, grievous though these were; it was by the onslaught on two principles which had hitherto been thought fundamental to the academic ethos. The first was the principle that university research should be governed not by considerations of commercial profit but by disinterested academic curiosity. This was crucially weakened by the insistence that publicly-funded university research should be largely guided by the requirements of the national economy. The second was the idea that an academic career should be pursued not for the sake of financial reward but as a vocation worthwhile for its own sake. This was weakened by the insistence on differential salaries and performance pay. Hitherto, academics had been content with their unremarkable stipends because their worth was not judged, either by their peers or by the nation as a whole, in terms of the size of their pay-packets. Under Thatcherism, academics, like everyone else, were encouraged to rate themselves and all their activities in strictly financial terms. It was particularly bitter for dons to be told that their worth henceforth was to be seen in terms of monetary reward at the same time as the value of those rewards fell well behind those earned by their non-academic peers and their own pupils a few years out of college. This hardly made long-term sense even economically: if everything was to be valued monetarily, first-rate academics would no longer be willing to work for the modest salaries with which formerly they had been content. I once complained to a Permament Secretary in the Department of Education and Science that in introducing to academic life the concept of performance pay, the government was killing a goose which had laid many golden eggs. I am afraid he had not the faintest idea what I was talking about.

More than once in these years, when I lamented in private to Conservative politicians the harm Mrs Thatcher's government was doing to universities, I found a measure of agreement that the policies were damaging. 'But', my interlocutor would continue, 'in this matter Oxford has a lot to answer for.' 'Surely,' I would reply, 'no admirer of Mrs Thatcher could suggest that her policy in respect of the nation's higher education system could be influenced by pique at Oxford's refusal of an Honorary Degree?' At that point, the discussion usually came to an abrupt end.

18

Books and Bookmen

THE BODLEIAN LIBRARY is one of the most august institutions of Oxford, founded by Duke Humphrey of Gloucester in the fifteenth century and refounded by Sir Thomas Bodley at the end of the sixteenth. It has one of the finest historical collections in the world, and as a Library of Legal Deposit is entitled to a free copy of every book published in the UK. It has long been presided over by the Curators, a venerable body which meets, under the chairmanship of the Vice-Chancellor, in a handsome panelled room at the foot of King James I's Tower in the Bodleian quadrangle. In 1985 I was elected a Curator, and began to take part in deliberations about the lending of books to exhibitions, the fixing of opening hours, the levying of charges. It was hard to avoid the feeling that the Curatorial Body belonged to the dignified rather than the efficient part of the University's constitution; still, as one of the senior Curators told me, 'It is a fine thing to be a Curator of the Bodley: you walk with head held higher.'

The Curators had survived several attempts at reform. For most of my time in Oxford the library system was governed under proposals emanating from the 1966 Shackleton Report, which sought to introduce a measure of order in place of what it called 'unplanned independence and enthusiastic rivalry'. Shackleton created a Libraries' Board, which was to give expert advice to the General Board on library issues, divide a University-wide budget between individual libraries, and co-ordinate common services – cataloguing, acquisitions policies and the like – across the library system. In the event, in a typical Oxford compromise, it was given financial responsibility only for eleven major central research libraries and faculty libraries; forty-two departmental libraries in the sciences continued to be funded from within departmental budgets, and of course all the College libraries retained their total independence. All libraries, even those funded by the Board, retained managerial autonomy.

In 1985 I became chairman of this Libraries' Board, and indeed it was in that capacity that I joined the Curators. The constitutional arrangements were decidedly odd. As chairman of the Libraries' Board I reported to the Vice-Chancellor through the General Board; on the other hand, the Libraries' Board determined the budget allocation to Bodley's Curators – who were chaired by the Vice-Chancellor. I soon discovered that this was not just a piece of Alice-in-Wonderland quaintness, but reflected the main problem of the library system, which was the relationship between Bodley and the other libraries.

'Bodley' now meant much more than just the historic buildings of Old Bodley and the hideous New Bodleian erected across the Broad in the 1930s. The Radcliffe Camera, the Radcliffe Science Library, the Rhodes House Library, the Law Library, and a number of Oriental libraries were all dependencies of the Bodleian. Together, they employed more than 400 staff and absorbed 80 per cent of the Libraries' Board grant. To achieve co-ordination between all these libraries, and to make cost-effective a system which was more expensive than that of any other university in the country, was a formidable task, made more difficult because any proposal for reform or co-operation was seen simultaneously by the smaller libraries as a Bodleian takeover, and by the Bodleian as a threat to its unique international status.

Eventually, co-operation was forced on the system by the advent of automation. When I was first a Curator, the catalogue consisted of printed slips pasted into guardbooks by a team of ladies on high stools; even the card index was regarded by many of the staff and readers as an unhealthy transatlantic innovation. Paradoxically, the Bodleian had been one of the first libraries to see the advantages of automated catalogues, and a team had been working for years on the computerization of the pre-1920 catalogues. But the pioneering work had been overtaken and outdated by technological developments, and Bodley had by now fallen far behind many comparable libraries.

The main task of the Libraries' Board and its staff during my years as chairman was to establish a programme for computerizing the library system and building up a unified catalogue. Pilot schemes were carried out in three faculty libraries and gradually a unified catalogue began to emerge. But the intermediate period was chaotic, and when I left the Board the Bodleian had four catalogues in operation: a print-out of the pre-1920, incompletely computerized catalogue; guard books for the years 1920 to 1983; index cards for the 1983 to 1986 period; and computer terminals for current titles. Much more work was needed, and still is, to integrate all the catalogues and complete the programme we launched in those years.

In 1986 I acquired responsibilities for the production of books as well as for their preservation and access, as a Delegate of Oxford University Press. OUP is not an institution separate from the University – it is its publishing arm, and one of the most important vehicles by which the University carries out its educational mission. There are people in many parts of the world who know nothing of Oxford except its Press; and OUP's dictionary-makers have brought the University as much prestige as any of its faculties. The Delegates form the committee which is responsible to the University for the running of the Press; and of all the University committees on which I have served, the Delegacy was the most rewarding as well as the most demanding.

The University Press was once housed in the Clarendon Building (between the Bodleian and Broad Street) – built from the profits of the publication of Clarendon's *History of the Rebellion*. It long ago moved to larger premises in Walton Street but the Clarendon Building still houses the Delegates' Room, where the governing body of the Press meets every alternate Tuesday in term beneath an ample but indifferent portrait of Queen Anne. The Vice-Chancellor takes the chair, and the sixteen delegates wear gowns. Each is chosen for expertise in a particular subject; I was the delegate responsible for philosophy, though at various times I had some involvement, with one or two others, in the oversight of texts in theology, Classics, and music.

The main task of the Tuesday morning meetings is to approve a list of academic titles to go to contract. The actual work of commissioning, drawing up contracts, copy-editing, book production and marketing is of course the responsibility of professional publishers. But each subject editor works closely with the relevant delegate, discussing possible authors and topics, and choosing referees for manuscripts submitted. For most of my time the philosophy editor was Angela Blackburn, energetic and dedicated; we worked easily together in spite of (or perhaps because of) our rather different views about what constituted good philosophy. The subject Delegate saw all significant correspondence between editor, author, and referees. When a proposal was ripe for contract, a one-page summary of the title, with projected print run and necessary investment, was put before a Delegates' meeting; only after their approval could a contract be issued. Every book was categorized as green, red, or amber, according to whether it was likely, unlikely, or uncertain to recover its cost in its first year.

It was possible, in a two-hour meeting, to deal with sixty books or more. If referees were unambiguously in favour, and subject editor and Delegate agreed on the merits of a book, it went through on the nod. Discussion was prolonged only if there was disagreement among the experts, or political implications to the issuing of a contract. No time was wasted, but simply reading the papers and listening to the reports gave each Delegate a sense of what was happening in the forefront of other disciplines.

After a year I was put onto the Finance Committee, in effect the Board of Directors of this multi-million-pound international business. The Finance Committee had a very different ethos from the full Delegates' meeting. No gowns were worn at the meetings held monthly on Tuesday afternoons, not in the antique splendour of the Clarendon, but in a glossy office in Walton Street. The Committee contained half a dozen Delegates, plus two outside members with business experience (in my time, Tim Rix and Martin Jacomb); these were in effect the non-executive directors while the executive directors were the professional publishers who headed the different divisions of the Press. Much of the business of the Finance Committee concerned not the academic monographs and serials which were the main concern of the Delegates' meetings, but the more profitable areas of schools' educational publishing, English as a Foreign Language, and reference and general books.

During the 1970s the financial position of the Press was at times parlous, and the University gave much thought to how it could meet its commitments in the event of the Press being unable to satisfy all its creditors. During the 1980s, in the later years of George Richardson's period as chief executive, and particularly after Robin Denniston became Academic Publisher, the financial situation improved enormously, and the Press expanded and began to produce healthy annual surpluses, part of which were passed on to assist the University, the rest used to fund future investment. A project such as a new edition of the *Oxford English Dictionary*, or the *Dictionary of National Biography*, needs substantial investment over many years before any return will be seen.

The most important event during my time on the Finance Committee was the publication of the Second Edition of the *OED* in 1988, the culmination of five years' work and £8 million of investment. This was not a new edition, compiled as a single venture on unified principles; rather, it was an amalgamation of the original *Dictionary* begun by Sir James Murray with the several *Supplements* more recently edited by Robert Burchfield, plus 5,000 new words which had entered the language in the last few years. None the less, it was a magnificent achievement, and its twenty handsome volumes, plus the electronic version on CD-ROM, are the most treasured possession which I retain from my time as a Delegate. The same year saw the fourth edition of the highly profitable *Oxford Advanced Learner's Dictionary of Current English*, which became the most widely-used reference book for learners of the language. Overall turnover in that year was just under £120,000,000, with a surplus before tax of £9,500,000, and in subsequent years both turnover and surplus showed a large increase.

Before becoming a Delegate I had imagined that the Press's academic publishing programme was run at a loss, subsidized by more profitable operations of general and educational publishing. In fact, I discovered, the academic programme itself showed a modest annual surplus. This made some of us delegates uneasy, at a time when academic books were becoming more and more expensive for the hard-pressed academics who bought them, and a decision was taken at the last Finance Committee meeting I attended, that academic books should no longer attempt to show a surplus but should be published at cost. This had a benign effect on academic book prices in this country, and helped to halt a series of many years of price rises above the level of inflation.

OUP has a large number of branches overseas. The largest is OUP (USA), bigger in its own right than any American academic publisher. There are branches also in India, Canada, Australia, New Zealand, Malaysia, Singapore, Hong Kong and eastern and southern Africa. In 1988 Sir Roger Elliott, who had recently become the Chief Executive of OUP, having been chairman of the Finance Committee for thirteen years previously, asked me to assist him in reaching a decision whether the Press should continue to operate in South Africa; my Balliol experience was, perhaps, thought to be relevant. (After many unsatisfactory skirmishes with Barclays about the activities of their South Africa branch, as related elsewhere, Balliol finally closed its account in February 1986 and moved to the Co-Operative Bank. Shortly afterwards, Barclays decided to sever their connection with South Africa. I wondered whether the College should then return its custom – but the bursars found the service from their new bank so superior that they stayed put.)

Many of the staff of OUP, and some of the delegates, were uncomfortable that the Press maintained a South Africa branch, and felt it should be closed down as long as apartheid lasted; others were well aware that the Press was performing a valuable service in producing badly needed textbooks for black schools. The Finance Committee was genuinely uncertain how to proceed, and we decided to take advice from some of the most senior opponents of apartheid. Roger and I went to see Archbishop Tutu when he visited London, and I telephoned Oliver Tambo, then in Sweden.

The advice we received was conflicting. The Archbishop, who used then to refer to himself as 'Mr Sanctions', saw the issue in terms of the

economic boycott: the Press's presence in South Africa was a violation
of this, and therefore should be brought to an end. Tambo, on the other
hand, gave priority to the educational needs of the majority community,
judging the matter in terms of the academic, rather than the economic,
boycott. The ANC had at one time favoured an academic boycott; but
it was now, he told me, about to announce a relaxation of this policy
which would be ample to accommodate the Press's activities.

In the light of this we decided to keep the branch open, but to set up
a local advisory committee in South Africa to alert the Trustees to any
undesirable political implications of their publications. One of those
who accepted an invitation to join this committee was Wieland Gevers,
now Cabinet Secretary to the Mandela government. Archbishop Tutu,
when I reminded him in 1994 of the advice he had given, agreed with
hindsight that it would have been a remarkable piece of bad timing if
OUP, having operated throughout the years of the Nationalist government, had pulled out just on the eve of a new South Africa.

My first contacts with the ANC had begun not long before this OUP
consultation. In 1985 a South African friend, Ann Yates, who had long
lived in Oxford, suggested some of us should start an organization to
help train exiled members of the ANC for the kinds of job they would
be doing once they began to take their rightful part in the government
of their country. I was initially sceptical. Was there any likelihood of the
ANC exiles having a part in running South Africa in the foreseeable
future? Even if there was, would they welcome any intervention in their
affairs by amateurs in Oxford? But Ann persisted, and converted to her
project others with real experience of the struggle against apartheid,
David Astor and Anthony Sampson, who in 1986 began discussions
with Oliver Tambo; the project began to take shape.

We quickly discovered that the ANC were not short of members who
were, in an academic sense, highly trained – in Lusaka alone there were
some 2,000 Ph.Ds, many of them from Eastern European universities.
The problem was finding an opportunity for them to validate and exercise these qualifications in an appropriate professional capacity, in
advance of their eventual return to South Africa. The ANC called it 'the
parking problem', and Tambo and his colleagues welcomed our offer to
assist. The Southern African Advanced Education Project was set up in
1986 'to provide practical training and experience for black South
Africans and to prepare people against the day when they would be
needed for key roles in a new South Africa'.

A Trust was set up, chaired by James Cornford; I became one of the
founding Trustees, and was happy to provide accommodation in Balliol
Lodgings for committee meetings and other SAAEP gatherings. I

invited Adelaide Tambo to luncheon in the College to finalize some details before the Trust deed was signed, and she was very pleased about the way in which we intended to proceed. But at the end of luncheon she asked me, 'Are you not worried about working closely with the ANC? Don't you feel you might lose your job?' 'How do you mean?' I asked her. 'Well, Mrs Thatcher doesn't like us very much, you know.' I responded that I didn't like Mrs Thatcher much, either, but that fortunately the government had not yet arrogated to itself the power to hire and fire the heads of Oxford colleges.

Ann Yates became the first director of SAAEP, and what she and her colleagues were able to achieve went far beyond the initial hopes even of the optimists among the Trustees. SAAEP Fellows, chosen on advice from the ANC and other anti-apartheid organizations, were funded for professional qualifications, or found placements with local authorities, national utilities, community sports organizations, newspapers, radio broadcasting stations. Private industry, at first rather suspicious of the ANC, became more welcoming to our Fellows after the Cummins Engine Company showed the way. Group courses were set up for future civil servants and diplomats; on one occasion it seemed as if almost the entire overseas representation of the ANC was assembled in Wadham College. The Trustees and officers of SAAEP worked hard at fund-raising, and found it was not difficult to fire the imagination of benefactors, both public and private. Contrary to Mrs Tambo's fears the government, or at least the Overseas Development Agency under Chris Patten, proved itself very sympathetic once it learned what SAAEP was doing. By the time I ceased to be a Trustee, in 1992, SAAEP had an annual income of about £1 million, and in addition to group courses had sponsored nearly 200 individual Fellows on tailor-made training and work experience courses of between three months and two years. When the Trust was wound up in 1995, 700 individuals had benefited from its practical programmes.

Events in South Africa moved much faster than any of us had imagined, and many SAAEP Fellows were able to return home and make their contribution to the new order of things. In the first free elections in April 1994, five Fellows were elected to the National Assembly, six to provincial assemblies, and nine were among the first appointments to the new multiracial civil service.

But in 1987 that all seemed a long way away, and my attention was taken up more with the problems of rich and poor in Oxford University than with rich and poor in South Africa.

The wealth of the different colleges in Oxford varies greatly, and there has long been in operation a system of taxation of the richer for the benefit of the poorer, overseen by a committee of Council called the College Contributions Committee. This consists of representatives of the richer, donor colleges, balanced by representatives of the poorer, recipient colleges; it is normally chaired by the head of a college somewhere in the middle of the league table.

Balliol answered to this description, with an annual income in the mid 1980s of about £2 million. In an article in the *Financial Times* at the end of 1985 I claimed that, considered as a business, the College was pretty efficient:

> If Balliol is judged in managerial terms, I do not think it need be ashamed of its record. Workplace relations are excellent: our academic staff work hard and happily for half the salary their skills could command elsewhere; our administrative, technical and domestic staff have not lost a single hour through industrial action in recorded history. In the detestable jargon of productivity, we can claim, perhaps not with any great pride, that in 1985 we processed 501 students in plant which in 1935 catered for 274.
>
> We have a pupil–tutor ratio of 10.9 to 1. Moreover, the amount we have to teach our pupils increases year by year, as new discoveries are made, new theories propounded, new evidence brought to light. One of our economics tutors says he now has to teach his pupils for their preliminary examination the amount of material he had to cover for his finals papers two decades ago. The increased teaching burden has not inhibited scholarship and research; during the past academic year we produced between us nineteen books and many papers in learned journals.

Efficient or not, Balliol was certainly neither very rich nor very poor; accordingly, I was asked to chair the College Contributions Committee in 1987. Since previous agreements were about to run out, the Committee was asked to review the whole taxation system, to see whether it should be ended or whether a new generation of taxes should be imposed.

We invited colleges which felt they were still insufficiently endowed to submit their case, along with detailed accounts. The bursars of the wealthy All Souls and Merton, who were members of our committee, scrutinized these accounts with great care. Heads and bursars of petitioning colleges were invited to give evidence, and vivaed ruthlessly to discover whether any income was being understated or concealed, and how far current poverty was the result of inefficient management or injudicious investment. Never having been a bursar, I found it a most educational experience to chair these eyeball-to-eyeball confrontations between donor bursars and beggar bursars.

In the end, even the hardest-nosed members of our committee were convinced of the case for another round of taxation, partly to remedy the chronic under-endowment of some of the poorer colleges, but also to cushion the government cuts in University grant-in-aid which were being passed on to the colleges in the shape of reduced funding for joint appointments. The burden of new taxation would fall predominantly on six wealthy colleges; All Souls and Merton, represented on our committee, were behind our recommendations; St John's and Christ Church were willing to go along with them; Queen's and Magdalen, however, set their faces against the rates of tax we had proposed, proving impervious to persuasion. At a cold December meeting the Vice-Chancellor's pleas to the Bursar of Magdalen to accept the proposals were met with an offensive rebuff.

Though Council had the power to fix the tax rates without the consent of the colleges, its proposals might be defeated in Congregation, if objecting colleges wheeled out all their members to vote against. Even if the proposals were carried, the colleges might go to law against the University. The possible outcome of this was uncertain; but the case would be costly. So we gave in, and accepted a compromise tax rate somewhere between our original position and Magdalen's – it was one more example of Oxford's vulnerability, in the absence of a Senate of Colleges able to bind its members, to obstruction by maverick institutions.

A happier instance of co-operation between colleges and University was the launching of Campaign for Oxford. Initially it was feared, with good reason, that the colleges might oppose a central University funding appeal as likely to reduce contributions by alumni to individual colleges. By assiduous courtship of Heads of Houses, Sir Patrick Neill persuaded all to sign a document inviting contributions to the Campaign.

In 1988, however, the University passed up a great opportunity. All fund-raisers know that it is helpful to pin an appeal to a historic event, such as a centenary. No one knows when the centenaries of Oxford's foundation occur, since no one knows when the University was founded, and indeed there may be no single event which can claim to be its foundation. But there is one which is undoubtedly the first dated event in its history: Gerald of Wales, fund-raising for a Crusade, visited Oxford in Lent 1188, and tells us that there he read his works to the assembled doctors of all the faculties. I suggested to the Vice-Chancellor that he should therefore declare 1988 the eighth centenary of the University, and make the Campaign a Centenary Appeal.

The Vice-Chancellor took advice from the learned Sir Richard Southern, who proclaimed Gerald of Wales a notorious liar. Not wishing to put out a false prospectus, the Vice-Chancellor vetoed my proposal for an eight-hundredth-anniversary celebration. It was, I think, a pity: even if Gerald didn't actually read his works in Oxford, his words are evidence of the existence of the University at that time – it is no use boasting, even falsely, of a visit to a University if that University does not exist.

Gerald's History of Ireland, the work in question, still repays reading. It begins as follows: 'The two islands of Britain and Ireland are so close to each other that on a fine day from this side you can see the other side. But from the other side, because of the greater distance, it is not possible to see this side.' Whatever has happened to Oxford University in the succeeding eight centuries, it is clear that the Irish joke has not changed.

19

Visitors and Chancellors

THE PATRON SAINT of Balliol is St Catherine of Alexandria. She is also the patron saint of all philosophers, having, according to legend, refuted the arguments of the 300 pagan philosophers sent by her imperial suitor Maximian to convert her from Christianity. Balliol's dedication to St Catherine seems to have arisen from the devotion of the Lady Dervorguilla, and her feast day, 25 November, has for many centuries been celebrated with a banquet in the College, open since 1897, unlike most College feasts, to students as well as dons. Each year a guest of honour is invited to address the gathering, and a final-year scholar proposes the health of the guest, customarily in a form which falls well short of flattery.

In the years of student revolt we at High Table would wait, in some trepidation, to hear the scholar's speech: it was a marvellous opportunity for insult beyond the bounds of convention, or for political barracking from the junior tables. But though we often held our breath, successive feasts passed off without incident, and the most controversial speech heard on a St Catherine's night dinner came not from the scholar but from the invited guest.

In November 1985 the guest of honour was Denis Healey. It was at the height of the AIDS scare, and some dons worried whether it was safe to continue with the St Catherine's night tradition of passing a silver loving cup from hand to hand and mouth to mouth to drink the toast *Floreat Domus de Balliolo*. I made inquiries of the chaplain and the College doctor. The chaplain told me that no case was known of AIDS being spread by the use of the Communion cup in Anglican churches; the College doctor said that though there were seventeen diseases you could catch from a loving cup, AIDS was not one of them. I therefore instructed that the custom was to continue as usual – but rashly told Denis of the inquiries I had made and the reassurances I had received. When his (excellent) speech was drawing to a close he said, 'And now it is time for the loving cup. The Master tells me that there is a one in seventeen chance of catching AIDS by drinking from it: but such is my trust in the Master's heterosexuality that I am happy to share it with him.' Next day I received angry letters from gay and lesbian groups in the JCR protesting about the insult to their sexuality. (A year later the minority groups got their revenge: the JCR passed a motion outlawing 'frolicking and pseudo-affectionate activity' – intended, I was told, to curb rampant heterosexuality among junior members.)

In the same month I paid a flying visit to Rome to join my former classmates at the English College in celebrating the thirtieth anniversary of their (and my) ordination to the priesthood. The festivities were presided over by Jack Kennedy, now Rector of the English College. In December Nancy and I were invited to Arundel Castle to celebrate the enthronment of my old friend Cormac Murphy O'Connor as Bishop of Arundel and Brighton.

Christmas that year was a worrying time, since Robert had reached the stage of applying to university. The period during and after Cambridge interviews was, Nancy wrote to her mother, 'the worst part of our parenting since Charles's dyslexia'. But by the time the boys and I went skiing in January we were able to celebrate his admission to read mathematics at Trinity College.

Every Oxbridge college has a Visitor with jurisdiction over the Head and Fellows and students, empowered to settle disputes between them. Most colleges have a Visitor specified in the statutes: Oriel, for instance, has the Queen as Visitor, St John's has the Bishop of Winchester. Balliol is unusual among the colleges of Oxford in enjoying the privilege of electing its own Visitor, and it has been customary to elect a senior Balliol judge. When I first came to the college the Visitor was Lord Pearson of Minnedosa; for most of my time as Master, Lord Kilbrandon. According to the Statutes a new Master must be presented to the Visitor of the College before he can exercise any of the powers of his office. When I was taken by the Senior Fellow from the Chapel to the Lodgings to greet Jim Kilbrandon, in order to be made an honest Master, it was the beginning of an extremely happy relationship, both personally and throughout the judicial and political issues described elsewhere.

If things go badly in a college, the powers of the Visitor are very important. Only he can resolve disputes between Master and Fellows about interpretation of the Statutes, for instance. But just as a happy country has no history, so a happy college has no Visitations. We were proud at Balliol that at no time during Kilbrandon's Visitorship was he ever called upon to resolve a dispute among its members. But he was always ready with informal advice when consulted on legal issues; provided our procedures were honest and open, he would always argue for simplification and the abolition of red tape.

At the end of 1985 Jim announced that the time had come for him to retire. It did not take long to think of an appropriate successor. Tom Bingham had proceeded from distinction to distinction in the law ever since, as a young barrister, producing a much admired report on sanctions-busting in Rhodesia. He was now one of the most respected High Court judges, and though it was a little unusual for the Visitor to be younger than the Master, I had no hesitation in proposing his name to Governing Body, where it was received with acclamation. At a luncheon at Buck's in February I secured the endorsement of Harold Macmillan, who was our most senior Honorary Fellow as well as Chancellor of the University. Tom was formally elected by the College in April, to take over in October.

In the spring of 1986 I went to Pakistan as the Azfar Visiting Fellow. Kamal Azfar had gone home to a career at the Bar after reading PPE at Balliol in 1958–60. He was the Sindh Minister of Finance during the government of Z.K. Bhutto, but retired into private life during military rule in Pakistan. He had endowed a visiting Lectureship, in memory of his brother, which was to bring a Balliol Fellow to Pakistan each year.

Shortly before our departure one of Robert's teenage friends took his own life, and as Nancy did not wish to leave our son alone at such a time, I travelled by myself.

On arrival at Islamabad I was, for the first time in my life, delivered to the VIP Lounge, but hardly had time to savour the pleasures of walking swiftly past the immigration queue when I discovered the downside of VIP treatment: since you do not collect your own luggage, the odds on its being lost increase. My suitcases were nowhere to be found. By the time I had filled out the necessary forms, passengers who had gone through the normal procedures were well out of the airport.

Kamal Azfar arrived to rescue me, and we flew on to Lahore, where I was given a change of underwear so that I could at least be clean when I went to buy replacement clothes. Western dress was hard to find, so I settled for a shalwar. It was not a bad costume for visiting the delights of the city – the Shalimar gardens, the Badshahi Mosque, the Lahore Fort. It was my first encounter with Mogul architecture, and I was overwhelmed. Most enchanting of all was a visit to the Tomb of Jahangir. We arrived after closing time, and were allowed in only after bribing the custodian. But it was money well spent. The tomb must be beautiful at any time, but it was awesome in twilit solitude, the silence broken only by the screeching of kites.

Later that night we flew to Karachi, and Kamal installed me in the Sindh Club, a massive relic of the British Raj, with a beautiful garden and the grandest (but now driest) bar I have ever seen. The next day I was to carry out the duties of the Azfar Fellow – newspaper interviews, followed by the Jawed Memorial Lecture. To my great relief, my own clothes arrived from Islamabad just in time for me to face the 400-strong audience.

I addressed the topic of my lecture – the relationship between Church and State – at an abstract level of theology and philosophy, and was careful to draw all my concrete examples from Christian contexts, but I knew the subject was currently one of burning concern in Pakistan. Translated into Muslim terms, the burden of my lecture was the importance of drawing a distinction between personal devotion to Islam, and the Islamization of the institutions of state. In the discussion afterward, journalists pressed me to make the very applications to Sharia law which I had been careful to avoid in the lecture. Kamal had warned me of the minefield; to judge by the newspaper reports the next day, I had managed to tread through it without causing any explosion.

Immediately after the lecture I was driven to an audience with the Governor of Sindh. A no-nonsense military man, he urged me, on my return to Britain, to ensure that the BBC broadcast no more reports on riots in Pakistan, which, in his view, only contributed to civil disorder. I did my best to explain that I neither could, nor would wish to, alter the policy of the World Service. Even so, I was loaded with gifts on my departure.

At Kamal's house I met his wife Naheed, who in a remarkable way combined a vigorous business career with the old-fashioned skills both Western and Eastern males continue to expect from their wives. The dinner party over which she presided included Christians and Muslims, Parsees and Hindus, princesses and diplomats, politicians and academics, businessmen and mystics. The most vivid impression I took away from that evening, and from my entire time in Karachi, was of the high literary culture of the political class in Pakistan. Over dinner, poems were recited and critically discussed in several languages. I recited some Gerard Manley Hopkins, but felt out of my depth once the discussion turned to a comparison between his work and that of Iranian lyric poets.

My brief after-dinner speech fulfilled the obligations of the Azfar visit; henceforth, my time in Pakistan was sheer holiday – but it contributed a great deal to my education, and never has a lecture been so handsomely rewarded. I was to be driven into the Karakoram Mountains, up the newly completed highway, with Kamal as my guide. From

Islamabad we drove to Taxila, to the museum where the coins and arte-facts of the Buddhist kings who were descendants of Alexander the Great's generals record the marvellous encounter of Greek and Indian culture in the last centuries before Christ. From there we drove to a motel in Swat, the former kingdom of the Wali immortalized by Edward Lear.

Next morning we were taken to the palace of the current Wali who, though deprived of his kingdom, still held court with an establishment of 30 guards and 70 servants. An elderly, courtly, country gentleman, he welcomed us to a copious breakfast. I exclaimed over the bee-shaped honey pot, thinking it the work of skilled local craftsmen. 'Yes,' said the Wali proudly, 'I ordered it specially from Mappin and Webb.'

Having paid our respects to his grandfather's shrine and visited his summer palace, we took our leave of the Wali and headed towards the Shangla Pass. We soon left spring behind in the beautiful Swat plains, driving up a winding road through mud, snow and rocks to the junction at Basham where, over lunch, we had our first breathtaking view of the Karakoram Range. By evening we reached the Shangri-La Motel at Chilas where my room had a spectacular view over the Indus river.

Our next day's journey took us through desolate moonscape to Janglot. Here, the nature of the road changed. The Karakoram Highway follows the old Silk Route through the Indus valley to China, through terrain of high military significance where in the nineteenth century the three Emperors of Russia, China, and India (i.e., Queen Victoria) strove to obtain supremacy over Afghanistan. In the present century its strate-gic importance has been derived from the corridor linking Communist China with Communist Russia. When the highway was planned, American engineers invited to tender for its construction looked at the chasms it would have to cross, and declared it impossible. The Chinese Army stepped in to fill the gap, and from Janglot up to the Khunjerab Pass, where Pakistan joins China, the road bears the marks of Chinese workmanship, particularly in the decoration of the bridges over gorges. Many lives were lost in the building of the road, but the Chinese Muslims in the construction teams were told that if they died they would go straight to Paradise since they were involved in a holy enter-prise, or Jihad.

After the parched drive from Chilas through Janglot it was a delight to reach Gilgit, which resembled a village in the Langdales, raised to the power of ten. From Gilgit to Karimabad the drive was miserable, but well worth the pain: Hunza, of which Karimabad is the capital, turned out to be a fairy-tale kingdom, full of blossom and greenery after the desert, with still-sleepy poplars looking, at this time of year, like quills on a hibernating porcupine. The people of Hunza, though small in stature, were cheerful and stately, and wore the most beautiful embroidered cloaks.

After Gilgit the Karakoram Highway goes on to the Chinese border at Khunjerab. Soon after leaving Gilgit, however, we were told that the road was closed for military reasons. We returned to Gilgit through enchanting rows of lights illuminating the hillside in honour of the birthday of the Caliph Ali, the great Shi'ite feast.

On our way back to Chilas we had our first real view of Nanga Parbat, facing the Karakoram Range, twice as high as anything I have ever seen in the Alps. Since the tree-line here is also twice as high as the Alpine tree line, the mountain did not *look* any higher than Mont Blanc; but even so I was happy to worship it from the banks of the Indus, where Kamal and I picnicked and discussed the pros and cons of his returning to public life in the Pakistan government.

The descending drive was something of an anticlimax. At Thakot the Chinese contribution to the highway ends, and the surface deteriorated. Our driver, a veteran of service in both British and Pakistan armies, told us the British Imperial administration had been the most efficient one in his lifetime – would he have said the same if Kamal's guest had been a senior Pakistani official? We had a delicious meal in Abbottabad, named after Sir James Abbott, first deputy Commissioner of the province, and much beloved of Muslims. Kamal tried to persuade me that he had been a Balliol man, but in fact he joined the Bengal Artillery at sixteen.

We returned, not to Islamabad but to Rawalpindi, where we were entertained to dinner, with a number of distinguished guests from three continents, by the Speaker of the National Assembly, elected to his post in the teeth of President Zia's disapproval. At this dinner I made the mistake, after a very hot curry, of sipping the drinking water. This destroyed my comfort on the flight back to Heathrow early the following morning, but once restored to health I regarded my visit to Pakistan as one of the most remarkable experiences of my life.

As a consolation prize for missing the Pakistan trip I took Nancy to Venice for a brief holiday at the end of the Easter vacation. There we read of the American bombing of Libya and the shelling of Lampedusa. Charles subsequently went to a sit-down protest outside the American Embassy in Grosvenor Square, sent off full of instructions such as 'write the telephone number of the Legal Advice Centre on your arm'; but the event passed off peacefully with no arrests. The most visible consequence of the Libyan action was a comparative absence of American tourists in Europe that year. Later in the spring I was awarded an honorary degree by Denison University in Ohio. Asked to give the Commemoration Address, I took the opportunity to explain why the American action had been unpopular with many of their allies, and also to urge my audience not to be afraid to come to Britain as usual. I echoed Mrs Thatcher: 'We miss your friendly faces.'

The spring of 1986 saw a stream of distinguished foreign visitors to Oxford: I helped to entertain the Prime Minister of Israel, the King of Spain, the Speaker of the Pakistan Assembly, and the Secretary General of the United Nations, Perez de Cuellar. The most memorable of these visits, however, was during the official visit to Britain of Hu Yaobang, the General Secretary of the Central Committee of the Communist Party of China. The Thursdays of official and state visits are customarily left free of London engagements, for an expedition at the discretion of the visitor, and Secretary Hu expressed a wish to spend his free day being entertained in Oxford. Sir Patrick Neill, the Vice-Chancellor, quickly sensing that this had the potential for being a very sticky occasion, decreed that so important a visit must be hosted not by a mere Vice-Chancellor, but by the Chancellor (Harold Macmillan, now Lord Stockton) himself. This was a neat piece of footwork: it meant that the responsibility for the entertainment fell not on his college, All Souls, but on the Chancellor's – Balliol.

So it was fixed that we would entertain the Chinese party in Balliol Hall on Thursday, 10 June. I had a full week: I was bidden to the official dinner at 10 Downing Street the day before (no doubt so that I could see how this kind of thing should be done) and to another at the Chinese Embassy the day following (no doubt in gracious return of hospitality).

Our Bursar and staff were sure that the dinner would be worthy of the occasion, but the Foreign Office began to take a keen interest in our preparations. They insisted that food and drink and company were not enough. We must also exhibit the riches of British culture: they would provide a team of first-rate actors and musicians to entertain the guests for an hour after dinner.

From the outset, we at Balliol were very dubious about the wisdom of this, not wholly reassured even by the calibre of the actors – Jeremy Irons, for instance, had been commissioned. There was to be a programme of verse and music to illustrate the eleven ages of man.

The arrangements at the Downing Street dinner were admirable, Mrs Thatcher a warm and affable hostess. I took the occasion to ask the advice of Mr Denis Thatcher. Did he think it a good idea to end the morrow's proceedings with a cultural event? He listened wide-eyed to the proposed programme. 'Get it stopped!' he said. 'I have done this job for seven bloodstained years, and I can tell you that the last thing you want when you are on a foreign tour is an hour of culture late at night, in a language you don't understand.'

Delighted by the sound sense of these remarks, I telephoned the FCO next morning to tell them the cultural event must be cancelled: I had had instructions, I said, from 10 Downing Street. But my bluff was quickly called. Would I mind telling them exactly who in Number 10 had given those instructions? The cultural event was to go ahead as planned.

The dinner was as prickly as expected. All communication was through an interpreter. The Chancellor, indeed, seemed to get on well enough with the aged Hu Yaobang, who was refreshed at frequent intervals from a bottle of ginseng. But I was next to Li Peng, whom I found very difficult. At one point I risked a joke. I hoped, I said, that official visits to Balliol did not bring bad luck: the Speaker of Pakistan who had been with us lately had lost his job shortly after returning home. I could tell from the interpreter's face that this had gone down extremely badly. I had to stammer that of course no such outcome could possibly be imagined in the case of the present distinguished visitors.

At last dinner ended, all of us, guests and hosts, were ready for bed. But no, there was the cultural event. By the time we got to the third age of man our guests were becoming visibly impatient. The Chancellor leant behind his neighbour to whisper, 'Can we not summon the Proctors' men and eject these strolling players?' A hapless University official was deputed to negotiate with the entertainers, who eventually agreed to cut the eleven ages to six. Jeremy Irons, insulted, bounded down the steps of the Hall, brushing aside autograph hunters. The Chinese guests leapt into their official cars the instant the actors disappeared. The Vice-Chancellor and I collapsed on the sofa in the Lodgings. 'Do you think', I asked, 'that we have done more harm or good to Anglo-Chinese relations?' 'We won't know', he said, 'until we open tomorrow's newspapers and find out whether or not they have declared war.'

The next day, however, I was very courteously entertained to an elegant but rather more expeditious dinner at the Chinese Embassy, an occasion marred only by Mr Thatcher losing his footing, at a early stage of the evening, on the over-polished floors. It was a poor reward for his wise, if neglected, advice earlier in the week.

The Chinese dinner was one of the last great occasions attended by Lord Stockton as Chancellor. He was prevented by a chest infection from opening the Dellal Building on the Master's Field later in June and

Lord Kilbrandon deputized for him, as I did at the centenary celebrations at St Hugh's.

He was able to attend the Balliol Society Dinner at which Lord Kilbrandon handed over to Sir Thomas Bingham the Visitorship of the College. We were delighted that our high opinion of Bingham was apparently shared by the Lord Chancellor, who had just made him a Lord Justice of Appeal. At the dinner, I recalled my long friendship with the retiring Visitor.

> It has been one of the great privileges of being Master that gradually I became a personal friend of the Visitor. From time to time we would share in the pleasant task of entertaining the Chancellor on his visits to the College. The Visitor, however, was a man of more regular hours than myself. I well remember one night when he withdrew, shortly after midnight, leaving me with the Chancellor to gossip into the small hours. 'That is the trouble with judges,' said Lord Stockton. 'No stamina any more.'

The summer of 1986 was a busy one. For his gap year before Cambridge in October 1987 Robert had been accepted as a staffer in the office of Senator Paul Sarbanes of Maryland. We went, as a family, to stay with Nancy's parents during the summer, then Nancy and I drove to Washington to deliver Robert into the formidable corridors of the New Senate Building. We also paid another visit to Bill Coolidge and learnt of his plans to arrange a series of academic exchanges between Balliol and Massachusetts Institute of Technology.

In July, Nancy and I had been invited to Buckingham Palace during the State Visit of the new President of Germany, Dr Richard von Weizsäcker. I had first met him while he was still Burgomeister of Berlin, at a luncheon organized by the Foreign Secretary, Sir Geoffrey Howe. Surprised to be included, I discovered that Dr von Weizsäcker regarded himself as an old member of Balliol. Flattered but slightly puzzled, I later asked for the College archives to be searched to discover in what way Balliol could claim him as an alumnus.

We could not find any record of Dr von Weizsäcker's having been matriculated as a member of Balliol. I was saddened, as I wished to propose him for an Honorary Fellowship, and we had a rule that no one but a former alumnus could be elected. However, it seemed that at the suggestion of his uncle, a friend of A.D. Lindsay in the 1930s, he had spent Trinity Term of 1937 as a guest of a Balliol/Trinity chemistry lecturer, visiting the College for tutorials in English, international law, and history. All of us on Governing Body were admirers of the new president, and after an animated discussion we decided it would not be a disastrous precedent if we opened the Fellowship to heads of state who believed – even if not quite accurately – that they had once been junior members of the College. Accordingly, and to universal acclaim, President von Wiezsäcker was elected an Honorary Fellow in 1987.

President Cossiga of Italy was also a lover of Oxford. A keen scholar and admirer of the works of Cardinal Newman, he delighted in spending time at Oriel; but he also liked to visit Balliol, aware of its important, if ambiguous, role in the Oxford Movement. As we took our coffee after luncheon in the Lodgings during a visit he paid to the College in November 1986, a group of students with a banner could be seen in the quad below. The President wondered which Italian political issue had caused the demonstration; I explained that it was a purely local grievance. For security reasons, Governing Body had decided to end the policy of leaving the front gate open all night. The JCR objected, and the banner read 'Keep Balliol Open'. The President seemed pleased, if rather puzzled, that they appeared to wish to enlist him as an ally.

When Nancy and I entertained the President at home, at The King's Mound, he wrote a most gracious thank-you letter, comparing his visit to Erasmus's to Sir Thomas More's house in Chelsea. I was immensely flattered; Nancy, remembering Erasmus's unflattering description of Dame Alice ('neither a girl nor a pearl'), was less inclined to boast of the compliment.

Sadly, during the last months of 1986 Lord Stockton's health continued to decline. When first I became Master he had been an occasional visitor to the Lodgings, whether as one of the oldest alumni of Balliol, or as Chancellor of the University. In the latter capacity he had presided over the celebrations of the eightieth anniversary of the foundation of the Rhodes Scholarships, and had charmed alumni from all over the word by the vigour of his intellect, the shrewdness of his judgement, and the impishness of his wit.

As the years went on, he became a more and more frequent guest in my Lodgings. While John Sparrow was Warden of All Souls, Macmillan had commonly been his guest, but he did not find the All Souls Lodgings so congenial after Sparrow's departure. 'Can't move anywhere without meeting young ladies with tennis rackets,' he complained, referring to the daughters of Warden Neill, whom he nicknamed, rather unfairly, Mr Quiverful. When first I became Master, Nancy and I had planned to entertain him at home, at The King's Mound, and had indeed furnished one bedroom after what we imagined was his taste; but he preferred the quasi-bachelor establishment in the old Lodgings, and became a very regular guest, whether attending University or College functions.

After College dinners he would sit on for hours in the common room, surrounded by dons and students and old members; perhaps at twelve or one he would progress to the Lodgings, but he was always reluctant to go to bed and often he and I would sit and talk alone for another hour or two, of books and people, of heroes and villains of history and of common friends at the present time, and perhaps most of all of men and women who were history to me but still living as friends in his memory. We shared an admiration for the novels of Anthony Trollope and the sermons of Ronald Knox; and as the night drew on he would talk as if I too could remember those Edwardian years which were for him the golden days of Balliol.

He took a keen interest in the history of the College. I once told him that the portrait of Lord Lindsay showed signs of decay, and had more than once needed to be returned to the artist, Lawrence Gowing, for a recolouring of the nose, which exhibited an embarrassing tendency to turn red over the years. 'Ah,' he said, 'what a pity Balliol is not in Naples: there would be constant pilgrimages to see the Miracle of the Rubrefaction of the Master's Nose.' Late one evening he said to me, 'Master, you will be remembered as the Jowett of the twentieth century.' No doubt, on similar occasions, he made the same compliments, *mutatis mutandis*, to the other Heads of Houses of his University.

After a long, late night he could be capable of rising smartly for early chapel. But on other occasions, especially if he had a second Oxford engagement on a succeeding evening, he might lie abed until the afternoon. I recall one such day when I was giving a small pre-luncheon party to celebrate the achievements of another of our Honorary Fellows. The noise of this decorous festivity must have penetrated across the landing of the Lodgings into the bedroom, for suddenly there shuffled into the drawing-room a familiar figure in dressing-gown and slippers. Lord Stockton took a chair in the middle of the room and quickly became the centre of attraction. As the official guest of honour was taken away to luncheon, Lord Stockton looked around the room with sober satisfaction. 'What a magnificent scene of debauchery,' he said. 'Master – Chancellor all unbraced – empty champagne bottles as far as the eye can see.'

I felt a sense of personal loss when he died at the end of 1986. I had been one of the last Oxford friends to visit him in his final illness at Birch Grove; I was one of three pro-Vice-Chancellors to represent Oxford at his funeral, and I read the lesson from First Corinthians at his memorial service in the University Church of St Mary's on 7 February 1987.

No sooner was the old Chancellor dead than speculation began about his successor. In the car back to Oxford from the country funeral, the Vice-Chancellor and the pro Vice-Chancellors (who included Lord Blake) mentioned a number of names. Archbishop Runcie? Sir Edward Heath? Lord Scarman? Lord Jenkins? Lord Carrington? We waited to see who would put their hats into the ring.

Quite early on, Roy Jenkins let it be known that he would like to stand. I greeted the announcement with enthusiasm; Nancy and I had known the Jenkinses since the 1983 luncheon to celebrate the founding of the Social Democrats with a Balliol party leader. I was sure Roy would be a popular candidate, and I was very happy to endorse him.

But before I could do so, news was brought that Ted Heath also intended to stand. This was sad news. I was fond of Ted and admired the magnanimity he had shown to a Balliol which had sorely tried his patience, but I was sure he had no real chance of being elected, and did not want him to be wounded yet again after all he had had to suffer during the Thatcher government. I approached a number of his close friends, urging them to dissuade him from standing; but to no avail.

This altered the situation. If among the serious contenders for the Chancellorship there were to be not one but two Honorary Fellows of Balliol, then neither I nor the College could officially endorse one or the other. In the circumstances Governing Body decided that the appropriate course was for the College, remaining neutral between the candidates, to offer each of them, impartially, such assistance as they might require from the College Office. This was not of course intended to prevent individual Fellows and members from campaigning vigorously for the candidate of their choice, and both Heath and Jenkins found eloquent champions among our Fellows and Honorary Fellows.

During the Chancellorship election Balliol was the subject of much press interest. For instance, the *Independent* wanted to know whether Balliol was running buses for their old members to vote? No, Balliol was confident their old members could get from London without the College's assistance. Was the University shut down so that all could campaign for the candidates? No, all was normal and the main topic of conversation was the government cuts in academic funding.

The third candidate for the Chancellorship was Lord Blake, the Provost of Queen's. He was encouraged to stand by the Vice-Chancellor, who believed, quite mistakenly, that he would be seen as an academic, non-political candidate. In fact, Blake was seen as the Thatcherite Conservative candidate, a counter-weight to Heath, who was drawing a great deal of support from Labour dons. The situation was complicated, but the political realities not really altered, when at a late stage Downing Street began to advise Conservative members of Convocation to vote for Heath as the party member most likely to win, a move which deeply wounded Lord Blake but had little effect on the eventual outcome. I summarized the contest, in a suitably partisan tone, in my annual letter to Balliol old members.

> The Chancellorship struggle was an uneven one if viewed – and how else is there to view it? – as a contest between Balliol and the rest of the University. The third serious contender, Lord Blake, was Provost of Queen's and an Honorary Student of Christ Church. This meant, naturally, that for his war-chest he could feel entitled to draw upon two of the richest colleges in Oxford. Balliol, a comparatively poor College, had two candidates to support single-handed and must face the prospect of a divided vote amongst its alumni. None the less, as the world now knows, the College emerged tri-umphant. Some three out of four votes cast were for Balliol candidates, and the Rt Hon. Roy Jenkins became the fifth Balliol Chancellor out of the last eight holders of the office. As he thanked his supporters in the OCR in the evening of the election, he told them that he was doing so on the exact spot where in 1939 he had made his acceptance speech as President of the Balliol JCR. When the result of the election was declared, the College's impartial support for its two candidates was metaphysically transmuted into unani-mous welcome to the successful candidate.

I was delighted by Roy's election, though I sympathized with his rival's disappointment. Ted was taking tea with his supporters in our Lodgings when the result was declared; and the embarrassment was heightened when our son Charles, who had been deputed to run from the Proctors' office to communicate the result as soon as the votes were counted, confused the figures and mistakenly told Ted he had come second (not, as it turned out, third) in the overall vote. Later in the evening the Chancellor-Elect celebrated with his supporters at a cham-pagne party in the Old Common Room.

By tradition, a new Chancellor is entitled to award a dozen or so hon-orary degrees shortly after election. On 20 October Lord Jenkins con-ferred degrees on the King of the Belgians, President Cossiga of Italy, and a number of other statesmen and academics. It is an agreeable custom that a new Chancellor honours the Head of his own Society; I was delighted that the new Balliol Chancellor conformed to this custom and made me a Doctor of Civil Law. After the festivities the College offered dinner in Hall to the Chancellor and Officers of the University and to the honorands and their friends. It was the grandest and most colourful occasion in Hall since Harold Macmillan's ninetieth birthday in 1984.

When Jenkins was elected after such a distinguished career as parlia-mentarian, cabinet minister, and president of the European Community, it would have been reasonable to wonder whether he might not treat the Chancellorship as a dignified sinecure, and take a relaxed attitude to its duties. In the event, nothing could have been further from the truth. He has been a most hard-working Chancellor, never turning down a serious social invitation from the University or its colleges, and willing to support in the most energetic way the fund-raising activities which, for better or worse, have become such a central part of University life in the 1990s. He and the University have both lived up to the implicit bargain struck when he was elected, as he recorded in the last paragraphs of his own autobiography, *A Life at the Centre*: 'Since my election, the University has taken up a quarter of my working life. I regard this as wholly satisfactory, since it has provided fully a half of my happiness.'

20

Arthur Hugh Clough

At a luncheon one day in the Lodgings at Balliol at which Graham Greene was a guest, the conversation turned to the question: since, to the unbeliever, faith is only a delusion, why do those who have given up their faith feel a sense of loss? Greene quoted the words,

> Of all the creatures under heaven's wide cope
> We are most hopeless who had once most hope,
> We are most wretched that had most believed.

I did not recognize the quotation and was told it came from *Easter Day* by Arthur Hugh Clough. I knew of Clough only the two poems everyone knows, *The New Decalogue* and 'Say not, the struggle nought availeth'; but Greene's quotation struck me, and I was anxious to read more. Dan Davin, the Oxford publisher, was at the luncheon and later sent me the OUP edition of Clough's poems, since when the volume has been one of my favourites.

Easter Day, a long poem in some thirty irregular rhyming stanzas, begins with a passionate denial of the Resurrection of Christ, couched in the words in which it is proclaimed in the final chapters of the Gospels and in the fifteenth chapter of the first Epistle to the Corinthians:

> Christ is not risen, no,
> He lies and moulders low;
> Christ is not risen.

The poem sets out to state, as concretely as possible, what is involved in denying the Resurrection of Jesus, drawing out the consequences of its non-occurrence for the life of would-be Christians. It can be taken as a paraphrase of St Paul's words, 'If Christ be not risen . . . if in this life only we have hope in Christ, we are of all men most miserable'; however, unlike Paul, the poet takes the 'if' clause to be true.

Eat, drink, and die, for we are men deceived,
Of all the creatures under heaven's wide cope
We are most hopeless who had once most hope,
We are most wretched that had most believed.
Christ is not risen.

Eat, drink, and play and think that this is bliss!
   There is no Heaven but this!
   There is no Hell;
Save Earth, which serves the purpose doubly well,
   Seeing it visits still
With equallest apportionments of ill
Both good and bad alike, and brings to one same dust
   The unjust and the just
   With Christ, who is not risen.

What should Christians do? Service to the dead Christ must be replaced by service to our living neighbours; idle gazing into heaven must give way to workaday life.

Easter Day, with its chilling use of Gospel language to negate the Gospel message, is the most powerful of Clough's religious poems. But I soon came to realize that Clough's talents were many-sided, and that he wrote best when he was dealing with quite different topics. His two longest poems are novels in verse. The first, the *Bothie of Tober-na-Vuolich*, is a lively account of a Long Vacation reading-party, bubbling with cheerful good humour, leading to a happy ending in which the hero goes off to marry his love in New Zealand. The second, *Amours de Voyage*, is an epistolary novel in hexameters and elegiacs telling of the indecisive love-making of an Oxford student, Claude, who on the Grand Tour arrives in the Rome of Mazzini's 1848 Republic, makes friends with the daughter of some English tourists, is caught up in the siege of the city by French troops, and loses contact with his female friend just at the moment when he has come to realize he loves her.

The merit of these two poems is widely recognized (*The New Oxford Book of Victorian Verse* devotes forty pages to Clough, and includes almost all of *Amours*). But both poems spoke to me for personal reasons: I shared the poet's enthusiasm for mountain reading parties, and for the city of Rome and its history; and then, of course, Clough was a Balliol man.

In the nineteenth century Balliol was a remarkable nursery of poets. At the end of the previous century, it was in Balliol (by staircase XV, where now the JCR meets) that Robert Southey plotted with his Cambridge friend S.T. Coleridge the foundation of a transatlantic socialist republic or pantisocracy. However, Southey's poems have not worn as well as his fairy tale *The Three Bears*, and it was in the middle years of the century that Balliol educated the poets of which it is most proud: Clough (1837–42), Arnold (1841–5), Swinburne (1856–9), and Hopkins (1863–8). The century went out with Belloc (1891–5) – not in the same league as the great quartet, perhaps, but certainly more often quoted nowadays than Southey. Browning was made an Honorary Fellow of the College by his friend Benjamin Jowett, but this was late in his life, and he could not say, as Belloc did (in lines still often chanted in the College, but most commonly at least half in jest)

> Balliol made me, Balliol fed me,
>   Whatever I had she gave me again;
> And the best of Balliol loved and led me,
>   God be with you, Balliol men.

It was not only Clough's poems that fascinated me; his life, too, was full of interest. He was born in 1819, the son of a Liverpool cotton merchant, and lived in South Carolina from his fourth year until he was sent to Rugby under Dr Arnold. He was outstanding as a schoolboy, and spent much of his vacations with the Arnold family. In 1836 he won a scholarship to Balliol, and after taking up residence there in 1837 he remained in Oxford for the next eleven years. Though he disappointed his tutors by obtaining only a second class in Schools in 1841, he was elected to a Fellowship at Oriel the following year and became a colleague of John Henry Newman. He collected a brilliant group of friends and pupils, including the Arnold brothers, Matthew and Thomas. In 1848 he resigned his tutorship, unwilling any longer to subscribe to the religious test of the Thirty-nine Articles. He travelled to France, where he saw the revolutionary Paris which preceded the Second Empire, and to Rome, where he was an eyewitness of the seige which he described in *Amours*. Gradually, he moved from Anglicanism into Unitarianism, and his final religious position seems to have been agnostic.

After leaving Oriel Clough had little success in finding or holding down jobs. In 1852, having become engaged to Blanche Smith, he sailed to Boston to look for work; again he was unsuccessful, but he was warmly welcomed by Boston literary society. Eventually his friends in England found him a post as examiner in the Education Office which he held from 1853 to 1861. In his last years he wrote little of lasting value: much of his time was spent in assisting his wife's cousin, Florence Nightingale, in her campaign to reform military hospitals. In 1861 his health broke down – perhaps, as some of his admirers believed, because he had been overworked by Florence – and he embarked on a foreign tour. He died, in Florence, in 1861. Many of his poems were first published by his wife after his death, and the elegy for him, *Thyrsis*, which Matthew Arnold wrote was for a long time better known than any of his own poems.

By 1985 I had become familiar with all Clough's writings and much that had been written about him. When my autobiography was well received, Sidgwick and Jackson asked whether I would write something else for them – a book on agnosticism? Agnosticism in itself, I replied, was rather a dull topic, but I would be willing to write a book on one particular agnostic, namely Clough. They asked me for a single sheet explaining why; I drew attention to the parallels and differences between Clough's life and that of Gerard Manley Hopkins (the two being, in my view, the most interesting of Balliol's Victorian poets).

Both were from middle-class Anglican families, and both were educated in the same disciplines in the same institution. Though Clough was the elder by a generation, they shared a number of friends and were influenced by several of the same people. During their time in Oxford they both underwent a religious development, but in opposite senses: Clough moved from Anglicanism towards Unitarianism and eventually agnosticism, while Hopkins moved from Anglicanism to Catholicism and found his abiding vocation as a Jesuit. How could such different endings be reached from a common starting point?

On receiving this, Sidgwick and Jackson said, 'Ah, *now* you've got a book!', and so *God and Two Poets* was commissioned. The two halves of the book set quite different tasks. Clough's religious poetry had, not unnaturally, received much less critical attention than his more substantial works, and close reading was often sufficient to offer original insights into its interpretation. But so much had been written about Hopkins that it was almost impossible to discuss his poetry, and much of his prose, without merely repeating what had already been well said by many a scholar and critic. All I could do was bring some aspects of his work into sharp relief by contrasting them with corresponding aspects of Clough's work.

I outlined the basic facts of the biography of each poet, but the structure of the book was dictated by the life of Clough rather than that of Hopkins. Thus, the first comparison I made between the poets' works was between Clough's undergraduate sequence 'Blank misgivings of a mind moving in worlds not realised' and the sonnets of desolation of the last years of Hopkins' life. A chapter about prayer, on the other hand, compared some of Clough's mature poems with some of Hopkins' juvenilia.

Hopkins, in his 'Wreck of the *Deutschland*', contrasts the conversion of St Paul and that of St Augustine. He prays:

Whether at once, as once at a crash Paul,
Or as Austin, a lingering-out sweet skill,
    Make mercy in all of us, out of us all
Mastery, but be adored, be adored King.

I used this as a text to narrate the conversions of the two poets: Hopkins' a climactic Pauline change, Clough's a lingering-out, gradual disillusionment with the Church of England. Both, on their spiritual journeys, came under the influence of Newman: Clough of the Newman of Oriel, Hopkins of the Newman of the Birmingham Oratory.

In four chapters I compared the thought of the two poets on topics which exercised them both: scripture, original sin, the sacramental system, and the relation between religion and politics. In the final chapters (the ones which Clough scholars, reviewing the book, have found most worthwhile) I considered Clough's unfinished verse drama *Dipsychus*, the text of which I reconstructed afresh from the ambiguous evidence of the manuscripts and early editions. There was no real point of comparison for this in the work of Hopkins, but in an epilogue I returned to the comparison between the two poets and ventured the value judgement that though Hopkins was undeniably superior as a craftsman of verse and as an observer of nature, Clough could claim equal honour as a religious poet.

The texts I had studied provided the theme of a reading party I took to the chalet in 1987 with Balliol's chaplain, Canon Hinchliff. With a group of theologians, philosophers, and undergraduates reading for the honour school in English, we discussed Faith and Doubt in Victorian literature. That reading party stands out in my mind not for the theologico-literary evenings, nor even for the spirited performance of Clough's verse drama *Adam and Eve*, but rather for the fact that the chalet's loo was out of action for most of the week, and we had to make use of a hollowed-out armchair poised above a pit under the larches, often holding (for the weather was not always kind) an umbrella. The party continued in good humour, displaying a social fortitude which would have won the approval of the Victorians, whether believers or doubters.

God and Two Poets appeared in 1988, to rather mixed reviews: approved, on the whole, by theologians, commonly patronized or lambasted by the literary establishment.

Many of the manuscripts of Clough's poems are in Oxford, mostly in the Bodleian, but some in Balliol College Library. One day while working on my book I asked a librarian to bring me a manuscript of one of the poems. He misunderstood what I was asking for, and brought me instead a set of journals which Clough had kept during his years at Rugby, Balliol and Oriel. Until that moment I had not known of their existence, still less of their presence in Balliol, though I soon discovered they were known to scholars and had been used, for instance, by Lowry in his edition of the correspondence between Clough and Matthew Arnold. But they had never been published, and proposals to edit them had proved abortive.

When I studied them, the problems of publication became clear. Though they were easily legible (except at times of emotional stress), they were often cryptic and allusive, full of quotations and remarks in Latin and Greek, and very repetitive. What they revealed, for the most part, was not the workings of poetic intelligence but the writhings of religious melancholia. A full transcription of the diaries, a very difficult task, would have found few readers.

None the less, I formed the project of publishing an edition of the Oxford diaries. I was familiar with the Balliol environment within which Clough had written, and had been brought up on the same Classical and biblical texts; moreover, I had read most of what had been written about the Oxford Movement which provided the backdrop for much of his religious musing. I was convinced that by leaving out the quotations from other writers, the indecipherable or unintelligible jottings, and the repetitious passages of self-reproach (for example, on late rising in the morning) I could produce a manageable edition which would be welcomed by those interested in Victorian literature, religion, or psychology.

I made a proposal to OUP, who naturally enough were initially rather wary of the idea of a truncated edition of a primary text; however, both their readers agreed that in this exceptional case a selective publication was the correct decision. Any spare time in my last years at Balliol was devoted to transcribing and editing.

The diaries had been given to Balliol in 1972 by Miss Katherine Duff, the poet's great-niece. The copyright belonged to her, so when I had reached an appropriate stage in the transcription I went to see her, to show her the transcripts and ask her permission to publish them. She received me graciously, and gave me permission in very generous terms. She was delighted to hear that the diaries could now be published. 'I hope you are going to put in all the sexual bits,' she said. 'An earlier proposal for publication planned to leave them out.'

The principal 'sexual bits' were a chronicle of masturbation, guiltily recorded by Clough in a series of large asterisks. There were also accounts of visits to a mysterious Susan of Woodeaton, and a Bessy

Gray at Shotover. But what the diary most brings to life is the heated emotional, if not explicitly sexual, relationships which could grow up between tutors and pupils in Victorian Oxford. William Ward, Balliol's mathematics tutor and an erratic ally of Newman during the heyday of the Oxford Movement, made the most outrageous demands on Clough's time and emotions when he was a second-year undergraduate. I found this astonishing, as one of the things Ward was most famous for was having forfeited his Balliol Fellowship by rushing into matrimony; indeed, I had been a friend of his grand-daughter, Maisie Ward, towards the end of her life. Ward's marriage must have been a great relief to Clough; but he in his turn, when a tutor at Oriel, filled his diary with emotional fantasies about his own pupils.

The diaries presented a difficult task to the typesetter, even though I did not attempt to make the printed page anything like a facsimile of the original, and proofs were the better part of a year in materializing. But when the book eventually appeared in April 1990 it was a satisfactory volume, handsomely illustrated, and with few surviving errata. This time I (if not always the young Clough) was very handsomely treated by the reviewers.

They often said (whether in blame or praise) that *God and Two Poets* was a very personal book; and indeed I do feel a considerable personal identification with Clough, or rather with his brand of agnosticism. I know of no poet, and of very few philosophers, who have wrestled as he did with the problem of the inconceivability of God.

St Anselm, in his celebrated ontological argument, defined God as that than which no greater can be conceived, and as being himself beyond conceiving. But if we cannot conceive him, how can we talk about him? Few philosophers have described the paradox of talking about the inconceivable godhead as Clough did. His poem of 1851, 'Hymnos Aymnos' ('a hymn, yet not a hymn'), begins by saying that we look for God in the shrine of our inmost soul; but that any attempt to embody him in words leads to triviality or nonsense. Silence – inner as well as outer – is the only response to the ineffable:

> O thou, in that mysterious shrine
> Enthroned, as we must say, divine!
> I will not frame one thought of what
> Thou mayest either be or not.
> I will not prate of 'thus' and 'so'
> And be profane with 'yes' and 'no'.
> Enough that in our soul and heart
> Thou, whatso'er thou may'st be, art.

The agnosticism is radical: the *via negativa* is rejected as firmly as the *via positiva*. Not only can we not say of God what he is, we are equally impotent to say what he is not. In the final stanza of the poem Clough pushes his agnosticism a stage further. Perhaps there is no way in which God dwells – even ineffably – as an object of the inner vision of the soul. Perhaps we should reconcile ourselves to the idea that God is not to be found at all by human minds. But even that does not take off all possibility of prayer.

> Do only thou in that dim shrine,
> Unknown or known, remain, divine;
> There, or if not, at least in eyes
> That scan the fact that round them lies.
> The hand to sway, the judgment guide,
> In sight and sense, thyself divide:
> Be thou but there, – in soul and heart,
> I will not ask to feel thou art.

21

Farewell to Balliol

FROM TIME TO time people told me I was likely to become the Vice-Chancellor of Oxford University. It was first suggested in 1983, when a candidate was being chosen to succeed Geoffrey Warnock in 1985. I doubted whether the electors would wish to have two philosophers in succession, and in any case those who thought I was the likeliest candidate must have been assuming that the Warden of All Souls, a QC with a busy London practice, would not wish to be considered. Fortunately for Oxford, Sir Patrick Neill was willing to let his name go forward, and he was Vice-Chancellor from 1985 to 1989.

The next election was due to be held in the spring of 1987. Again, there seemed a possibility that I might be chosen, although it would create a problem: hitherto, the Vice-Chancellor had always been a Head of House, and I had undertaken to resign from the Mastership of Balliol not later than 30 September 1990, only one year into the next Vice-Chancellorship. Friends in Balliol had foreseen this, and in Hilary Term 1985, while I was on leave, the College voted *nemine contradicente* that I should not feel bound by my undertaking to resign, but should be free to accept the Vice-Chancellorship if approached by the electors in 1987.

However, between 1985 and 1987 my name began to be mentioned in a different connection. I had not been very active in the affairs of the British Academy since joining it in 1974, until in the early 1980s I became chairman of its philosophy section. The philosophers were frequently at odds with the Academy's President, Owen Chadwick, and with its governing Council, which though theoretically elected each year by the AGM was in practice self-perpetuating. Once, as a democratic gesture, I put up a candidate as an alternative to the Council slate and he was roundly defeated. Michael Dummett and I proposed a motion at the AGM in 1983 that there should be a joint meeting with the Royal Society on scientific and ethical issues related to nuclear weapons. For reasons which neither of us found wholly convincing, Council failed to set up such a meeting. Partly in consequence, Michael Dummett resigned from the Academy, thus ceasing to be a thorn in Council's flesh; I was dealt with by the time-honoured alternative, being myself appointed to Council in 1984. In 1985 Sir Randolph Quirk, then President, asked me to be one of his two Vice-Presidents, and early in 1987 sounded me as to my willingness to let my name go forward for consideration as his successor. I was very flattered, but told both him and Peter Brown, the Academy's Secretary, that I would prefer to keep my options open until the future Vice-Chancellor of Oxford had been nominated.

When the Oxford electors met in the spring of 1987, however, they decided to depart from the custom – which was not a requirement of the Statutes – that only Heads of House should be considered. Instead, to the great satisfaction particularly of the scientists in the University, they elected the Professor of Zoology, Sir Richard Southwood. Naturally I felt some personal disappointment, but I wasted no time brooding. My family tell me that in fact I was more downcast when I failed in my application for All Souls.

Once the Vice-Chancellor's name was announced, I told Randolph I would be happy to be considered for the Presidency of the Academy. But I also had to look for another job, and after the headship of a college the kind I would want was likely to be one with a long lead-time, so it was not too early to begin. Almost at once something ideally suitable was advertised: the Wardenship of Rhodes House. This was attractive in several ways. I already knew what the job involved, having been for many years a Balliol colleague of the previous Warden, Bill Williams; I had friends among many former Rhodes Scholars who had been members of Balliol; the intercontinental travel which formed an essential part of the job was something Nancy and I were experienced in and enjoyed; finally, we could remain in Oxford amid friends, and still do justice to family commitments either side of the Atlantic. Moreover, I could continue to serve the University on Hebdomadal Council and as a Delegate of the Press.

To my pleased surprise, Balliol's Governing Body voted once again that I should not feel bound by my undertaking to resign early, and a delegation led by Roger Lonsdale, speaking for, it seemed, the overwhelming majority of Fellows, asked me to stay on as Master. Very touched, I did not give an immediate response, but promised to do so in the following Michaelmas Term. I considered withdrawing my application to the Rhodes Trustees; however, it was clear that to continue as full-time Master (and not at the same time as Vice-Chancellor, handing over the governance of my college to an acting head during my term of office) would have been against the spirit of my undertaking, and reflection did not alter my view that it would be bad for the College and bad for me to continue as Master until the normal retiring age – a total of 21 years. Among Heads of Houses in Oxford I was already very senior; looking at the University diary for the current year, I discovered that, setting aside the Vice-Chancellor, there were only four Heads of Houses who had held office longer than I, and of those two already had successors appointed.

So I let my Rhodes application go forward, and was placed on a short-list of three and interviewed by the Rhodes Trustees. After answering their questions about how I saw the job and its duties, I was asked what I would feel about being identified with the name of Cecil Rhodes, given some of the misdeeds which tarnished his memory. I replied guardedly that though I was no unqualified admirer of the Founder, I had known and admired many Rhodes Scholars. Only later did I think of the appropriate answer: that someone who had for many years borne the name of a robber baron like John de Balliol could have no reason to jib at bearing that of Cecil Rhodes.

I was offered the post, and before any public announcement I informed the Balliol Fellows at a College meeting in November. Thanking my colleagues for offering to allow me to continue as Master, I spelt out the reasons why I preferred to abide by my undertaking. I gave notice that I now intended to resign the Mastership at the end of the academic year 1988/9, and that I had accepted appointment as the next Secretary of the Rhodes Trust and Warden of Rhodes House. I added the following remarks:

> The Rhodes Trustees normally ask an incoming Warden to take up employment under the Trust a year before becoming Warden. This is to enable him to travel round the world and meet the selection committees for the Rhodes Scholarships. I told the Trustees that I thought it would be unfair to Balliol to give no more than ten months' notice of my departure. As it happens, the College has given me sabbatical leave for Michaelmas Term 1988, to take up a Visiting Professorship at Williams College, Massachusetts. I shall be able, during that period, to travel about the US to meet the American selection committees. The committees elsewhere I shall be able to meet by travelling during the vacations of the academic year 1988/9. Accordingly, I hope to carry out all the duties of Master of Balliol until October 1989.
>
> I have been very happy as Fellow and Master of Balliol. I have experienced the extraordinary loyalty this College inspires in all those who have been connected with it. I love the College, and I shall always regard whatever good befalls it as a personal joy to me, and whatever ill comes to it as a personal grief. I have loved living among the Fellows and count it a great privilege to have been a member of a Common Room so free from enmities and petty squabbles. I have appreciated the consideration I have always received from

the Fellows since I have been Master, a considerateness which I know, from conversation with other Heads of Houses, is by no means to be taken for granted.

There is no College in Oxford whose head I would have been more proud to have been, and I would like to end by thanking those who elected me to this magnificent job. *Floreat Domus de Balliolo.*

Many Fellows were kind enough to say that we would be much missed, and many people in Oxford outside Balliol were much puzzled by my decision. I was very glad that I had had minuted nine years earlier my intention to hold the Mastership for a fixed term, so that I could prove that my retirement was not due to any disagreement with the Fellows, or disenchantment with the College. The Fellows treated me with extraordinary consideration. The Senior Fellow was empowered to tell me that they wished to offer me on retirement the choice of an Honorary Fellowship (which has customarily been offered to retired Masters) or a Professorial Fellowship (which would carry a continuing place on Governing Body). I was deeply touched, and well aware of the attractions of remaining in the College full time on the back benches, but continued to think it would not really be wise, or fair to my successor. I accepted with enthusiasm the offer of an Honorary Fellowship, since it entitles one to the pleasures of a Fellowship, such as participation in common room life, without the duties. I opened negotiations with some other colleges with a view to securing a Professorial Fellowship to hold in conjunction with the Wardenship of Rhodes House, and was honoured to be offered one at St John's.

By the beginning of the academic year 1987/8 both The King's Mound and the Lodgings were in a poor state of repair. The King's Mound needed a new kitchen and thorough rewiring, while in the Lodgings a bath from the undergraduate floor above was gently sinking through the floor and ceiling into our quarters. The College moved us for the term into Eastman House, on Jowett Walk, which is provided for an annual visiting professor from the US. For 1987/8 this was the pianist and musicologist Charles Rosen, who because of professional engagements was not to take up his duties in Oxford until January 1988.

At the end of term we moved back to The King's Mound, and enjoyed our new kitchen and refurbished rooms. We also visited Rhodes House to see our future quarters. We were favourably impressed, and thought Pevsner's judgement of the architecture unduly harsh: 'The building is an oddity, but it has personality enough to arouse affection in some.'

In December I visited two remarkable old members. On 8 December Robert Wilberforce, who had come to the college in 1908, reached his hundredth birthday. I attended his birthday party, and told him that Governing Body had elected him to a Fellow Commonership – an antique status revived for the occasion. In the Christmas vacation I gave some lectures in Oslo University and was invited to luncheon with King Olav. He was now eighty-six, and losing his sight, but it was the unseasonably warm weather, not his infirmity, which kept him from his customary energetic skiing.

In April King Olav paid a State Visit to Britain, and we were invited to the State Dinner in the Banqueting Hall at Windsor, beneath the Waterloo portraits. The atmosphere was much less formal than at Buckingham Palace. We were moved through the courses very briskly in order to ensure that the Queen's after-dinner speech hit the right slot on the BBC. In the drawing rooms afterwards chamberlains with white staves were still discreetly marshalling queues to talk to the monarch, but junior members of the Royal Family circulated freely. At one moment when we were talking with Archbishop Runcie a young man clapped him on the back and said, 'How are you, Archbish?' It was the Duke of York, who told me I was the wrong Dr Anthony Kenny: the real one was the Duchess's gynaecologist. The Duke went on to say that Windsor was shortly to be closed for rewiring, a job likely, he claimed gloomily, to take six years; it was this work that shortly after set on fire the historic hall in which we had just been banqueting.

After I had announced my resignation, there was no sense of diminuendo; on the contrary, my life at Balliol seemed to move forward accelerando and crescendo. In May 1986 I had proposed a long-term planning commission to set out the College's goals for the next decade, to identify its strengths and weaknesses and pinpoint threats to its well-being and opportunities for its development. The commission, chaired by Jasper Griffin, presented an interim report in March 1988; already it was clear that a number of its recommendations would be implemented only in my successor's time. With the aid of the Senior Tutor and the Archivist, I undertook a thorough investigation of the many minor Trusts associated with the College, set up by wills and deeds over the centuries. The administration of these had been overhauled and streamlined by Don Harris some two decades earlier, but in a number of cases complications had occurred in the meantime, and it was quite a task to get them all untangled.

In Trinity Term I was again, as in 1971/2, a Gifford Lecturer, this time in Glasgow. In this, the centenary year of the lectureships, the Committee invited a team to discuss theological, philosophical, historical and scientific issues concerning the relationship between human beings and the world they live in, with respect to the natural theology which was the motive behind Lord Gifford's foundation. With Archbishop Habgood of York, John Barrow the cosmologist, Richard Dawkins the evolutionist, John Roberts the historian, and Don Cupitt, Dean of Emmanuel College, Cambridge, I was invited to contribute to a set of lectures on 'Humanity, Environment, and God.' My own were entitled 'The Kingdom of the Mind'. We gave our lectures in series (unlike the 1971 team which had lectured in parallel), so that there was no discussion between the different lecturers. The book which eventually appeared is, accordingly, a set of brief monologues rather than a co-operative discussion.

I found it more rewarding to discuss natural theology with Al Plantinga, who had himself been giving Gifford Lectures in Aberdeen and was now spending Trinity Term in Oxford to give the Wilde Lectures. Another visitor to Balliol who was a congenial member of the SCR was George Soros, who gave an interesting set of seminars on the philosophy of investment, in which he discussed the ideas to be found in his book *The Alchemy of Finance*.

My family, too, were busy during the term. Nancy was learning the part of Dido in Purcell's opera; Robert was studying for the examinations at the end of his first year and dashing back from Cambridge to take driving lessons; Charles was working for a demanding quartet of A-level subjects (maths, physics, history and English); the ageing Stigger was paying frequent visits to the vet and had an operation on his ear. At the end of term Robert rushed home to pass his driving test, then set off for a summer in Boston spent running the computer program for the city's free taxi service, The Ride.

Towards the end of term, South African investment once more began to trouble Governing Body. The JCR presented a petition, signed by the great majority of members, requesting 'that the College prohibit further direct investment in those British firms most heavily involved in South Africa until such time as the apartheid system is abolished or until those firms withdraw completely from operations in South Africa, to the extent that such a prohibition is not in conflict with the College's fiduciary responsibilities'. The JCR also requested the College to sell securities presently held in these firms 'as soon as alternative investments of equal or greater expected yield become available'. Of the firms listed in the JCR Report, Balliol had shares in BP, Shell, Plessey and RTZ.

It proved impossible to have the issue referred to both our Investment Committee and our Shareholder Action Committee before the end-of-term Governing Body meeting, but I pointed out that if the College postponed a decision it risked an accusation of bad faith from junior members. I quoted a recent survey made by Mark Orkin (Balliol

1971–73) of black attitudes to disinvestment: 26 per cent of respondents urged unconditional disinvestment, while 49 per cent thought foreign firms should invest in South Africa only if they recognized trades unions and actively pressured the government to end apartheid. Having studied the correspondence between the JCR and the companies named, I came to the conclusion that while BP and Shell had taken reasonable steps to fulfil the Orkin conditions, RTZ was in a quite different position. Accordingly, I urged, as a pledge of good faith to the JCR, that the College should dispose of its holdings in RTZ and return to the other companies and the general issue at a later meeting. Governing Body voted, by a majority, in favour; but the Bursar insisted on it being minuted that the motion had been put on my personal initiative.

Trinity ended, as always, with the festivities of Encaenia. The University conferred a degree by diploma on President von Weizsäcker. Because he was now an Honorary Fellow of Balliol, it fell to Nancy and me to pilot him and his staff through the ceremonies and garden party. The public orator, choosing his words with skill, described him as 'an Oxford man, and indeed a Balliol man, since he once studied at Oxford and was taught by fellows of Balliol'. We gave a small party in the Lodgings to present German students in Oxford to the President. He recalled how he had hoped to be a Rhodes Scholar, but when he was of an age to apply, the German scholarships had been abolished. In Oxford as a visiting student in 1937, he said, he was so ashamed by what was happening in Germany that he did not wish to attach himself formally to any Oxford institution.

On this hot summer's day I steered the Presidential party rather carefully through the College, lest the more formal of the German diplomats might feel the state of undress of junior members in the garden quad inappropriate. In fact, what most struck our visitors was the absence of graffiti on the College walls. No German university had achieved that in recent years: how did we manage it?

The week of Encaenia ended with a College celebration of the publication of the History of Balliol by John Jones. John, chemistry tutor, Dean and Archivist, had been working on the College's past and present history for a decade: he had edited the current edition of the *Balliol Register*, compiled a hand-list of the College archives, and now produced an elegantly written and illustrated 300-page volume far surpassing, in accuracy and comprehensiveness, anything previously written about the College. 'John destroys several cherished Balliol myths in his book,' I wrote in the year's Master's Letter, 'but illustrates in his own person the myth of effortless superiority.'

In introducing the book I described how, outlining the College's history to visitors, as a Master often must, I compared particularly the Eighties of each century since the College's foundation.

In 1288, the silver jubilee of John de Balliol's foundation, the first scholars of Dervorguilla's foundation would have been completing their course in Arts. In the 1380s, Oxford was ringing with the disputes surrounding the recently-dead Wyclif, and the version of the Bible long attributed to him was circulating – though scholars now seem to believe that, like other Balliol tutors from time to time, he has been given credit for an achievement which was really that of some of his pupils. The 1480s saw the completion of the College's medieval buildings, and in 1488 John Morton, the first Balliol Cardinal, was beginning his career as a minister of Henry VII. 1588 was the year of the Spanish Armada, the result of a policy plotted by the best-known and best-hated Balliol man of his generation, the Jesuit Robert Persons.

Guests standing in the Master's Lodgings might be told that they were within fifty yards of the sites of two other decisive events of the English Reformation. A cross in the road to the south marks the site of the burning of the martyrs Latimer, Ridley and Cranmer, while across the quadrangle to the north-west the JCR stands on the site of the Catherine Wheel Inn where the Oxford branch of the Gunpowder Plotters met to scheme. Collectively, the burning of the bishops, the Spanish Armada, and the attempt to blow up King, Lords and Commons branded Papists, in the eyes of many generations of Protestant Englishmen, as the great enemies of Church and King.

The Protestant Reformation was consummated by the Glorious Revolution of 1688, to which Balliol's modest contribution was the provision of hospitality for the Whig peers who came to Oxford to vote against the succession of the Catholic James in the debate on the Exclusion Bill of 1681. The silver they left as a house present still survives in the Senior Common Room.

The 1780s were a quiet period in the College's history. The Mastership of Theophilus Leigh – 59 years – was coming to its end. I like to fancy that latterly he was perhaps visited by his niece Jane Austen – she was ten when he died – and that perhaps she admired the handsome Chippendale chairs he left in the Lodgings and which stand there to this day.

By 1888, Balliol was very much the College we know today. Benjamin Jowett was seventy, and had five more years to live: he had presided over the erection of a new Hall, completed a reforming Vice-Chancellorship, and seen Balliol pupils carry his ideals to the most distant parts of the Empire. He had devoted the year to an edition of Plato's *Republic*. In the Lodgings, in my time, hung two portraits of Jowett, one either side of the dining-room fireplace: to the left, a young face, serene, almost debonair, drawn by Richmond; to the right, a copy of Watts's portrait showing the worn features and hooded glance of the old Master. The contrast could be pointed out to visitors as an indication of the toll taken by service as Master of Balliol.

There was no lack, however, of candidates willing to take on the job as my successor. From a distinguished field the fellows chose the Nobel Laureate Baruch Blumberg, from Philadelphia.

My final year as Master left me somewhat breathless, since I was also already in the service of the Rhodes Trust. Michaelmas Term was spent on sabbatical at Williams College, a liberal arts college in western Massachusetts. Nancy and Charles had spent part of the summer in the US but returned to Oxford for the term, and Robert was back in Cambridge, so I was alone in the handsome house the college provided. In October, a letter from the British Academy asked me to confirm that I was willing to stand as President; Council was taking longer than expected over its deliberations. At weekends I travelled around the continent, from California to Newfoundland, meeting groups of Balliol alumni, former Rhodes Scholars, and members of the selection committees who choose between Scholarship candidates. I made two weekend dashes back to Oxford, for the Balliol Society at the beginning of October, and to preside at my last St Catherine's dinner. I finished my courses at Williams in December, and was back in time to see Charles play Andrew Aguecheek in *Twelfth Night*, to encourage him in his application to King's, Cambridge to read economics and to sympathize with him in his rejection. Arrangements were set in train for his gap year: he was to spend the first half teaching in a Church of England school in Zimbabwe, near Bulawayo, the second half as a staffer in the office of Senator David Boren of Oklahoma. The following Christmas, he was accepted to read history at Peterhouse, Cambridge.

During the Christmas vacation of 1988 we celebrated my mother's ninetieth birthday, and the Council of the British Academy resolved to propose me to its membership as its next President. I returned to College for Hilary Term to be faced, once again, with the issue of disinvestment. During my absence I had effectively been censured for proposing the sale of the RTZ shares without having taken the advice of the appropriate committees. Meanwhile, the issue of ethical investment had been dramatically affected by the decision in a lawsuit between Arthur Scargill and the Trustees of the National Union of Mineworkers. The Court held that it was unlawful for charitable trusts to take investment decisions on ethical grounds, except where the ethical issue was closely related to the central purposes of the Trust; thus, a Quaker Trust could adopt a policy of never holding stock in armament manufacturers. Despite eloquent JCR argument, it was hard to see that the overturning of apartheid was an intrinsic element of Balliol's educational purposes.

Apart from this, Hilary was a normal Balliol term for me. Nancy was busy organizing a second performance of *Dido and Aeneas* to raise funds for the Ashmolean Museum, but took time off, which she later regretted, to be interviewed for a volume entitled *Establishment Wives*. In Cambridge, Robert switched courses from mathematics to management studies. In the Easter Vacation Nancy and I travelled round the world eastwards, from Pakistan, India, Singapore and Hong Kong to Los Angeles, Vancouver, Pittsburgh and Ithaca, making the acquaintance of Rhodes constituencies wherever we went.

Meanwhile, in Britain I acquired a new responsibility, as chairman of the executive committee of the Society for the Protection of Science and Learning, a charity which assists foreign academics prevented for political reasons from obtaining or keeping employment in their own country to find suitable work elsewhere. It was originally set up to help academic Jewish refugees from Nazi persecution, and had supported some very distinguished scientists and scholars in the 1930s. Sadly, the need for such an organization had long survived the demise of Nazism.

My first involvement with the Society arose through Julius Tomin's departure from Prague in the autumn of 1980. Invited by Balliol in 1979 to give a brief series of endowed lectures, he had declined on the grounds that it was unlikely he would be allowed to return to Czechoslovakia if he accepted; we were therefore surprised when we learnt of his decision to come in September 1980, but both Balliol and King's College, Cambridge welcomed him, providing hospitality and a stipend in addition to the lecture fee.

While he was in England, however, some remarks Tomin made about the Polish workers' strike were taken as provocative by the Czech authorities, his citizenship was revoked, and he could not return home. I made strenuous efforts to have his citizenship restored, enrolling the support of prominent British figures who had influence with Husák's government; the Czech authorities professed themselves willing to restore it on certain conditions, but these Tomin, no doubt for good reason, was unwilling to comply with. Those of us responsible for inviting him here accepted that in the circumstances it was our duty to see him provided with funds after the stipends from Balliol and King's came to an end in April 1981, until he could become self-supporting.

At this point I approached the Society for the Protection of Science and Learning, and they continued to support Tomin as long as their rules allowed, until August 1982; but he made no attempt to find a job.

A number of friends offered help in finding him suitable work, but for reasons which remain unclear he has refused to make any realistic applications, preferring to live on welfare.

During my chairmanship of the SPSL, from 1989 to 1993, we were called on to help a number of academics from Muslim countries who were the victims of Islamic fundamentalism. No more than the end of Nazism did the end of the Cold War bring to an end the ideological persecution of academics.

Trinity 1989 was a term of parties, and of farewells. A lunch in Hall presided over by Carol Clark to mark the tenth anniversary of the admission of women to the College was attended by ten years' intakes of Balliol women and one Balliol baby (fortunately female). Many festivities were held in our honour. 'Everyone is being extraordinarily nice to us,' Nancy wrote to her mother. 'They see us as people with a terminal illness. Everyone knows there isn't really life after Balliol.' The SCR presented us with several handsome pieces of silver, while the members of the JCR Committee baked us an enormous goodbye cake, modelled as a replica of the college; it was too large to fit through any door, but quickly vanished into the mouths of junior members assembled for a farewell party in the Quad.

For our part, we contributed to the purchase of a new eight for the boat club, to be named *Nancy Kenny*, and presented eleven silver napkin rings to the SCR, one for each year of my Mastership. There had never, in my time, been enough napkin rings for all the Fellows, so that possession of one was a prized mark of seniority. A colleague told me that he was surprised one day at lunch to find a ring beside his place. He pointed out to our Spanish butler that he was not yet sufficiently senior, and must have been given someone else's ring by mistake. 'Is quite all right, sir,' was the answer; 'Professor of Surgery, he drop dead eleven-thirty this morning.'

On the final Sunday of term I preached in Chapel, for the first and last time. Among other things, I had this to say:

> Several of my predecessors would have regarded preaching as one of the main duties of a Master. If so, it is one which I have sadly neglected. This is my very first appearance in this pulpit, on the very last Sunday when I am attending Chapel as Master. The reason is that I am not a believing Christian. When I was elected Master I asked the Chaplain whether he would object to my attending Chapel. He replied that quite a number of regular Chapel attenders would not regard themselves as believers; and that the Chapel community regarded attendance by unbelievers as something to be encouraged rather than frowned upon.
>
> It is upon those terms that I have attended Chapel from that day to this.

Some of you may wonder what right a non-Christian has to attend service in Chapel, let alone to ascend the pulpit. For my part, I have to say that I should have thought worse of successive chaplains if they had debarred me from this community on the grounds that I was unable to recite the Christian creed. For it seems to me that this is not only a Christian Chapel, but a College community. And in my view the most important function of the Master of the College is to be a symbol of the College as a community.

A collegiate university is unique in being an assemblage of communities. In these days of colleges with over five hundred members perhaps it is romantic to speak of a college as itself being a community. A college like Balliol at any given time is rather a set of overlapping communities . . .

The duty of a head of college, as I conceive it, is to help to relate these communities to each other and to be a symbol of the college's interest and identification with each of them. In an ideal college Fellows as well as students are identified with each of these communities. But when Fellows are too busy or too distracted, the Head of House should do his best to show that the college has an interest not just in the studies, but in all the creative activities of its junior members.

If for no other reason, I think that a Head of House should be present in Chapel to show the college's interest in this, one of the most important of the collegiate communities. But it would, of course, be insulting to suggest that the presence of a Master in Chapel should be simply on a par with his presence by the boathouse cheering on the second Eight. There is nothing insincere in appearing on the towpath without being a rowing man; there would be something indecent in appearing in Chapel if one regarded religion simply as a spectator sport. The Master of the College is, after all, according to the statutes, to be appointed by the Fellows because they think he is, 'in their judgement, most fit for the government of the College as a place of religion, learning and education'.

Does this mean that a non-Christian Master either should not be appointed, or should avoid the Chapel? On the contrary: at a time when the majority of members of the College are not Christians, the presence of a Master who is an unbeliever – or, as my successor will be, a member of a non-Christian faith – is an important symbol that the College as a community transcends, but has a deep interest in, this most important of all the smaller communities which make up the larger body.

The Long Vacation of 1989 was the busiest I have ever had. On 6 July I was elected President of the British Academy; I was committed to a programme of travel to New Zealand, Australia, Zimbabwe and South Africa to make the acquaintance of Rhodes constituencies there; and I was due to take over as Warden of Rhodes House on 1 September. So, effectively, for much of the summer I had three jobs.

The Rhodes tour gave me the opportunity for a final reunion, as Master, with Balliol men in the southern hemisphere. Perhaps the best-known in Australia at the time of our visit was young Warwick Fairfax. After the death of old Sir Warwick, he attempted to gain control of the *Sydney Morning Herald*, the flagship newspaper of the John Fairfax Company, which at that time was managed by his elder half-brother, James, also a Balliol alumnus. Warwick was poorly advised, and made an excessively high bid, which forced him to sell off all the other assets of the family company to pay back the banks from which he had borrowed. All this was bad news for young Warwick and for the firm, but good news for the original shareholders in John Fairfax, which included Balliol and James Fairfax. The Balliol Fairfax Fellowship – which I had held as a tutor – was funded by a holding of John Fairfax shares; these now nearly trebled in value, enabling the College to set up a second Fairfax Fellowship. Nancy and I visited James Fairfax in Sydney, partly to admire his magnificent art collection, but also to invite him to contribute to some new College building plans. He did so, handsomely, and an elegant quadrangle skilfully tucked into a corner of Holywell Manor now bears his name.

We returned in time to move into Rhodes House in the last days of August. During September I was, dizzily, both Master and Warden. I continued to carry out my Balliol duties; the last, on the last day of the month, was to address the members of the Balliol Society at their annual dinner. I did so in the following words:

> I rise for the last time as Master of Balliol to welcome the members of the Society. On this occasion it gives me comfort to know that when at midnight I cease to be Master, and indeed leave the employment of the College altogether, I shall continue for life to be a member of this Society.
>
> Tonight we have present no fewer than three Masters of Balliol: one past, one present and one future. Never before have there been three Masters at one dinner; not, indeed, since the Reformation have there been three Masters alive at the same time.
>
> I am, I understand, the 63rd Master. I was not always so: I began as the 62nd Master. When I became Master, if you looked at the list and started with Walter de Foderinghay I was number 62. But then John Jones began to take time off from organic chemistry to write the College history and found another Master before Walter, one Robert of Abberwick of whom no one had ever heard. So all the rest of us got bumped, I became 63rd, and Barry [Blumberg] will be the 64th.
>
> Benjamin Jowett once wrote 'The head of a College . . . is married to the College and has a duty to his family.'
>
> Unlike Jowett, when I became Master I was already very happily married. So I could never call the College my wife: rather, perhaps, my mistress; sometimes a very demanding mistress. Like a Neapolitan grandee of the last century I kept two establishments: a humble one at The King's Mound with

my wife and my legitimate children; a grander one in the Broad with all the children of the College as my brood. My wife was very tolerant of this state of affairs. She did not begrudge my devotion to my college-mistress: indeed she played a great part herself in cherishing and adorning this mistress.

I have been often asked: How can you bring yourself to leave the Mastership of Balliol for the Wardenship of Rhodes House? I must confess that to someone like myself, the Mastership of Balliol represents a summit of human ambition. If, twenty years ago, a fairy godmother had appeared and told me that I could become either Master of Balliol or Warden of Rhodes House, but not both, I would have chosen, without hesitation, the Mastership. But I have had a more generous fairy godmother. As an American Balliol Rhodes Scholar put it to me, 'Aren't you a lucky man to have in succession the two best jobs in Oxford?'

My years in Balliol have been years of great happiness, and my years as Master the happiest of all. For twenty-five years I have enjoyed the privilege of belonging to an incomparable society of Fellows – intelligent, witty, companionable, devoid of the malice which sometimes disfigures small and proud communities. I have been honoured as Master to be the representative of a world-wide community of Balliol men and women, remarkable for the distinction of its members and above all for the affection for the College which holds it together.

The Masters of Balliol have been, over the centuries, an undistinguished lot. Who remembers, for instance, Thomas Lawrence or John Hugate? Yet it was in their Masterships that Balliol men made two of the greatest contributions to modern civilization. In 1639, under Lawrence, a Cretan Balliol man, Nathaniel Conopius, introduced into England the drinking of coffee. In the 1360s, under Hugate, John Wyclif invented the lockable loo.

The two most important events in my time were both things with which I had nothing to do. The first was the admission of women to the College. I welcomed this greatly; but the decision was taken as the result of years of planning and persuasion by Christopher Hill. The second was the election of Barry Blumberg, who will become Master at midnight tonight.

Barry's election is a landmark, not only because of his own conspicuous merits but because he is the first scientific Master of Balliol. (So, at least, I believe – but who knows what alchemy Walter de Foderinghay and Robert of Abberwick may not have got up to in the Lodgings after Compline?) After 63 Arts Masters it is high time the Sciences got their turn.

Barry's entry to the College has not been without difficulty. As an alien, he needed a work permit. We sent his CV with our application; but the authorities clearly had a high view of the qualities needed to run the College. 'We see he has a Nobel Prize,' they wrote back, 'but what makes you think he is up to the job?' Our Senior Fellow listed Barry's many virtues, and eventually permission was granted. But the Home Office is cautious: his permit is for one year, renewable on good behaviour. So I invite you all, when toasting the College in the familiar words, to drink to Barry's good behaviour.

Index